Bringing Peace Into the Room

Daniel Bowling
David A. Hoffman

Bringing Peace Into the Room

How the Personal Qualities
of the Mediator Impact the
Process of Conflict Resolution

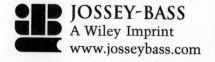

JOSSEY-BASS
A Wiley Imprint
www.josseybass.com

Published by Jossey-Bass
A Wiley Imprint
989 Market Street, San Francisco, CA 94103-1741   www.josseybass.com

Jossey-Bass books and products are available through most bookstores. To contact Jossey-Bass directly call our Customer Care Department within the U.S. at 800-956-7739, outside the U.S. at 317-572-3986 or fax 317-572-4002.

Jossey-Bass also publishes its books in a variety of electronic formats. Some content that appears in print may not be available in electronic books.

Library of Congress Cataloging-in-Publication Data

Bringing peace into the room : how the personal qualities of the
mediator impact the process of conflict resolution / Daniel Bowling and
David Hoffman, editors.— 1st ed.
    p. cm.
Includes bibliographical references and index.
  ISBN 0-7879-6850-1 (alk. paper)
1. Conflict management. 2. Mediation. I. Bowling, Daniel, 1943- II.
Hoffman, David A., 1947- III. Title.
  HM1126.B75 2003
  303.6'9—dc21
                                    2003011730

Printed in the United States of America
FIRST EDITION
HB Printing   10 9 8 7 6 5 4 3 2

Contents

*To Beth, Jessica, Jacob, and Lily, my home team: thanks for
your patience with this project and for understanding how much
joy there is in trying to turn ideas into words and vice versa.*
David A. Hoffman

*To Thelma, Robin, and Jessica: three generations of uniquely
gifted women whose love has created the shelter necessary
for me to discover that life keeps breaking our hearts open
until we have the courage to allow our hearts to stay open.
The joy and grace of this great gift is the doorway to presence.
Thank you for your presence in my life.*
Daniel Bowling

Introduction

$\cdot\;\cdot$

This book originated with a shared inquiry about what makes us effective, or ineffective, as mediators. The two of us had come to dispute resolution as a career and a calling—an opportunity to make the world a better place. We had begun to realize how much our ability to influence the parties to a dispute in a positive way depended on the personal qualities we brought with us into the room. We also began to realize that those qualities have certain changeable dimensions and others not-so-easily changeable—something like a landscape that one views at dawn, with colors that may vary from day to day or minute to minute but an overall shape that is slow to change.

Each of us sought in our own way to understand what qualities of *being* as opposed to *doing* were influential in mediation. We were trying to look beyond the skills training each of us had pursued to find those qualities of heart and spirit that, on our best days, helped us open doors to peaceful resolution.

Our inquiry began during our work together on a complex, multiparty conflict involving approximately two hundred claims, arising within a spiritual community founded in the early 1970s. The conflict erupted over charges of serious, repeated sexual abuse and abuse of power by the community's spiritual leader. This mixture of sexual and spiritual abuse creates thermonuclear conflict. As we watched the conflict spin toward a destructive court battle, we were forced to confront our own limitations and came to realize that our engagement with such conflict required something more than our normal skills and techniques.

Gandhi is often quoted as saying, "We must be the change we want to see in the world." Our immersion in the conflict that embroiled the spiritual community called upon us to embrace change within as a necessary means to fostering change in the community. Out of the painful, difficult, but ultimately successful struggles of that community toward resolution, we learned first-hand how life-altering our work could be not only for the parties but also for the dispute resolvers.

Talking with Colleagues

To further explore what it means to *be* dispute resolvers—to "be the change we want to see in the world"—we offered a workshop several years ago at the annual conference of the Society for Professionals in Dispute Resolution (SPIDR, which has now merged with other organizations to become the Association for Conflict Resolution). In the workshop, we asked attendees to consider which of their personal qualities were helpful—and which unhelpful—in their work as dispute resolvers. We generated two long lists and then role-played two mediations, in which some of the best and worst qualities were acted out. It was an amusing and enlightening exercise.

What we have learned over many years of pursuing this inquiry—from the workshop, discussions with colleagues, and our experience as workaday mediators—is that our complexity as human beings makes it impossible to prescribe a single correct way to be a mediator. Recent efforts by some mediation theorists to define a correct form of mediation have been met with resistance by many practitioners who believe—as we do—that mediation cannot be so easily constrained. A variety of styles, techniques, and methods of mediation have proven to be effective, in large part because so much depends on hard-to-define, and therefore hard-to-prescribe, personal elements. Mediators need to find an individual style that is congruent with their personal qualities and plays to their strengths, rather than imitating the styles of others. Such a truly authentic style will certainly borrow from others, yet its very authenticity requires constant grounding in self-reflection and self-awareness.

Thus we—and the other contributors to this book—provide no rules, guidelines, or advice that can be applied to all mediators as to what personal qualities are best. "Bringing peace into the room"—our shorthand way of describing what we mediators can do when we are at our best—does not necessarily mean that mediators should behave or live in a certain peaceful way. The peace that we seek to foster can take many shapes, just as each of us has his or her own way of developing the qualities that foster it. Some mediators succeed in bringing peace into the room with a manner that is excitable, blunt, or—like the "trickster" figures described by Robert Benjamin and Michelle LeBaron in this book—more akin to a wise guy than a sage.

Writing About Our Work

After our workshop, we decided to collaborate on an article in which we tried to integrate our experience with insights from other mediators and scholarship from such diverse disciplines as psychotherapy and quantum physics. Two years and twenty-five drafts later, we published in the *Negotiation Journal* the article with which this volume begins. Our editor at Jossey-Bass, Alan Rinzler, asked us to expand our article into a book-length discussion, but we decided that we were more interested in hearing what other mediators might say on this subject. We felt certain then—and we believe the essays in this volume bear out our confidence—that a variety of views on this subject would be of more value than simply expanding the description of our own views. This is a subject that lends itself to a variety of approaches—none of them necessarily right for everyone.

Purpose of This Book

These chapters were written for the ever-growing community of mediators in the United States and beyond who are seeking to enhance their ability to be dispute resolvers by moving beyond knowledge and skills to deeper levels of engagement in their work. Information and technique can carry one only so far. The next task after knowledge and skills are acquired is developing a sense of identity with the role and responsibility of being a mediator—whether that role is conceived as healer, shaman, trickster, aikido master, or problem solver.

Looking beyond information and technique, each of the contributors has addressed the question of whether there are, in fact, personal qualities that can help us bring peace into the room. Each has answered with a description of those qualities—dimensions of our being that are not static but that instead develop over time with life experience, mediation experience, and the experience of looking deeply within.

As you read these chapters, you may be nestled in a comfortable chair or couch, but if there is a consistent theme in the varied perspectives of the contributors it is that truly becoming a mediator is not an armchair experience. It requires engagement, commitment, and intention. Mediation is not for the fainthearted; to become good at it requires facing our demons and faults, while building on our strengths. We can read about it, but, as Oscar Wilde once said, "Anything truly worth learning cannot be taught." In short, these chapters were written with the understanding that they are simply guideposts for fellow pilgrims, seeking to learn—as we, the authors, continue to learn—by reflective practice and more reflective practice.

Although each chapter espouses an emphatic point of view, all of us—reader and writer alike—are seekers on this path, and the authors do not claim that their path and perspective are somehow truer than those of others. Nor should any chapter be read as a claim of mastery by its authors. It is often said that we teach what we want to learn. So it is with what we and our fellow contributors have written here.

The chapters contributed to this book are the work of some of the most experienced and inspiring mediators in the field. We wish to share with you, the readers of this book, our heartfelt appreciation not only for the chapters they wrote but also for their leadership in the field of dispute resolution. Each of these writers has led by example—walking the talk, to use the vernacular—in their lives and work. We feel blessed to have them as colleagues and to have our own chapters included with theirs.

Our work on this book was a labor of love—love for the field of dispute resolution, for the people we serve in our work as mediators, and for the people who taught us how to do this work. The same is true for our contributing colleagues, and they have collectively agreed, along with us, to donate all royalties from this book to non-profit organizations that provide dispute resolution services or leadership for the field, or both.

Brief Description of the Chapters

Because the contributors were asked to write on themes discussed in what is now Chapter One, there may be some value for the reader in beginning there. Beyond that first reading, however, these pieces need not be read in any particular order. Each can stand alone but also resonates with the others as an endorsement of the proposition that we each carry within ourselves the ability to bring peace into the room.

In our initial chapter, "Bringing Peace into the Room: The Personal Qualities of the Mediator and Their Impact on the Mediation," we note that the training and development of mediators have focused primarily on enhancing mediators' technical skills and increasing their understanding of the theory behind the practice of mediation. We then focus on a third aspect of the development of mediators, namely, their personal development. We contend that a mediator's "presence" is more a function of who the mediator is than what he or she does; it has a profound impact on the mediation process. Drawing on analogies from the social and physical sciences, we suggest that the most subtle influences of the mediator's affect and manner may in fact be powerful influences in helping the mediator bring peace into the room. If this is true, then the development of our personal qualities becomes quite important. We suggest that "integration"—a quality of being in which the individual feels fully in touch with, and able to marshal, his or her mental, spiritual, and physical resources—is one way to describe what underlies presence. We conclude by describing the approach to mediation of an integrated or fully present mediator.

Ken Cloke's contribution, "What Are the Personal Qualities of the Mediator?" is filled with poetic and paradoxical questions. He invites us into a profound inquiry regarding the power of those questions to have an impact on the one who asks and the one who is invited to answer. He cautions against delineating a list of ideal qualities that are aspirational and encourages us instead to listen deeply within to discern what is crying out for change and development in our lives and in the conflicts with which we engage. He calls upon us mediators to embrace the daily challenge of daring to live whatever we speak and speaking only what we dare to live.

Peter Adler's Chapter Three, "Unintentional Excellence: An Exploration of Mastery and Incompetence," describes the path to mastery as a mediator. He suggests that the paving stones on that path are "gifts" (aka talent), "models" (examples of people using their gifts effectively), "repetition" (the determination to practice until effectiveness becomes second nature), "chunking" (the effort-less integration of multiple sources of insight), "critique" (openness to reassessment—in short, reflective practice), and "grace" (that ineffable moment when all of the parts in the symphony of practice come together). These components, according to Adler, are fused (and infused) by the "connective tissue" of imagination.

In a pair of chapters analogizing the role of mediator to that of trickster, Robert Benjamin and Michelle LeBaron explore the terrain of myth and folklore. In Benjamin's "Managing the Natural Energy of Conflict: Mediators, Tricksters, and the Constructive Use of Deception," he declares that the trickster (from every culture and era) is the prototype of the modern-day mediator. Mediators achieve resolution through effective management of the natural energy generated by conflict, rather than a rational, structured thought process. To achieve this effective management, a mediator must have an unusual array of personal qualities: being compulsive, marginal, voyeuristic, and confused. Benjamin suggests that a mediator must create dissonance in a party's thought process and tweak the dissonance to create space for a more encompassing thought. The skills needed for this work? To be a good storyteller and actor, perhaps a wise fool à la Lt. Columbo. Though such a figure is not a classical hero, a mediator can, by creating intentional and unintentional mistakes, bob and weave her way to resolution.

In "Trickster, Mediator's Friend," LeBaron acknowledges that the very concept of mediator as trickster makes some mediators uncomfortable because of our commitment to rationality and honesty. Nevertheless, according to LeBaron, the qualities of the trickster are necessary to accomplish effective conflict resolution. The trickster, like the mediator, crosses boundaries (both within and without), resides at boundaries, and stretches boundaries to uncharted territories. Mediators work as shapeshifters, fluid in their reaction to the issues in a conflict and adapting to the individual personalities of the parties. Mediation also requires creativity; a mediator must see issues in a new light and deliver them in a

favorable package to the other party. Last but not least, the mediator is a peacemaker, using his or her inherent talent as a trickster,
along with creativity and intuitive understanding, to bring peace
into the lives of others.

In Chapter Six, "Emotionally Intelligent Mediation: Four Key
Competencies," Marvin Johnson, Stewart Levine, and Lawrence
Richard consider whether the components of emotional intelligence,
as delineated in Daniel Goleman's book *Emotional Intelligence*, are
important for effectiveness in mediation. Goleman argues that one's
emotional intelligence, or EQ, is actually a better predictor for success in life than the more traditional IQ. The chapter describes the
specific competencies that make up EQ and suggests that they are an
excellent basis for both effective mediation and reflective practice.

Hoffman's Chapter Seven, "Paradoxes of Mediation," suggests
that among the personal qualities that mediators need to develop
is a high level of tolerance for ambiguity. He describes a set of
fundamentally irreconcilable tensions in the practice of mediation,
tensions that make our aspirations to perfect our practice futile. For
example, mediators try to be both fully present in the moment and
strategic at the same time—"to influence the future while simultaneously ignoring it." Likewise, we seek to be both empathic and
candid, qualities that are often in tension with each other. Some of
these tensions relate to our personal qualities and others to our
skills, but all of them present us with choices that, of necessity, lead
to flawed outcomes. Mediators cannot avoid these paradoxes;
instead, according to Hoffman, we should embrace them, while at
the same time pursuing a reflective practice that leads us to progressively better results.

Lois Gold's chapter, "Mediation and the Culture of Healing,"
focuses on applying to conflict resolution certain practices and
principles from the healing arts with roots in the "perennial philosophy." She describes how people in conflict lose all context for
their lives and delineates the principles of healing practices that can
be applied through mediation to support parties in rediscovering

context for their lives. She urges mediators to discover how to create the space for parties to reveal their very best selves and presents techniques and practices for creating a healing environment. She underscores the importance of developing presence and offers four specific practices: (1) coming from center, (2) compassion, (3) connection to central and governing values and higher purpose, and (4) congruence. She concludes by outlining practical strategies for augmenting the healing and peacemaking potential of mediation.

Sara Cobb's Chapter Nine, "Creating Sacred Space: Toward a Second-Generation Dispute Resolution Practice," argues for the importance of the mediator as moral witness. Most descriptions of mediation, she notes, focus on the secular and instrumental aspects of the process: addressing the parties' needs and interests, and maximizing joint gains from bargaining. Missing from these descriptions is the moral dimension, which often has the greatest impact on the resolution, because it creates a "sacred space" in which the parties achieve greater understanding of themselves and others. The mediator is a participant, along with the parties, in creating the moral frame in which each party's story is told. Thus, the personal qualities of the mediator, and particularly his or her own moral framework, shape the outcome.

Jonathan Reitman takes a deeply personal approach in his chapter, "The Personal Qualities of the Mediator: Taking Time for Reflection and Renewal." Writing from his experience with intractable conflict in Bosnia and the Middle East, he discusses the importance of taking time to reflect on his practice and renew himself. He outlines the personal qualities to which he returns over and over as a result of this reflection and renewal, underscoring the importance to a mediator of courage, optimism, lateral thinking, and genuine curiosity.

In "Style and the Family Mediator," Donald Saposnek describes mediation as a union of art and science, informed by an intuitive understanding of human relationships and their "frictional" element. Developing such an effective mediation style, according to Saposnek, requires not only a grounding in the principles of mediation but also a holistic, systemic approach to the components of conflict. The personal qualities that enable a mediator to practice in this way involve an ability to be comfortable with conflict, calm while managing the intensity of the parties' commitments to their separate views, and flexible and open to the parties' perspectives. Perhaps most importantly, effective mediation requires the mediator to establish a trusting relationship with each party and remain compassionate and sympathetic throughout the process.

In Chapter Twelve, "Tears," David Hoffman describes his reaction to emotional moments in his life and in his work as a mediator and arbitrator. None of us, he suggests, is immune from the feelings that arise when we encounter other people's joys and misery. As dispute resolvers, we must walk the line between professional detachment and authentic human connection; according to Hoffman, we should not be ashamed of showing how moved we are by the feelings of others.

In the final chapter, "Mindfulness Meditation and Mediation: Where the Transcendent Meets the Familiar," Daniel Bowling recounts his own experiences with meditation—both the challenges and the illumination. He discusses the history and benefits of this practice, including the ability of meditation to enhance mediator presence from a deeper sense of being. He encourages the practice of "mindfulness meditation" or other forms of contemplative practice because, in his view, they are uniquely relevant to developing the personal qualities necessary for the practice of mediation. He describes the conjunction of meditation and mediation as the place where the transcendent meets the familiar—the present moment of now. He concludes by urging mediators to use the presence acquired from contemplative practice to take on, and assist their clients in taking on, the seemingly monumental challenges of conflict resolution.

To give the reader an opportunity to reflect on a chapter in the light of individual experience, at the end of each we include reflective practice suggestions. These suggestions are intended to highlight aspects of each chapter that, in the editors' view, bear on the over-all themes of this volume. Our purpose was not to summarize the chapters or to suggest, by highlighting one issue, that other points in a chapter are somehow less important. Simply put, we offer these reflective practice suggestions to underscore the fundamental point of this book: development as a mediator is not an armchair experi-ence. We hope our comments will suggest ways to engage experi-entially with the ideas presented in this volume and encourage the reader to develop his or her own reflective practice approaches. In our experience, it is through our commitment to reflect on our work, who we are being through our work, and the path of devel-opment we wish to follow as mediators, that we continue to evolve as mediators and expand what we offer in service to our clients.

A final word. We and our fellow authors welcome your response to what we have written. Contact information is included with each contributor's biographical information. Each of us views these writ-ings as part of an ongoing conversation in the field of dispute reso-lution, and we invite your participation in, and expansion of, that conversation. We see this conversation as essential for opening the door to another dimension of our practice—a dimension that may have been forgotten in our professions of origin—in which who we are becomes as important as what we do. We claim no certainty regarding the contours of this dimension or the path that leads there. Its existence, however, is grounded in our experience. We offer these chapters with the hope that they are useful to you as you find your own path toward uncovering your authentic style and per-sonal qualities, as together we learn what it means to be a bearer of peace in a deeply conflicted world.

Acknowledgments

We are grateful for the help and support we received from numer-ous people in connection with this book. First and foremost, we wish to thank the contributors for the chapters you provided. It was a pleasure working with you on this book, just as it has always been in working with you as colleagues in the field of dispute resolution.

Our editor at Jossey-Bass, Alan Rinzler, has been an enthusiastic supporter of this project from its inception. His sound judgment, ready availability to address questions of all kinds, and his seriousness about deadlines have kept the book on track.

Our colleagues who attended our first session on this topic, at the 1997 Conference of the Society of Professionals in Dispute Resolution in Orlando, and who encouraged us with their enthusiastic and thoughtful responses contributed enormously to our decision to continue the inquiry that has led to this volume.

A stalwart crew at the New Law Center office in Boston—Diane DiLeo, Melissa Filgerleski, and Stacey Bran—handled a variety of editing and logistical tasks with resourcefulness and care. We also benefited from excellent research and editorial assistance from law student intern Bhavani Murugesan.

We also wish to thank the many fellow mediators—too numerous to list individually here—who have contributed to the ideas expressed in this book. We feel lucky to have entered a field in which collaboration and a sense of community combine to make newcomers to the field—such as we were, not that many years ago—feel welcome. Thank you for holding the door open for us.

Daniel Bowling
David A. Hoffman

1

. . . .

Bringing Peace into the Room

The Personal Qualities of the Mediator and Their Impact on the Mediation

Daniel Bowling and David A. Hoffman

Empirical studies of the mediation process consistently show high rates of settlement, as well as high levels of participant satisfaction (for an example, see McEwen and Maiman, 1981). These favorable results seem to occur regardless of mediation styles or the philosophical orientation of the individual mediator (evaluative versus facilitative, transformative versus problem solving). Indeed, the history of mediation as well as our own experience show that mediation sometimes works even when the mediator is untrained.[1] Is there some aspect of the mediation process—wholly apart from technique or theory—that explains these results?

Some might say that mediation works because it creates a safe forum for airing grievances and venting emotion (that is, it gives people their "day in court"), and this can be done even with an unskilled mediator. Others might point to the use of active listening and reframing—skills that many people have, whether or not they have had any formal mediation training. Still others may focus on the use of caucusing and shuttle diplomacy—again, techniques that do not necessarily require specialized training.

We believe all of these techniques are important. We also believe that mediation training is vitally important as a means of enhancing our ability to do those things that for some people may come naturally but for most of us require training and practice.

However, there is a dimension to the practice of mediation that has received insufficient attention: the combination of psychological, intellectual, and spiritual qualities that make a person who he or she is. We believe that those personal qualities have a direct impact on the mediation process and the outcome of the mediation. Indeed, this impact may be one of the most potent sources of the effectiveness of mediation.

We do not profess to know precisely how this happens or why it happens, although this chapter does suggest a framework for examining these questions. Because the ideas we present are not based on empirical studies or controlled experiments, we cannot prove their validity. They have evolved from reflection on our own experience as mediators and observation of the work of other mediators. We hope these ideas stimulate further inquiry.

Bringing Peace into the Room

The observation that led us to write this chapter can be simply stated and may even seem self-evident: as mediators, we have noticed that, when we are feeling at peace with ourselves and the world around us, we are better able to bring peace into the room. Moreover, doing so, in our experience, has a significant impact on the mediation process. What may be more complex and difficult to explain is how we, as mediators, can maintain a sense of peacefulness while working with people who are deeply enmeshed in seemingly intractable conflict. Often the disputes that we deal with in mediation trigger feelings in us about conflicts in our own lives. However, we believe that successful mediators have an ability to transcend those conflicts, or perhaps to use the insight derived from them, to help the parties in the mediation reach a genuine resolution of the dispute that brought them there. This ability arises, in our view, not so much from a particular set of words or behaviors but instead from an array of personal qualities of the mediator that create an atmosphere conducive to resolution.

In an effort to make sense of these observations, we have found very useful and pertinent analogies from research in the physical and social sciences, and in particular the field of psychology. Research in these fields is useful not so much because it furnishes a definitive answer to the question of how personal characteristics influence the mediation process but because it offers what we believe are useful metaphors for the processes we observe in mediation, and useful frameworks for thinking about the interactions of mediator and client.[2] Some of the scientific theories we describe here are considered controversial; others are well established. We are not seeking to prove, nor do we vouch for, the validity of this scientific research. Instead, we look to that research, as part of an exercise in reflective practice (see Lang, 1998), to see if it affords useful insight into the mediation experience and thus a deeper understanding of the qualities that will make us better mediators.

Three "Stages" of Development

Our starting point is to reflect on how we ourselves developed as mediators. For us, and for many of our fellow mediators, the process seems to involve three major "stages." Although we describe these aspects of our development sequentially, for some mediators they may occur in a different order, overlap, or occur to some degree simultaneously.[3]

First, as beginning mediators, we studied technique. We learned, among other things, active listening, reframing, focusing on interests, prioritizing issues, and helping the parties generate options. We learned to demonstrate empathy as well as impartiality; how to diagnose settlement barriers; and how, with any luck, to bring a case to closure. We looked for opportunities to practice these skills. A period of apprenticeship ensued, involving, for some of us, co-mediation with more experienced colleagues, observation of other mediators, and opportunities for debriefing and peer supervision.

The second stage of our development involved working toward a deeper understanding of how and why mediation works. In seeking an intellectual grasp of the mediation process, we hoped to find the tools with which to assess the effectiveness of various techniques; identify appropriate professional and ethical boundaries; and better understand what we were doing, why we were doing it, and the meaning of the process for our clients. These intellectual inquiries, encompassing both empirical and theoretical research and normative discussions of mediation practice, increased our effectiveness as mediators and enhanced the personal satisfaction we derived from this work.

The third stage of our growth as mediators is the focus of this chapter, and we consider it to be the most challenging frontier of development. For us, the third aspect begins with the mediator's growing awareness of how his or her personal qualities influence (for better or worse) the mediation process. It is at this stage that we begin to focus on, and take responsibility for, our own personal development as mediators. It is about *being* a mediator, rather than simply *doing* certain prescribed steps dictated by a particular mediation school or theory. Mediator David Matz recently wrote, in a paper titled "The Hope of Mediation": "In addition to what a mediator does, there is the matter of what a mediator is. Spirit emanates from being, just as articulately as it does from doing. More specifically, it is the mediator's being, as experienced by the parties, that sends the message" (Matz, 1999, p. 17).[4] Our conception of this third task is developmental; it is based on the premise that gaining mastery is an ongoing process.

An example of the differences among these stages of development can be seen by looking at a particular feature of the mediation process—for example, reframing. In skills training (first stage), mediators are taught how to restate and reframe the parties' accounts in a way that helps them feel heard and understood. Further reading and study (second stage) might demonstrate the reasons reframing is an effective technique. At the level of personal development (third stage), the mediator develops the ability to reach a deeper level of personal connection with the parties, so that the reframing resonates with authenticity.

Very little has been written about this third stage in the process of becoming a mediator, although we believe that it is a vital aspect of a mediator's development. Likewise, little is known about the personal qualities of mediators and how they affect the mediation process. More is known about what makes people effective psychotherapists and lawyers (see, for example, Kottler, 1991; and Ryan, 1996).

Personal Qualities of the Mediator

More than a decade ago, mediators William E. Simkin and Nicholas A. Fidandis (1986) catalogued what they believed to be the necessary qualities for an effective mediator. We assume, for purposes of this discussion, that these qualities, and the others discussed in this chapter, are not entirely innate and can be developed. Simkin and Fidandis included in their list, which was no doubt partly tongue-in-cheek:

- The patience of Job

- The sincerity and bulldog characteristics of the English

- The wit of the Irish

- The physical endurance of a marathon runner

- The broken-field dodging abilities of a halfback

- The guile of Machiavelli

- The personality-probing skills of a good psychiatrist

- The hide of a rhinoceros

- The wisdom of Solomon

Another writer (Boulie, 1996) suggested, in a more serious vein, that successful mediators are empathetic, nonjudgmental, patient, persuasive, optimistic, persistent, trustworthy, intelligent, creative, and flexible, and that they have a good sense of humor and common sense.

Such catalogues of qualities—which are anecdotal, not scientific—help us identify some of the characteristics that we may want to foster in ourselves and look for in other mediators. However, we believe there is some deeper and more fundamental quality that the most effective mediators have: a quality that may include such attributes as patience, wisdom, or wit but that involves other attributes that are not in these lists. As we try to identify that quality, we focus on both the subtle influences of the mediator (those that may operate beneath the level of conscious awareness), and those where the mediator's influence is readily apparent.

Placebo Effect

As a starting point, we note that the success of mediation is not always the result of the mediator's personality or the skill with which he or she practices mediation. Some disputes are resolved even if the mediator is not present (or in spite of the mediator's presence, if he or she is not particularly skillful) simply because the parties to the dispute have sat down at the table, figuratively or literally, to discuss the matter. In the legal arena, the mere process of getting two lawyers to open their files on a case simultaneously and focus on them often produces a settlement.[5] A certain number of such settlements occurs whenever a court-connected event (such as a motion hearing or a status conference) brings the parties and counsel together. In cases of this kind, mediation is simply an event that brings the parties together for a discussion that, even without the mediator, might resolve the case because the circumstances are ripe for settlement.

The Mediator's Interventions

The most direct and obvious impact that the mediator has on the mediation process comes from the techniques he or she uses to influence the course of negotiations. These interventions, based on the mediator's assessment of the obstacles to settlement, might involve giving the parties an opportunity to vent emotional reactions to the dispute, encouraging the parties to focus on interests rather than positions, or helping the parties generate options for settlement.

These basic techniques, and others, are widely used by mediators, but with varying results. Some of the variation is certainly attributable to differences in the cases themselves. Disputes vary, and the parties themselves display an infinite variety of personal characteristics, which may foster or impede settlement. Likewise, however, the personal qualities of the mediator influence the effectiveness of his or her interventions.

The "Hawthorne Effect"

A useful analogy for the process we are describing comes from the social sciences, in a phenomenon known as the "Hawthorne effect," a term used to describe the changes people make in their behavior when they realize they are being observed. This phenomenon was recognized by sociologists who conducted an experiment in the 1920s and 1930s at Western Electric's Hawthorne plant on the outskirts of Chicago (see Gillespie, 1991). The researchers wanted to know whether increasing the illumination of the factory would increase the workers' productivity. After determining the benchmarks of worker performance, the researchers turned up the lights and found that productivity increased. To confirm these results, they then reduced the level of illumination below the original level and found, to their surprise, that productivity was higher than the benchmark levels. They concluded that it was their presence, not the changes in the factory's lighting, that had caused the change in worker productivity.

This insight parallels physicist Werner Heisenberg's discovery in the 1920s of the "uncertainty principle": that the observation of particles influences their behavior. The application of this principle to mediation is clear. If factory workers (or indeed subatomic particles) behave differently when observed, how much more so individuals in conflict who have sought out the assistance of a mediator?

Some mediators, however, have observed what might be described as a "negative Hawthorne effect": parties who seem to negotiate *less* productively if a third party is present. One explanation for this phenomenon is that the parties may have other goals and other agendas, apart from settling the issues that ostensibly brought them to the mediation, which they feel safe in pursuing only when a third party is present. Another explanation is that what may appear to be a negative Hawthorne effect could, in fact, be positive. For example, in some cases explosive personal issues (such as the emotional distress caused by an abrupt termination of employment or the discovery of infidelity in a marriage) cannot be discussed productively without a third party present, and the seemingly unproductive discussions that take place in the mediator's presence are nevertheless more productive than they would be without the mediator. Moreover, even discussions that appear to be destructive in nature may be needed to achieve a resolution in a particular case. In any event, it seems likely that the presence of the observer influences the parties' negotiations for good or for ill.

Of course, mediators do much more than simply observe the parties' negotiations. One might suppose that the active intervention of the mediator would override or transcend any subtle influence that arises from the process of observation. However, it is the influence of another person's presence, whether that person is actively intervening or not, that we wish to focus on. It may be difficult, if not impossible, to isolate from the complex web of interactions that portion of the mediator's influence that arises from his or her observation of the parties. What is significant, however, is that mediators, by their mere presence, influence the parties.

The Mediator's "Presence"

This brings us to the heart of our thesis: there are certain qualities that the mediator's presence brings to the mediation process that exert a powerful influence and enhance the impact of the interventions employed by the mediator. The term *presence*, of course, has at least two meanings here: (1) the fact that the mediator is physically present and (2) the qualities that his or her physical presence brings into the room. It is the second meaning we are interested in as we explore how the mediator's presence influences the mediation.

As part of that exploration, it is important to recognize that the personal qualities of the *parties* may influence the mediator, just as the mediator's personal qualities affect the parties. Trying to understand the effect of the mediator's presence, without considering the impact of the parties on the mediator (what could be called a reverse Hawthorne effect), is to look at only half of the picture. In traditional psychoanalytic terms, a similar phenomenon might be described as countertransference, the term used to describe feelings evoked in the therapist by the client. (For a useful discussion of transference and countertransference in negotiation, see Fukushima, 1999.) Just as it is important for a psychotherapist to be aware of those feelings so that they do not inappropriately influence the course of treatment, mediators need to be aware of the feelings evoked in them by their clients and the nature of the dispute in order to make productive use of those feelings. In Gestalt psychology, the phenomena we are examining would be viewed as being comprehensible only by looking at the whole set of interactions of the parties and the mediator, the qualities that each brings to the process, and the changes wrought by those interactions. Gestalt psychologists assert that "living organisms . . . perceive things not in terms of isolated elements, but as integrated perceptual patterns—meaningful organized wholes, which exhibit qualities that are absent in their parts" (Capra, 1996, p. 32).

These analogies from the field of psychology point to the utility of considering mediation from a systemic perspective, one in which we shift our focus from the interests of the individual parties to the set of interactions and relationships of the parties and the mediator. On the basis of systems theory, "The essential properties of an organism, or living system, are properties of the whole, which none of the parts have. They arise from the interactions and relationships among the parts. These properties are destroyed when the system is dissected, either physically or theoretically, into isolated elements. Although we can discern individual parts in any system, these parts are not isolated, and the nature of the whole is always different from the mere sum of its parts" (Capra, 1996, p. 29). Central to this way of looking at mediation is the recognition that the mediator is not extrinsic to the conflict (any more than the therapist is wholly separate from the issues addressed in therapy).

Such an approach is, to some extent, at odds with prevailing norms in the mediation field, in which the independence (or separateness) of the mediator is viewed as professionally appropriate, perhaps even necessary, if one is to be effective. These norms are expressed in ethical codes that articulate a vision of mediation in which mediators, for the most part, have no prior connections with the parties and maintain a stance of rigorous impartiality.

The view that mediators need to maintain a certain distance from the parties may stem from the professional norms of psychotherapy, law, and other disciplines where ethical principles require the professional to avoid personal involvement that might impair the ability to render independent professional judgments.

However, the values and norms of those other professions may not be completely applicable in the context of mediation. One important difference in the professional roles is that a psychotherapist or lawyer must, in some cases, take responsibility for directing the client's actions by giving professional advice. Most codes of ethics for mediators proscribe offering professional advice. For example, the *Massachusetts Uniform Rules on Dispute Resolution*, section 9(c)(iv), states that "a neutral may use his or her knowledge to inform the parties' deliberations, but shall not provide legal advice, counseling, or other professional services in connection with the dispute resolution process."

We are not suggesting abandonment of neutrality or impartiality; far from it. However, being neutral or impartial does not mean that conflict resolvers are separate from the conflict systems they are seeking to help resolve. Because mediators are inextricably involved in the conflicts they mediate, impartial may not be as accurate a description of the mediator's role as the term "omnipartial," which has been proposed by mediator Kenneth Cloke (see generally Cloke, 1994).

While reconceptualizing the process as one in which the mediator is personally involved—being influenced by the process as much as influencing it—the mediator must manage the tension between his or her own objectives and those of the parties. The mediator has a professional duty to the clients, whose interests and needs are of paramount importance. Yet at the same time, the mediator cannot fully serve the clients without being cognizant of (1) the evolution of relationships between and among the participants in the mediation, including the mediator, and (2) the impact of the mediation process on the mediator himself or herself.

We are not suggesting that the mediator redirect the attention of the parties from their needs or interests to his or her own. However, we are suggesting a departure from what we believe is the norm in much of the training of mediators with respect to managing their own feelings in the mediation process. Mediators are taught, for the most part, to contain whatever feelings they may have about the parties to maintain neutrality and communicate, by word and deed, their impartiality. We suggest that the feelings the mediator experiences may be important and useful material that the mediator can use—albeit judiciously—in helping the parties reach a resolution. In using such an intervention, a mediator must also maintain appropriate professional boundaries so that purely personal matters are not interjected into the process.

We are also suggesting that the mediator use his or her own self-awareness by adopting a deeply reflective practice, including the careful observation of the impact that the mediation, the conflict, and the parties have on her or him. Through such a practice, outside the mediation room, the mediator may substantially aid his or her progress in the third stage of mastering mediation to develop those personal qualities desirable for assisting in the resolution of conflicts. In doing so, mediators should seek to increase their awareness of how they resolve conflict in their own lives in order to lessen any unintended impact of unresolved personal conflict on the mediation process.

Subtle Influences

If we accept the view that, notwithstanding impartiality, mediators are inevitably engaged in creating a relationship with the parties—a relationship in which their personal qualities influence the parties' ability to negotiate successfully—we are led inevitably to the next question: What are the qualities in the mediator that contribute to a successful relationship with the parties, one that supports reorganization of this conflict "system"?

The field of psychology suggests some tentative answers to the question. In drawing on insights from psychology, we do not wish to blur the boundaries between mediation and the practice of psychotherapy. (For a useful discussion of the boundaries between these two fields, see Dworkin, Jacob, and Scott, 1991; and Kelly, 1983.) However, there are many useful points of comparison in the work done by therapists and mediators.

In traditional Freudian psychoanalysis, one of the earliest forms of Western psychotherapy, the therapist was trained to be a "blank slate," rather than attempting to project his or her personality into the process or foster a personal relationship with the patient. The analyst does not even face the patient during their sessions together. The blank-slate approach, in which it was important for the therapist *not* to disclose personal information or points of view, was believed to create the optimal setting for transference, which was considered an essential process for healing (see Kovel, 1976).

Modern psychotherapy has begun to move in another direction, with the therapist taking a more personal role in the therapeutic process (see O'Connor, 1993). Indeed, some schools of psychotherapy have moved to the point of teaching that positive identification with the therapist is beneficial (see Fierman, 1997). Norcross and Guy (1989) write: "Multiple and converging sources of evidence indicate that the *person* of the psychotherapist is inextricably intertwined with the outcome of psychotherapy. There is a growing recognition, really a re-awakening, that the therapist him or herself is the focal point of change" (p. 215). Other schools encourage the therapist to model appropriate behavior. Psychologist Jeffrey Kottler notes that modeling does not mean portraying an unflawed personality but instead "balancing omnipotence and humanness": "Modeling takes the form of presenting not only an ideal to strive for, but a real live person who is flawed, genuine, and sincere" (1991, p. 29).

Proponents of the techniques of neurolinguistic programming (NLP, admittedly, a controversial school of psychological inquiry) have also studied how subtle features of the communications between therapist and client—such as breathing rate, body language, speech and language patterns, the use of metaphor, and eye movements—have an impact on the therapeutic process (see O'Connor,

1993). One of the conclusions that flows from this work is that the therapist cannot truly be a blank slate, because even the most subtle aspects of our presence influence those around us, and we believe (based on our experience with mediation) that this conclusion applies to mediators as well. Indeed, research in the biological sciences has shown that we humans influence each other even by the chemicals our bodies emit.[6]

What these recent trends in psychotherapy have in common is their focus on how the behavior, affect, or manner—the presence—of the therapist influences the therapeutic process, wholly apart from the nature or structure of the therapeutic interventions. An assessment of the personal characteristics of psychotherapists suggests that there are qualities successful psychotherapists have in common, characteristics that may be relevant to the success of mediators as well. Kottler considered the personal characteristics of pioneers in the field of psychotherapy (Freud, Jung, Adler, and Rogers), as well as less prominent but nonetheless successful clinicians, many of whom employed radically different therapeutic techniques. He examined these characteristics because he was puzzled by the fact that, although there were numerous theories of treatment, each competing for hegemony on the basis of greater effectiveness, empirical research failed to show differences in treatment outcome that could be correlated with the technique used by the psychotherapist. One of Kottler's hypotheses was that there might be certain traits that successful therapists have in common and that these characteristics might be better predictors of success in treatment than the methodologies the therapists employed.

Kottler identified several qualities in therapists that appear to correlate with successful treatment. Among the most significant was a characteristic Kottler calls "personal power" or "force of personality"—not power over another person but rather a quality he equates with "charisma." Kottler concluded that, to explain the success of the best psychotherapists:

The answer is not totally confined to what effective therapists *do*, but also involves who they *are*. The common thread running through the work of all great therapists is the force of their personalities and the power of their personas. They are the kinds of people who radiate positive energy. They are upbeat, enthusiastic, witty, and quick on their feet. They have good voices and are highly expressive in using them. Most of these highly successful practitioners are simply interesting and fun to be around. And they exhibit qualities that other people want for themselves. . . . [Despite their apparent differences in style, they] have all been doing essentially the same things—that is, being themselves and allowing the force and power of their personalities to guide what they do. All the theorists invented styles that made it possible to play on their strengths [Kottler, 1991, pp. 73, 76].

The quality Kottler describes as personal power is similar to a trait discussed earlier: the mediator's presence. Mediator Gary Gill-Austern, describing presence as the essential characteristic that a mediator must bring to the table, defines it as "that quality of human action and behavior that addresses the moment, . . . that quality of service that is so alive as to be grace-filled and which transforms its agent into a harbinger of that which heals; that quality of being that loses itself as it meets the other" (see Gill-Austern, 1994). Therapist and mediator Lois Gold (1993) describes presence as composed of several characteristics:

- Being centered
- Being connected to one's governing values and beliefs and highest purpose
- Making contact with the humanity of the clients
- Being congruent

These qualities, she asserts, increase our effectiveness as mediators and enable us to harness the healing potential of the mediation process.

"Centering" is a process familiar to anyone who has ever tried to throw a clay pot on a potter's wheel. The first step is to press against the clay from each side until the spinning mass rotates smoothly and can then be shaped (see Richards, 1962). Centering the clay is similar to what we as mediators do when we begin a mediation: we bring a certain atmosphere into the room, through our personal presence, which has the effect of centering the mediator and the others in the room. An essential element of congruence is genuineness, communicated in part by the degree of authenticity of feeling that is present between individuals. For example, in conversation, we often know on an intuitive level whether an individual is truly *there* with us and communicating openly, honestly, genuinely. Another important aspect of congruence is the ability to behave in a manner that is appropriate for the particular clients we are serving. It is not that we as mediators fundamentally change who we are. It is rather that we accord our clients the respect of behaving in a manner that creates safety and inclusion for them as individuals, regardless of their background, appearance, or station in life.

"adaptive" authenticity

Another term for these qualities is "integration," which we would define as a quality of being in which the individual feels fully in touch with, and able to marshal, his or her spiritual, psychic, and physical resources, in the context of his or her relationship with other people and with his or her surrounding environment.[7] Others have used the term "mindfulness" to describe this quality. As discussed in the writings of Jon Kabat-Zinn (1994), mindfulness can be defined as "living in harmony with oneself and the world."

In our work as mediators, integration comes in part from developing a strong identification with our role: the transition from feeling that "I am someone who mediates" to realizing that "I am a mediator"—from seeing mediation as work that we *do* to seeing it as an integral part of our identity. An equally vital component of integration, from the perspective of mediation, is the constant awareness of our connection with the people whose conflicts we mediate. This approach to mediation parallels the development of heightened engagement by some modern practitioners of psychotherapy, who are moving away from an atomistic model of the separateness of therapist and patient to a more systemic model emphasizing engagement and relationship.

The New Sciences

Just as developments in the field of psychology suggest useful analogies for thinking about the personal qualities of mediators, developments of the past century in the physical sciences suggest new ways of looking at the *impact* of those qualities on the mediation process. In the sections that follow, we discuss a range of scientific developments and their potential usefulness as a lens for examining the mediation process.

Quantum Physics

We have already alluded to Heisenberg's well-known uncertainty principle. Heisenberg's theory was part of a series of discoveries that undermined previously settled views that the behavior of matter was fully explained by the laws of Newtonian physics. A fundamental premise of the Newtonian view was that matter could be analyzed by breaking it down into its constituent parts, and the interaction of those particles of matter could be accurately measured and explained. However, this view was challenged by quantum theory, which is broadly defined as an approach in physics to study and understand the fundamental and universal laws relating to matter and its movement (see, for example, Bohm, 1983). Quantum physicists concluded that electrons, which were supposed to be the smallest parts of matter, also showed wavelike properties, and conversely, light waves sometimes behave like particles of matter. Either of these outcomes depended, scientists concluded, on how one set up an experiment—on the interaction between the observing apparatus or individual and what is observed. As described by physicist David Bohm: "One can no longer maintain the division between the observer and observed (which is implicit in the atomistic view that regards each of these as separate aggregates of atoms). Rather, both observer and observed are merging and interpenetrating aspects of one whole reality, which is indivisible. . . . What is needed in a relativistic theory is to give up altogether the notion that the world is constituted of basic objects or 'building blocks.' Rather, one has to view the world in terms of universal flux of events and processes" (1983, p. 9).

Of course, the parties in a mediation do not behave like subatomic particles. But the impact of the observer on the observed and vice versa noted by Bohm is certainly consistent with what we see in the mediation room. There, the unique chemistry of mediator and parties produces differing results depending on who is in the room and the personal qualities they bring to the process. This framework is thus a useful metaphor when applied to the context of mediation.

Systems Analysis

Systems analysis offers another metaphor for thinking about this chemistry. Systems thinking became more widely known in the 1930s when ecologists began to explore living systems as wholes, rather than examining smaller and smaller parts of organisms. As noted above, the systems view seeks to explain the essential properties of an organism, or living system, as properties of the whole, arising from the interactions and relationships among the parts (Capra, 1996; see also Bohm, 1983; and Bohm and Hiley, 1993).

Systems analysis (which characterizes much of twentieth-century science) rejects the traditional analytic approach, which was based on the idea that all phenomena could be successfully studied as mechanistically determined events. A key element of such an analysis was the reduction of organisms and other matter to ever smaller components (see Davies, 1988). Systems analysis embraces contextual thinking, in which the properties of parts of systems are not entirely intrinsic to those parts alone, and can be fully understood only within the context of the whole system.[8]

One application of systems thinking can be seen in recent developments in the study of evolution (see Davies, 1988; Bohm, 1983; and Peat, 1991). As most of us learned in school, Darwin based his evolutionary theory on the ideas of chance variation and natural selection; neo-Darwinism expanded on those ideas by including the concept of *genetic* mutation, yet the theory remains grounded in the concept of natural selection (see Davies, 1988).

A new systems theory of evolution posits the existence of a second phenomenon in evolution in addition to natural selection: symbiogenesis. Symbiosis is the tendency of different organisms to live in close association with one another and often one inside the other. For example, our life is dependent on the bacteria that live in our intestines. Symbiogenesis is the process of living systems co-evolving with their environments, including the organisms in that environment. In other words, environments influence the evolution of living systems and vice versa (see Margulis and Sagan, 1986; see also Maturana and Varela, 1998; and Capra, 1996).

Scientists Lynn Margulis and Dorion Sagan theorize that the creation of new forms of life occurs through this symbiotic process, and that cooperation and mutual dependence among all life-forms is the central aspect of evolution: "The view of evolution as chronic bloody competition among individuals and species, a popular distortion of Darwin's notion of 'survival of the fittest,' dissolves before a new view of continual cooperation, strong interaction, and mutual dependence among life forms. Life did not take over the globe by combat, but by networking" (1986, pp. 14–15).

In the context of mediation, systems thinking (and such concepts as symbiogenesis) reminds us of the interdependence of the parties and mediator. This may seem obvious. However, much of the training mediators receive points in the opposite direction, with an emphasis on the competing interests of the parties in conflict resolution. One example of this tendency in almost all mediation training today is the emphasis on the parties' BATNAs (an acronym for "best alternative to a negotiated agreement"; see Fisher, Ury, and Patton, 1991). To be sure, mediators encourage parties to look at their underlying interests and seek opportunities to maximize those interests jointly through mutually advantageous exchange. Yet there is a deeper link between and among the parties and the mediator, and systems thinking suggests how, even during the relatively brief period of a mediation, we influence each other's interests, goals, and needs. In other words, each episode of conflict resolution is an opportunity for personal evolution, undertaken in cooperation with those around us.

The phenomenon of symbiogenesis offers a model of mediation in which the participants (including the mediator) grow, evolve, and change symbiotically. Many mediators have had the satisfying experience of participating in a mediation that resulted in an emotionally charged, cathartic resolution that deeply affected everyone involved in the process—that indeed left them "changed" by the experience. This type of growth (or coevolution) is powerful because of its mutuality; it cannot be accomplished alone. Moreover, it is unlikely to happen unless the mediator is attuned to opportunities for growth and change and able, because of his or her personal qualities, to support them. Looking at the process of mediation more broadly, one could even describe its increasingly widespread use as an evolutionary change that is leading our world toward higher levels of cooperation and mutual dependence.

Self-Organization Theory

Self-organization theory grew out of the early years of cybernetics. Scientists studying the capabilities of computers did an experiment in the 1950s in which they built models of binary, or simple on-off, networks (Capra, 1996). One such network had lamps that were designed to turn on and off at the connecting nodes in response to a bulb turning on or off at an adjacent node or nodes. The scientists activated this network by turning on certain random bulbs and were amazed to discover that after a short time of random flickering, ordered patterns emerged. They even observed waves and repeated cycles passing through the network. These networks, also known as Boolean networks, may lead, according to researcher Stuart Kauffman (1995), to an answer to fundamental questions regarding life emerging spontaneously from chaos to order through the collective, coherent dynamics of the coordinated behavior of the coupled molecules in such networks.

Russian scientists studying chemical reactions made an analogous discovery. These scientists mixed simple red and white chemicals and blended them so that they were in equilibrium. They then added other chemicals to the mixture of red and white, applied heat to the mixture, and tried other variables. The chemicals reacted by separating into red and white, but then restructuring themselves into beautiful swirling, spiraling patterns. The phenomenon, called the Belousov-Zhabotinsky reaction, demonstrates the ability of matter to restructure itself at an entirely new level of organization (see Wheatley, 1992; see also Wheatley, 1996; and Prigogine and Stengers, 1995).

These two phenomena—the process of random light connections becoming ordered patterns and the restructuring of matter into something new—and many other experiments led to the development of "self-organization" theory (see Capra, 1996; see also Kauffman, 1995). As this theory developed, it became clear that a distinguishing characteristic of a vital, living system is its ability to self-organize.

The field of biology offers a third set of studies examining self-organization. Autopoiesis, which means self-making (combining the Greek word *auto,* meaning "self," and *poiesis,* "making"), is a concept developed by Chilean neuroscientists Humberto Maturana and Francisco Varela. When Maturana and Varela studied the distinction between living and nonliving systems, they discovered that living systems were always composed of networks. Autopoiesis is a process that allows evolutionary change to happen within networks, by enabling these networks to "self-make." Within these living networks, such as the network of our cells or our organs, each component in the network helps produce and transform other components while maintaining the fundamental characteristics of the network (see Maturana and Varela, 1998). The cells in our own bodies are an example of the self-making process, as they break down and build up new structures, tissues, and organs in constant cycles, even as we maintain our fundamental identity, or pattern of organization. Capra writes: "Many of these cyclical changes occur much faster than one would imagine. For example, our pancreas replaces most of its cells every twenty-four hours, the cells of our stomach lining are reproduced every three days, our white blood cells are renewed in ten days, and 98 percent of the protein in our brain is turned over in less than one month" (Capra, 1996, pp. 218–219).

From their examination of this fundamental attribute of living systems, Maturana and Varela moved on to study the nature of the mind. They concluded that the mind is not a thing but a process. The mind is cognition, the process of knowing. They called this the Santiago theory. Cognition, according to the theory, is the process by which an autopoietic network, or a living system (the mind), self-organizes and self-renews (see Maturana and Varela, 1998; see also Capra, 1996). According to Maturana and Varela, this "process of cognition or knowing" or self-making ". . . compels us to adopt an attitude of permanent vigilance against the temptation of certainty. It compels us to recognize that certainty is not a proof of truth. It compels us to realize that the world everyone sees is not *the* world but *a* world which we bring forth with others. . . . The authors of the Santiago theory . . . assert that . . . there are no objectively existing structures; there is no pre-given territory of which we can make a map—the map making itself brings forth the features of the territory" (Maturana and Varela, 1998, p. 245; see also Capra, 1996).

One possible application of this theory for mediators comes in the early stages of the mediation process, when the mediator elicits from the parties an account of what happened—that is, what led them to enter the mediation process in the first place. The Santiago theory and the concept of autopoiesis suggest another way of understanding that step in the process. For many of us, our operating assumption is that there is some objective reality of what happened. We often try to discern that reality from the parties' accounts, even if the accounts are incomplete or self-serving. However, what we usually find is that the parties in conflict have vastly differing views of what happened. The Santiago theory suggests that for each of us reality is a unique creation (Maturana and Varela, 1998).

These theories suggest that every system (and thus every individual) has a history and process of organizing itself. Our worldview is a result of the completely different influences and experiences we have had in our lives and therefore a unique perception of reality. As our cognition does not take in and store an objective reality (which was the old mechanistic view), our accounts of "what happened," whether in a mediation or elsewhere, are a product of our own creation of meaning and order.

If reality is defined individually, these theories suggest that we as mediators "create" the conflict resolution process through our perception of the participants, the conflict, and our role in it as conflict resolvers. Just as our clients have created the conflict they bring to us and perceive that conflict through their particular worldview, so we as mediators perceive the conflict through a worldview that is a product of our own creation. Accordingly, who we are—that is, the personal qualities we bring into the mediation room—begins to take on larger significance. These qualities affect not only our impact on the parties and the conflict resolution process but also the manner in which that process assumes a reality for us as mediators (see Bohm, 1983). Mediation, in this worldview, has the features of an autopoietic system—one that, as described by Margaret Wheatley, is "not the fragile, fragmented world we attempt to hold together, but a universe rich in processes that support growth and coherence, individuality and community" (see Wheatley, 1992, pp. 18–19; and Maturana and Varela, 1998).

Chaos Theory

Another metaphor from the physical sciences that may be useful in thinking about our influence as actors in the mediation process is chaos theory, which involves the study of systems that appear so complex in their details as to defy description and explanation, such as turbulent rivers, weather patterns, and brain wave activity (see Peat, 1991; and Davies, 1988). Chaos theory has many startling implications, among them the concept that very subtle changes in one part of a complex system (such as atmospheric conditions) can cause enormous changes within that system as the ripple effect of the initial change mounts. This insight grew out of attempts by one of the founders of chaos theory, Edward Lorenz, to create a computer model that would predict weather. Recalling an ancient Chinese proverb that the power of a butterfly's wings can be felt on the other side of the world, Lorenz demonstrated that weather patterns are so sensitive to subtle changes that they defy accurate long-range prediction, leading him to inquire whether the proverb might be literally true (see Davies, 1988; and Kauffman, 1995).

For mediators, chaos theory suggests that the infinite complexity of the dispute resolution systems in which we find ourselves has the paradoxical effect of both limiting and extending our ability to influence that system. Our ability is limited by the number of variables at work; we simply cannot understand all of the layers of experience, meaning, emotion, and intention that the participants (including the mediator) bring to the table. However, we can take some measure of comfort from a description of chaos theory by one commentator, who writes that "you cannot direct a living system, you can only disturb it. In a system, the most we can do, when we are trying to serve, is to contribute a little twitch, be a little disturbance. . . . You cannot tell another human being or a human organization what to do and expect it to do it" (Wheatley, 1996, 23).

This is not to say that a slight "twitch" is all that we can do as mediators. Our interventions sometimes need to be more forceful, even blunt. However, in some cases, a slight twitch may be enough. In other words, the effectiveness of our interventions often arises not from their forcefulness but instead from their authenticity. When our actions as mediators—whether they are directed at mundane questions or questions that go to the heart of the matter— communicate a high degree of genuineness, presence, and integration, even the gentlest of interventions may produce dramatic results.

Implications for Mediation Practice

Taken together, the scientific theories we have briefly described here offer a new way of looking at our physical environment that emphasizes connection over separateness and interdependence over independence. These theories do not supplant the older theories from which they emerged. For example, scientists still build bridges and launch rockets using Newtonian principles and not those of quantum physics. Meteorologists go on predicting the weather using such tools as radar, notwithstanding the complexities of chaos theory. Among the common elements of the new sciences are that they (1) offer insights into phenomena that operate at a higher degree of subtlety than scientists had heretofore detected (for example, the behavior of subatomic particles) and (2) point to a higher degree of integration in the world's living (and nonliving) systems.

These common elements correspond to two themes we believe are relevant to the study and practice of mediation: (1) there are phenomena at work in mediation that operate on a level of subtlety that we have only begun to fathom and (2) mediation is a process that we can better understand as an integrated system than as a set of discrete interactions between and among individuals acting autonomously.

Both of these themes are relevant from the standpoint of the personal qualities of the mediator and their impact on the process.

For one thing, as shown by the psychologists' studies of neurolinguistic programming and the studies showing the impact of human pheromones, we as individuals influence each other in ways that are so subtle as to defy conscious detection or control. What this means for mediators is that once we have learned the basic principles and skills of mediation, and practiced them to the point where they feel natural, the next frontier of learning and development is within ourselves.

There are well-developed curricula focusing on the first two stages of mediator development—skill and theory—but we are not aware of any mediation training focused on personal development. Although it lies beyond the scope of what we are attempting to describe in this chapter, some consideration of the design of such a curriculum would, in our view, be worth undertaking. Just as there are many approaches to training in the areas of mediation skills and theory, we can imagine many possible approaches to training focused on the third stage of mediator development.

Second, our influence, and the influence of the parties with whom we work, sets in motion a process in which each participant's view of the conflict and each other is immutably altered. This is not a one-way street. The mediator's views and outlook may be influenced by the parties as much as the other way around. Far too often, when we attempt to understand or analyze the mediation process, we separate out the mediator, or the conflict partners, or the content of the mediation, or the kind of mediation, or the techniques used, or the particular mediation theory followed. A more fruitful approach may be to examine the process contextually, seeking to understand the relationships that are evolving and coming into existence as the process unfolds.

When we are mediating, if our approach is "I am the mediator, separate from the conflict, and my clients are here because they have a problem," we are not thinking about the mediation process systemically. The systems approach would involve thinking more along these lines: "I, as the mediator, am about to become a part of this conflict. How am I reacting to my clients? How are they reacting to me? How do I generally react to this kind of conflict in my own life? What qualities am I bringing into the midst of this conflict which will support its resolution?"[9]

The "Integrated" Mediator

Integration is a quality that we may never fully achieve but are constantly developing. It is a quality that, we believe, mediators should foster for two reasons. First, it is a positive model for the parties—bringing peace, if you will, into the room. In the words of Thich Nhat Hanh (1987, p. 1), "If we are peaceful, everyone in our family, our entire society will benefit from our peace." Second, by subtle means that are more easily described than understood, the "integrated" mediator's presence aligns the parties and mediation process in a more positive direction.

The Integrated Mediator at Work

As noted earlier, the mediation process can best be understood as a system in which the relationships of the parties to each other and to the mediator are in flux. Because of the fluidity of this system, and the parties' expectations that the mediator may be able to assist them in reaching a resolution, the mediator has an extraordinary opportunity to shape the direction of the parties' interactions and discussions.

As they consider the parties' accounts of their dispute, mediators distill in their own minds a vision of the dispute based on (1) their own perceptions of the parties (for example, their credibility, rationality, and objectivity, or lack of same) and (2) their own worldview. In short, mediators re-create the dispute, putting their own stamp on their vision of the dispute. This is unavoidable because each of us has our own experience of the world and our own perception of reality. What we see "is not *the* world but *a* world" (Capra, 1996).

The personal qualities of the mediator thus affect his or her ability to sort through the clutter of emotion, accusation, and recrimination that the parties bring to the table. The qualities we have described as integration enable the mediator to be aware (and accepting) of the limitations of not only the parties' partial (or what some might consider distorted) views but also his or her own partial views.

These same qualities help the mediator envision an integration of the parties' interests. Why? Because once mediators can experience their own views of the dispute as having a validity that is neither less than nor greater than that of the parties, they can begin to feel comfortable relinquishing their own vision of the right way or the best way to resolve the dispute, and abandon any intention of imposing that vision on the parties. Instead, the mediator seeks, as the first order of business, to establish a genuine relationship with the parties—a relationship that enables the mediator to reach a deeper level of understanding of the parties' views and objectives. Nonjudgmental awareness of the parties' needs thus constitutes the starting point for the mediator to use his or her influence, in a graceful and appropriate way, to guide the process toward resolution.

Imagine, if you will, a jigsaw puzzle in which the pieces can autonomously change their shape. The person attempting to solve such a puzzle has to continuously adjust his or her vision of how the pieces might align themselves to make a whole. Mediators are, in some ways, trying to solve such a puzzle. They seek to understand, with the same degree of detachment as the person solving the puzzle, the manner and extent to which the parties are willing to adjust their positions to fit those of the other parties, and yet paradoxically they can do so only by involving themselves in a deeply personal way with the parties.

Consider still another metaphor for the mediator's work: that of a medical doctor. Dr. Jerome Groopman, an oncologist and AIDS researcher at Boston's Beth Israel/Deaconess Hospital, is known as a physician of "last resort," a healer to whom other physicians send patients whose condition appears to be beyond treatment. Here is a description by Groopman of his diagnostic procedures, beginning with his conversation with a patient named Kirk:

> "I want to hear the story directly from you—not from the records—and in detail. . . . Then I'll examine you. From top to bottom. After that, we'll think this through together. . . ."
>
> In having him repeat his medical history and physical examination now for the fourth time, I wasn't performing a perfunctory ritual. . . . [E]ven if I discovered no new fact or physical finding, there was a journey taken when I listened to a patient recount his history and when I palpated his body. It was a journey of the senses—hearing, touching, seeing—which carried me into another dimension, that of intuition.
>
> I planned to walk deliberately along the milestones of Kirk's life . . . the extent of his education, the nature of his occupation . . . the status of his personal relationships, the vicissitudes of his prior and current illnesses and treatments—and for brief but illuminating moments I became integrated into his experience.
>
> After imagining his past through his retold history, I would be prepared to enter his present through the physical examination. My hands would press deeply into his abdomen to outline the breadth and texture of his inner organs; my eyes would peer behind his pupils to read the barometers of cerebral pressure and blood flow displayed on his retinas; my ears, linked by the stethoscope, would hear the timbre of his heart [Groopman, 1997, pp. 8–9].

The integrated mediator works in similar ways, taking the temperature of the room and the parties in it, diagnosing the causes of their dispute and their difficulties in resolving it, and trying to unlock the healing potential present in the parties themselves. To practice mediation in this way is a task of both mind and heart. It requires the mediator to integrate, in his or her relationship with the parties and their dispute, both cool detachment and profound engagement.

Personal Development

If it is true that we can increase our effectiveness as mediators by developing the ability to be authentically present and fully integrated within a conflict system, how do we develop those qualities?

This is a question that, in our view, must be answered individually. Some have found the answer in such practices as meditation, yoga, or religious discipline; some in psychological inquiry or other avenues of personal growth and self-discovery. In *The Seven Habits of Highly Effective People* (1989), Stephen R. Covey discusses the various techniques used by individuals to "sharpen the saw"—physically, mentally, emotionally, and spiritually. Philosopher Kenneth Wilbur gives this description of a process he found useful in reaching a higher level of self-understanding:

> My life is not simply a series of flatly objective events laid out in front of me like so many rocks with simple location that I am supposed to stare at until I see the surfaces more clearly. My life includes a deeply subjective component that I must come to understand and interpret to myself. It is not just surfaces; it has depths. And while surfaces can be seen, depths must be interpreted. And the more adequately I can interpret my own depths, then the more transparent my life will become to me. The more clearly I can see and understand it, the less it baffles me, perplexes me, pains me in its opaqueness [Wilbur, 1996, p. 93].

Developing these qualities requires focus and intention. As we focus on understanding and interpreting our own depths, we develop a greater ability to be present with a wider and wider variety of conflict. We develop a mastery over ourselves and therefore over the process of supporting the resolution of conflict.

Obviously there are many paths to greater awareness, and our purpose in discussing this aspect of personal development is not to advocate any one of them. However, we do suggest that the growing interest in this dimension of the mediator's work, as evidenced by the increasing number of articles on spirituality and mediation, reflects a significant direction in which our field is evolving (for example, see Zumeta, 1993; and Gold, 1993).

Most importantly, we need not wait until we are in a mediation to practice developing these qualities. One can, and perhaps should, focus on the development of these qualities in every aspect of one's life. Presence is a quality that can be developed in all areas of our life. In the heat of any personal conflict, one can work on developing the capacity to be present to every aspect of that conflict, while stepping aside from one's own point of view and learning to distinguish one's thoughts, from one's emotions, from one's perceptions, from our conflict partner's point of view, to embrace a broader, more integrated, view—in the words of Thich Nhat Hanh (1987), to "be peace." By developing the quality of our own presence in every aspect of life, we not only expand our capacity to bring that presence of peace into our work as mediators, we also develop our ability to fulfill our own life.

As we consider this form of personal development, we should not overlook the impact of the mediation process itself—the extent to which we are influenced by the parties, their dispute, and the manner in which it is resolved. If, as we contend, integration is a quality that we never fully achieve but develop over time, one of the benefits of our work as mediators is that it may foster such development. In most mediations, we encounter parties whose disputes do not differ radically from conflicts that have arisen in our own lives—that is, their issues are our issues. To be effective in such a setting, we must address our own need for growth, in our relationships with our clients and in our lives outside the mediation. A truly successful resolution of a mediation thus can become, for the mediator, a metaphor for the personal challenges in his or her life and a means for achieving a higher level of personal integration.

Conclusion

We have described three stages of development that we and many other mediators have taken on: (1) training in the basic skills of mediation, (2) developing a greater intellectual understanding of the process, and (3) developing the personal qualities that make us more effective dispute resolvers. We have also described some developments from the social sciences and physical sciences that offer useful metaphors for thinking about conflict and its resolution. These metaphors enable us to see more clearly how the mediator is inevitably part of the conflict he or she seeks to resolve. This way of understanding the dispute resolution process informs our view that the personal qualities of the mediator can be influential in shaping that process and its outcome.

The personal qualities that assist us in becoming better mediators are not the same for each of us, nor are our paths to achieving those qualities the same. We have attempted to describe in this chapter those qualities—self-awareness, presence, authenticity, congruence, integration—the development of which constitutes the "third task" in our progress as mediators. However, any attempts to describe these elusive qualities must always fall short of the mark. Understanding what the qualities are and why they work is always both highly personal and situational, a product of the moment and the people in it. Developing these qualities is a process of time, intention, and discipline, and it comes, in our view, not from intellectual inquiry or scholarship but from experience. To paraphrase Oscar Wilde, these are qualities that can be learned but they cannot be taught.

Reflective Practice Questions

As we noted in the Introduction, the reflective practice questions at the end of each chapter are intended to highlight aspects of the chapter that, in our view, bear on the overall themes of this volume.

1. What are the qualities in you that most contribute to bringing a peaceful presence into the room?

2. Have you experienced the mediation equivalent of the Hawthorne effect, or the quantum physicist's theory regarding the impact of the observer on an experiment? That is, when you serve as a mediator, do the parties appear to behave differently in your presence?

3. Do you agree with the view of mediation as a system that involves you, your personal qualities, your influence on the parties, and their influence on you? If so, what impact does the systems view have on your practice?

References

Angier, N. "Study Finds Signs of Elusive Pheromones in Humans." *New York Times*, Mar. 12, 1998, Sect. A, p. 22.

Bohm, D. *Wholeness and the Implicate Order*. New York: Routledge, 1983.

Bohm, D., and Hiley, B. J. *The Undivided Universe*. New York: Routledge, 1993.

Boulie, B. *Mediation: Principle, Process, Practice*. London: Butterworth, 1996.

Browde, I. "Mediators of the Future: Learning Guides." *Mediation News* (newsletter of the Academy of Family Mediators), Spring 1996.

Bush, R. B., and Folger, J. *The Promise of Mediation*. San Francisco: Jossey-Bass, 1994.

Capra, F. *The Web of Life*. New York: Anchor Books, 1996.

Cloke, K. *Mediation: Revenge and the Magic of Forgiveness*. Santa Monica, Calif.: Center for Dispute Resolution, 1994.

Covey, S. *The Seven Habits of Highly Effective People*. New York: Simon & Schuster, 1989.

Davies, P. *The Cosmic Blueprint: New Discoveries in Nature's Creative Ability to Order the Universe*. New York: Simon & Schuster, 1988.

Dworkin, J., Jacob, L., and Scott, E. "The Boundaries Between Mediation and Therapy: Ethical Dilemmas." *Mediation Quarterly*, Winter 1991, 9, 107–119.

Fierman, L. B. *The Therapist Is the Therapy*. Northvale, N.J.: Aronson, 1997.

Fisher, R., Ury, W., and Patton, B. *Getting to YES: Negotiating Agreement Without Giving In* (2nd ed.). New York: Penguin Books, 1991.

Fukushima, S. "What You Bring to the Table: Transference and Countertransference in the Negotiation Process." *Negotiation Journal*, 1999, 15, 169.

Gasset, J. O. *The Dehumanization of Art, and Other Essays on Art, Culture and Literature*. Princeton, N.J.: Princeton University Press, 1948.

Gill-Austern, G. "Staying the Course: An Apprenticeship in Mediation." Unpublished paper on file with the authors, 1994.

Gillespie, R. *Manufacturing Knowledge: A History of the Hawthorne Experiments*. New York: Cambridge University Press, 1991.

Gold, L. "Influencing Unconscious Influences: The Healing Dimension of Mediation." *Mediation Quarterly*, Fall 1993, 11, 55–66.

Groopman, J. *The Measure of Our Days: New Beginnings at Life's End*. New York: Penguin Books, 1997.

Hanh, T. N. *Being Peace*. Berkeley: Parallax Press, 1987.

Kabat-Zinn, J. *Wherever You Go, There You Are*. New York: Hyperion, 1994.

Kauffman, S. *At Home in the Universe: The Search for Laws of Self-Organization and Complexity*. New York: Oxford University Press, 1995.

Kelly, J. "Mediation and Psychotherapy: Distinguishing the Differences." *Mediation Quarterly*, Fall 1983, 1, 33–44.

Kottler, J. *The Compleat Therapist*. San Francisco: Jossey-Bass, 1991.

Kovel, J. *A Complete Guide to Therapy: From Psychoanalysis to Behavior Modification*. New York: Pantheon Books, 1976.

Lang, M. "Becoming Reflective Practitioners." Jan. 1998 [www.mediate.com/articles/reflect.cfm]

Margulis, L., and Sagan, D. *Microcosmos: Four Billion Years of Evolution from Our Microbial Ancestors*. New York: Summit Books, 1986.

Maturana, H. R., and Varela, F. J. *The Tree of Knowledge: The Biological Roots of Human Understanding* (trans. R. Paolucci). Boston: Shambhala (distributed by Random House), 1998.

Matz, D. "The Hope of Mediation." Unpublished paper on file with the authors, 1999.

McEwen, C. A., and Maiman, R. M. "Small Claims Mediation in Maine: An Empirical Assessment." *Maine Law Review*, 1981, 33, 237–268.

Norcross, J. C., and Guy, J. D. "Ten Therapists: The Process of Becoming and Being." In W. Dryden and L. Spurling (eds.), *On Becoming a Psychotherapist*. London and New York: Tavistock/Routledge, 1989.

O'Connor, J., with Seymour, J. *Introducing Neuro-Linguistic Programming*. Glasgow: Thorsons, 1993.

Peat, F. D. *The Philosopher's Stone: Chaos, Synchronicity and the Hidden Order of the World*. New York: Bantam Books, 1991.

Prigogine, I., and Stengers, I. *Order out of Chaos: Man's New Dialogue with Nature*. New York: Bantam Books, 1995.

Richards, M. C. *Centering: In Pottery, Poetry, and the Person*. Middletown, Conn.: Wesleyan University Press, 1962.

Ryan, P. *Profile of a Litigator: Personality Traits of the Personal Injury Attorney*. Sacramento: Droit, 1996.

Simkin, W. E., and Fidandis, N. A. *Mediation and the Dynamics of Collective Bargaining*. New York: BNA, 1986.

Wheatley, M. *Leadership and the New Science*. San Francisco: Berrett-Koehler, 1992.

Wheatley, M. "The Unplanned Organization: Learning from Nature's Emergent Creativity." *Noetic Sciences Review*, Spring 1996, no. 37, 20–21.

Wilbur, K. *A Brief History of Everything*. Boston: Shambhala, 1996.

Zumeta, Z. "Spirituality and Mediation." *Mediation Quarterly*, Fall 1993, *11*, 25–38.

2

What Are the Personal Qualities of the Mediator?

Kenneth Cloke

Self-Portrait
It doesn't interest me if there is one God
or many gods
I want to know if you belong or feel
abandoned
If you know despair or can see it in others
I want to know
if you are prepared to live in the world
with its harsh need
to change you. If you can look back
with firm eyes
saying this is where I stand. I want to know
if you know
how to melt into that fierce heat of living
falling toward
the center of your longing. I want to know
if you are willing
to live day by day, with the consequences of love
and the bitter
unwanted passion of your sure defeat...
—David Whyte

What are the personal qualities of the mediator? David Whyte's poem is probably the best answer because it reveals the hidden, subterranean soul of mediation, and leads us to where the magic begins, at the uncertain, *dangerous* edge of who we are and what we are doing.

The question is well worth exploring, partly because it is already the answer to a larger question, and partly because every thoughtful answer conjures up a set of deeper questions. In the end, neither the question nor the answer matters. What matters is the dance between them. What matters, in the words of physicist Richard Feynman (1999), is "the pleasure of finding things out."

The question "What are the personal qualities of the mediator?" already implies that mediation is a place where personal qualities matter; that there is no single correct answer to certain questions; that varying answers enrich our understanding of the meaning of the question; that learning can take place within the invisible field of a well-posed question; and that mediation is a process in which the answer to certain questions might make a difference.

Every question we ask is one that asks itself of us, just as every intervention in the lives of others intervenes in our own lives, often in subtle, unpredictable ways. Deep questions are not objects we manipulate, but forces that also manipulate us. By asking and answering questions in mediation, we do not merely mediate; we both *become* and *create* mediation.

Conflicts, like dreams, are made of desires and fears, honesty and deceit, passion and surrender, all of which lie beneath the surface and are revealed through a mediator's questions. Our willingness to answer these same questions ourselves gives us permission to search for the piercing, pivotal, dangerous moments that can change people's lives, and the courage to seek them out, even in our own lives.

To answer the question "What are the personal qualities of the mediator?" we first need to ask "What is mediation?" There may be an infinite number of correct answers to this question. Here are a few that reflect my experience. Mediation is a search for the invisible bridge that connects every living being with every other. It is a poem made of intention and vulnerability, of ecstasy and suffering. It is a reweaving of souls. It is an opening through which we are able to glimpse the other, naked and divine. It is a synchronization of heartbeats. It is a fierce, life-and-death struggle of each person with himself or herself. It is a design for creating a different future. It is a gentle, responsive exploration of the space between us. It is a breach in the myth of what we know to be true, leading to transformation and transcendence.

By defining mediation in these ways, we automatically initiate a deeper level of inquiry. We now need to ask, "What are the personal qualities of mediators that can result in such mediations?" and "What are the personal qualities mediators acquire as a *result* of mediating in these ways?" and "Is the nature of mediation a result of our personal qualities, or is it the other way around, or both?"

In my experience, we are privileged observers, intrepid explorers, and in some cases skillful navigators, of the tides and currents, forces and fields, twists and turns that intersect, overflow, and silently meander through the conflicts we mediate. We are better able to hear and help others navigate these tides and currents if we are able to hear and help ourselves.

Perhaps the first personal quality of mediators is the recognition that our "personal qualities" are fluid, and both a cause and an effect of what we do in mediation; that *who we are* is constantly being reinvented by what we do, just as what we do is constantly being redefined by who we are. I know that mediation has changed me, and that even though I brought a number of personal qualities that have aided me in its practice, I also brought a number that were useless or counterproductive. In the interaction between who I was and what I did, I discovered weak or insignificant qualities that suddenly became useful, simultaneously transforming both me and the way I mediated.

As with any craft, the more one practices the more skillful one becomes. Yet it is a conceit to think we are skillful or powerful enough to transform other people's lives without their active desire and willing participation, or that who *we* are matters most in resolving *their* conflicts. The fundamental reasons we are successful is that they want us to be. Often all we do is clear the obstacles to their communication and ask questions that lead them back to who they already are.

Nonetheless, there is a deeper truth concealed in the question. It is easier to assist conflicted parties in being authentic and centered with one another if we are authentic and centered, than if we are off-balance, inauthentic, ego-driven, or locked in conflicts of our own. The skills parties require most in mediation are the ones we *already* naturally possess but have often forgotten how to use—skills of honesty, empathy, intuition, and authenticity. These skills are less about unique personal qualities than the qualities of being a unique person.

As everyone is different, each of us approaches mediation in our own way, using our skills with numerous parties for various purposes, and thereby becoming new people, resulting in radically differing answers to the same question. For some of us, mediation means negotiating a cease-fire, while for others it is facilitating a settlement, ending a dispute, resolving the underlying reasons people are fighting in the first place, transforming the parties, dismantling dysfunctional systems, promoting compromise, encouraging dialogue, ending litigation, coaching parties to let go and move on, promoting forgiveness, empowering dialogue, recommending solutions, or achieving reconciliation.

Having said this, I believe there is a profound difference between the personal qualities of mediators who, on the one hand, simply want the conflict to go away because it feels frightening and dangerous, and are relieved when it is over; and those, on the other hand, who embrace each conflict because they recognize that the very qualities that make it frightening and dangerous also contain its deepest, clearest truths, and who are self-reflective when it is over.

The personal qualities of mediators also differ with each variety and type of dispute. In conflicts involving teenagers, for example, it is clear that the most effective personal quality of the mediator may be *being* a teenager oneself. Organizational disputes, business disputes, interracial disputes, legal disputes all call for qualities in the mediator that encourage trust and an ability to decode the subtle meanings of specialized forms of communication between the parties. According to this calculus, an angry, illiterate drug addict off the street could make a better mediator in certain kinds of conflict than a reasoned, respected jurist.

The personal qualities of the mediator also differ according to the question being asked. If the question is being asked, for example, by someone who wants to create a screening device that differentiates good from bad mediators, or to certify professionals by identifying criteria for inclusion, there will be a search for universal answers and objective measurements. But if the question is being asked by someone who wants to explore personal development, increase diversity in the profession, or identify a broad array of potentially useful mediation skills, there will be a search for qualities that are unique to each person and can only be measured subjectively.

Mediation, in my view, should not become the exclusive province of college graduates, professionals, or people with particular personal qualities. Rather, it is something we all need to know how to do. Nearly everyone can learn to mediate, from nursery school children to juvenile offenders, violent prisoners, illiterate peasants, political radicals, and corporate executives, all of whom I have seen mediate successfully. Mediation is a life skill and a social art in which everyone ought to be trained. In some distant, unimaginable future, mediation training might even be considered a human right.

If our reason for asking the question is our desire for acknowledgment or self-congratulation, or our desire to be better or more evolved than the parties with whom we mediate, the answers will be skewed, self-aggrandizing, and inflated. In truth, parties in conflict can be more open to feelings, more vulnerable and honest about what is not working, more capable of listening and creative in coming up with solutions than their mediators. We become less successful in resolving conflicts when we form too high an opinion of our own contribution in bringing it about.

If our reason for asking the question is to establish a norm, or a set of optimal personal qualities to use in training others, we need to recognize, as Oscar Wilde quipped (and as noted in Chapter One), that "nothing worth knowing can be taught." This does not mean it cannot be learned, but rather that certain kinds of learning take place from the inside out, not the outside in. Although instinct, empathy, and intuition, for example, can be observed, discussed, cultivated, and developed, it is extremely difficult to teach someone how to practice them. In addition, many of these personal qualities of mediators arise only through a long, deep, subtle process of self-examination that is not foreshadowed by the question.

For these reasons, we may want to pose another set of questions for mediators to answer, questions that concern our *values* and self-discoveries, the challenges we have faced, the struggles we have fought with ourselves, and often lost, and the questions posed by David Whyte's poem. For example, here are some of the values mediation seems to encourage, both in the parties and more gradually in ourselves:

- Valuing conflict as positive, seeing it as an adventure or journey, an opportunity for growth and change, an invitation to intimacy and relationship, and an opening for transformation

- Valuing diversity and difference, and rejecting stereotypes and assumptions of innate superiority and inferiority, correctness and heresy

- Valuing openness, honesty, and empathy in communication, process, and relationships

- Valuing agreement and commonality, oneness and humanity; and rejecting domination, coercion, humiliation, and suppression

- Valuing cooperation and collaboration as primary, and competition and aggression as secondary

- Valuing the satisfaction of everyone's underlying interests

- Valuing the integration of intellect, emotion, body, and spirit; of authenticity and integrity, and the unity of inner and outer

- Valuing the victory that is without defeat

- Valuing forgiveness, completion, and transformation

- Valuing perseverance, and refusing to leave *anyone* behind (Cloke, 2001)

By shifting the question and the dialogue that is prompted by it from a concern for personal qualities that seem innate, to values that are *developmental*, we challenge ourselves to continuously improve our capacity to act with integrity, to align our behavior with our values, and to become what we do. Personal qualities are what appear not only at the beginning but also at the end of the process, reflecting an internalization of values that takes place only *after* they have been lived in practical, day-to-day relationships with others. The place to begin is not with a set of ideal personal qualities to which we vainly aspire, but with the arduous practical struggle to mediate and live every day consistent with our values, ethics, and integrity. Only in this way can we find the answer to the questions framed by David Whyte's poem.

Reflective Practice Questions

1. Have you experienced, in your own work, "piercing, pivotal, dangerous moments" in the management of conflict, and how did those moments affect you?

2. Do you agree with the author's definition of mediation as "a search for the invisible bridge that connects every living being with every other, . . . a poem made of intention and vulnerability, of ecstasy and suffering, . . . a reweaving of souls"? Do you have your own definition?

3. The author emphasizes the mediator's values as a major factor influencing one's approach to mediation. How have your values influenced your work as a dispute resolver? How does the author's list of values compare with your own?

References

Cloke, K. *Mediating Dangerously: The Frontiers of Conflict Resolution.* San Francisco: Jossey-Bass, 2001.

Feynman, R. P. *The Pleasure of Finding Things Out.* Cambridge, Mass.: Perseus, 1999.

Unintentional Excellence

An Exploration of Mastery and Incompetence

Being Also a Rumination on Art, Craft, Career, Bungling, Skill Acquisition, Bell Curves, Baseball, Cooking, Surfing, Dentistry, Tree Trimming, and Why Mediators and Facilitators May Be Dangerous to Those We Are Trying to Help

Peter S. Adler

If you are reading this, the odds are pretty good that you are a mediator, facilitator, ombudsman, or arbitrator. I am too. Mostly I mediate and facilitate. Along with a few other colleagues with whom I am associated, I have been doing this work for about twenty-five years. I study it, practice it, and teach it and find a certain triangular nourishment in doing all three. Primarily, though, I consider myself a practitioner. My specialty is environment, health, and energy issues.

Over the years, I have worked on matters ranging from out-of-watershed bulk water transfers, siting of geothermal power plants, and creation of new telecommunication regulations. I have mediated many other more ordinary cases as well, inside and outside the court system, including disputes over broken promises, barking dogs, fights at weddings, and several especially nasty church and university feuds. Admittedly, plunging into other people's confusions is a peculiar, possibly aberrant way to make a living. Nonetheless, it is what I do, and by some fluke I like doing it.

The author is indebted to colleagues who critiqued early drafts of this paper, among them John Forester, Chris Honeyman, Paul Cosgrave, Robert Benjamin, and Kem Lowry.

Right Livelihood

When I was a graduate student in sociology, one of my professors assured me that I would one day have to choose between working in the world of action versus the world of ideas. Turns out he was wrong. The conflict resolution field combines both and does it beautifully. At its most elemental level, we try to help people get unstuck and solve vexatious and stubborn problems with a methodology that, when it doesn't work, has few serious side effects. When it does work, big things seem to happen. Agreements are made, relationships are improved, and people have new road maps for the future. Intellectually, people like you and me are privileged to study up close and personal the intricate ways human predicaments can be framed and tamed, how solutions can move from being exclusive to inclusive, how adversaries can turn the corner and become partners, and how people who mistrust each other deeply can ultimately face larger problems together.

Because conflict tends to be a sometimes nasty and venal crucible of human affairs, much of what we do is not just repugnant to other people, it is also—when they actually see what goes on—boring. Mediation is not the big theater most people think it is. More often, it is something akin to a doubleheader baseball game. There are a lot of innings with not too much happening, interrupted once in a while by a high-intensity moment when the bases are loaded and a flinty-eyed pitcher goes *mano a mano* with a great slugger. In evolutionary or biological terms (I have never met good metaphors that couldn't be mixed), multiparty and multi-issue mediation is a quintessential example of what evolution expert Stephen Jay Gould called "punctuated equilibrium."

In my practice, I tend to work in the background of public quarrels over natural resources, health, energy development, and social and economic policy. Most of the disputes I get involved in have a lot of parties, are laden with ideological differences, and are fraught with contentious politics and contested science. Usually, there is a legal or regulatory flap going on, or one that everyone recognizes is coming soon. In many of my cases and projects, businesspeople want to make or do something, nongovernmental organizations and community advocates oppose it, and government agencies are struggling to decide which public policies properly apply and in what combination.

I get involved in other conflicts as well. There are the usual business fights: the two corporate officers locked in mortal combat, the shareholder factions trying to wrestle control from each other, and the construction disputes where costs have started to outdistance potential profits. I have been in the middle of family-owned partnership dissolutions in which all sides were slowly descending into the abyss. There have been numerous organizational matters that challenge our best ideas about democracy: parliamentary impasses, strategic planning problems, leadership battles.

Surprisingly, all of these cases follow a certain pattern. People (usually, but not always, of good will) espouse divergent positions or interests. Each side seeks advantage. They clash. They attempt to work things out. They fail. They start demonizing each other. Communication channels get clogged or severed. Deep distrust starts to permeate every transaction. Matters radiate centrifugally or implode centripetally and the dispute escalates. Each side counts on threats, brinkmanship, and bluff to further its position. Finally, staring into the mirror of uncertainty and possibly an inferno of future conflict, someone says "Let's try to mediate." There is a shuffling of feet, small mutterings and throat clearings, a bit of denial and face saving, and finally people consent to sit down and negotiate. To paraphrase my colleague Howard Bellman, "Having made a big mess in the kitchen, they now want me to come in and cook them a nice omelette."

In this kind of melodrama, I have always thought my little part was fairly straightforward. I help people organize difficult, always touchy, and sometimes far-reaching discussions. If I can, I shepherd them through the substantive, procedural, and psychological maze they have created and bring some semblance of discipline to the processes of communication, negotiation, and agreement seeking. In some environmental cases, participants need a lot of help as they puzzle their way toward a reasonable juxtaposition of viable commerce, a healthy environment, and social equity. In other cases, matters come down to interpersonal dynamics and attributions (right or wrong) of avarice, revenge, or honor vindicated. In all cases, regardless of origins and dynamics, I follow Casey Stengel's dictum: "My job is to get all of these guys to hit a home run."

To do this, I try to have a variety of strategies at the ready. Sometimes matters require political disentangling. Other times it is all about way finding, coalition development, vision setting, cohesion building, deal making, and the bargaining out of impasses. Some of what I do seems counterintuitive to people outside our profession. With social workers, educators, psychologists, and others accustomed to endless verbal jujitsu, I try to narrow the issues and focus on problem framing and problem solving. With lawyers, engineers, and business professionals who are comfortable slapping down position papers, I may try to deposition their demands, widen the view plane, and focus on the communication of needs and interests.

Without meaning to boast, I think after twenty-five years of doing this kind of stuff that I now know something about designing good "issue-taming" processes, convening stakeholders, mediating differences of opinions, helping people build constructive working relationships, and infusing high-quality scientific and technical information into deliberations. All of this makes me (and you, if you are also in the trade) potentially incompetent and quite possibly hazardous to the very people we are working so hard to help.

For Whom the Bell Curve Curves

It really makes no difference if you are a grizzled veteran of hundreds of disputes, a newly minted conflict resolver emerging from the womb of the university, or a certified graduate of four 150-hour training programs. Consider this: your clients and participants are at risk from the best of your intentions. Not only that, you yourself are in jeopardy of deluding yourself that you are doing something helpful, that your failures are harmless, and that your successes are great victories. It turns out that the highest forms of proficiency and the lowest forms of incompetence are two ends of the bell curve, with the majority of us falling somewhere in between. Most of us, most of the time, are adequate and unexceptional. Stated differently, we get by.

Unfortunately for conflict resolvers, the bell curve isn't all that helpful if you want to locate or improve your mediation and facilitation skills with any precision. The hotshots can't really tell us what it is they do to be exceptional, and the nincompoops are blithely unaware that what they are doing doesn't work. Although most people think the difference between the two is self-evident ("we know it when we see it"), incompetence may actually be a little easier to ferret out. Cornell psychologist David Dunning says incompetent people tend to be supremely confident in their own abilities and oblivious to the fact that they are mucking things up. Through his research, Dunning found that the blunderers, bunglers, goofs, and ignoramuses among us are actually more confident in themselves than the people who do things well.

Dunning's work gets even more interesting because the incompetents turn out to be in double jeopardy. They not only screw things up but they also lack the reflective skills needed to change their patterns and make things better. Dunning says that this deficiency in self-monitoring skill "explains why the humor-impaired keep telling jokes that are not funny, day traders repeatedly jump back into the market and lose more money," and "the politically clueless continue holding forth at dinner parties on the fine points of campaign strategy" (Goode, 1999). Ambrose Bierce said it even better: "Ignorance ain't so much what you don't know as what you do know that ain't so."

At the other end of the spectrum, we have the more complicated business of "excellence," which the dictionary defines as "ability to an eminent degree" and "surpassing merit, skill, or worth." These definitions sound fine so long as they stay comfortably disembodied from what we actually do. In arenas where it is observably hard to obscure bad results (truck driving, fire fighting, newspaper printing), excellence is about measured performance that is superlative, meaning it is statistically far above the average, light years ahead of what incompetents do, and verifiable and replicable to other observers. All of which is a tricky bit of business when we talk about the stuff mediators, facilitators, and other people in helping professions seem to do.

This is not to say that many good people have not struggled mightily to deepen our understanding of what performance with distinction really is. John Gardner, former head of the Carnegie Corporation and a secretary of health, education, and welfare during the Johnson years, viewed excellence in his area of interest, education, as a set of "critical qualities of mind" conjugally wedded to "durable qualities of character" (Gardner, 1995). Dan Goldin, a longtime NASA administrator, used to argue for human and hardware systems that could be engineered around a "faster, better, cheaper" philosophy, with the implication being that this honed a version of excellence (Bergreen, 2000). Tom Peters, after describing an entire business strategy called MBWA ("management by walking around"), experienced what he himself called "a blinding flash of the obvious." He said that business excellence consists of caring for customers, taking care of your people, and constantly innovating (Peters and Austin, 1985).

In the world of conflict resolution, it has been our professional associations that have thought the hardest about all this. They have actually tried to embrace practical strategies for calibrating and achieving a core level of proficiency. The Society of Professionals in Dispute Resolution, the Academy of Family Mediators, and the Conflict Resolution Education Network, through their newly merged self, the Association for Conflict Resolution, have a fine history of producing standards, ethics, and best-practice statements. Like other professional groups (ranging from dental hygienists to plumbers to feng shui practitioners), mediators and facilitators have been trying to define themselves by what they aspire to do. In the process, excellence has been rendered down to the pursuit of certain core values—voluntarism, inclusion, confidentiality, diversity of opinion—followed by very detailed caveats and admonitions. All of this seems good for beginners and journeymen but not very helpful for people with a dozen or more years of mediation and facilitation experience under their belt.

There is, however, another approach. Beyond the bell curve and our statistical notions of excellence lies what Hawaiian cultural historian George Kanahele called "kina'ole" and what he sought to teach to the owners, executives, bartenders, maids, and bell caps in the island visitor industry. *Kina'ole* means "flawlessness" (Kanahele, 1993). In Old Hawaii, wrote Kanahele, when a warrior, craftsman, priest, or king's official performed a task in his or her line of work, it was expected to be done perfectly and without defect. The concept was something akin to continuously rising standards: doing the right thing, in the right way, at the right time, in the right place, to the right person, for the right reason, with the right feeling. *The first time*. All of which locates our work as mediators in the realm of "craft" as opposed to art and art form, and which brings us to the idea of "mastery."

Proficiency and Its Pathways

Years ago, I heard a description of the "four stages of skill development," which, no matter whether you are learning to play a violin, ride a bicycle, speak Hindi, ice-skate, or presumably mediate disputes, look something like this:[1]

1. Unconscious incompetence
2. Conscious incompetence
3. Conscious competence
4. Unconscious competence

Here's how it seems to work.

Imagine you are walking along a lovely beach one day and you happen to see someone surfing just offshore. It is a warm, bright morning. You stop and watch. Sunlight streams down and dances on the water. Seabirds are squawking and flapping above you. You gaze, mesmerized, as a certain surfer you have been watching steers his board into a wave, catches the leading edge of the wave's inner curl, rises to his feet, zigs and zags and dances down the slope of water, and then rides the break a few hundred feet until the power of the surge plays itself out on the flat of the shore.

Maybe it happens then or maybe it is a day or two later. You are bewitched, smitten with the idea that you can stand up on a stick of wood on top of the water and move with it. You go rent a board, drag it out in the water, fumble and bumble around in the baby surf, and eventually you crouch your way over a small ripple on your knees. You do it again. And again. Eventually you are in a half-standing, half-stooping position. At the end of the day, you have had a grand time goofing off at the beach, gotten fried from the sun, and caught your first few waves.

You could let all this go as an enjoyable one-day escape. Or you could be hooked. If it's the latter, what you have probably just experienced is the first stage of a learning trajectory, "unconscious incompetence." Basically, this is the "dumb and happy" stage of skill acquisition. You are enchanted with what you are experiencing, ignorant about real surfing skills, and oblivious to what you don't know. If you stay the course in your effort to surf, you will, with varying degrees of effort, move into a second phase of learning called "conscious incompetence."

At this point, you are aware of your lack of skills and resolved to learn more. In effect, you now know what it is that you don't know. So you study, practice, and plod your way through a series of recurrent surfing experiences. If you were trying to learn violin, this would be the equivalent of doing scales. If you were studying Hindi, it would be repeated and exaggerated pronunciation, practicing the reading and writing of script, and doing conjugations and declensions. If you were working on bike riding or ice skating, you would be spending a lot of time with skinned knees and elbows or sprawled out on the sidewalk with a cold and sore butt.

Comes a time, however, when you somehow move into a third stage, called "conscious competence." Although there are achievements that seem to mark the passage, it isn't always a clear transition. It just happens. With concentration and great expenditures of energy, you can perform the sequences and techniques that surfing requires. You know something about long boards and short boards, skegs and tethers, and how wax makes a difference to the traction your feet have on a wet piece of fiberglass. You can paddle out, wait for a set, catch a small wave with generally positive results, and have a pretty good time doing all this. Unfortunately, it is also very hard work. After each ride, you are exhausted.

Eventually, of course, things get easier and you cross another invisible frontier. For most people it takes years. For a few it might be months, and for a tiny minority it could be days. It might happen like this. One day you paddle out to a shore break, one that you've been surfing at for a while. You know the geography of this particular stretch of ocean, the reefs, sandbars, and seasonal ocean moods. On this day, you take on a bigger and more challenging wave. Maybe it's strategic or maybe it's just something you decide by impulse. Regardless, you catch it at exactly the right moment, impeccably carve a luminescent groove in the water, revel in the spectral blues and greens and the fluid forces of water in motion, and come out the other side, not tired but energized and exhilarated.

You are now in that place called "unconscious competence," the zone of human affairs where you can surf with a minimum of choreography and without thinking your way through every move. I think of this as mastery, a kind of unintentional excellence that is fluid and beyond the rational procedures and techniques of reason.

When you come to this moment, relish it, because it is usually fleeting. Very shortly, you will start the cycle over again, quite possibly with some new or kindred sport (windsurfing, parasailing, snowboarding), but also when you are confronted by some new aspect of surfing (a bigger wave, a faster set, a cleaner form, a whole new location) that devolves you back to previous stages, and possibly to the very beginning—the unconscious incompetence stage.

The role of the unconscious as a developmental element of competence and incompetence has long been suspected. Recent experiments, however, reveal just how important mental processes are that are normally inaccessible to our conscious self, in shaping professional judgments. In a battery of paper-and-pencil and card-game tests, psychologist Thomas D. Wilson has shown quite clearly that people divine or intuit the rules of the game well before they understand them intellectually. If true, the implications of this are potentially far-reaching. Rather than being some vast swamp of primordial memories and suppressed emotions that only therapists can decipher, the unconscious is probably more akin to Windows, DOS, Unix, or Palm OS. It runs in the background of our thinking, learns and adapts, evaluates circumstances, sets goals, detects threats, judges people, and deduces causes and effects, all below our normal waking radar systems (Begley, 2002).

This also suggests another way of thinking about mastery. Instead of being a condition, or stratum, or state, it is probably more like a succession of unconscious or semiconscious breakdowns and breakthroughs. Mastery isn't persistent and it isn't about continuous precision, though it may well be perceived that way by those who have not been exposed to the fundamentals. To the contrary, mastery is full of interruptions, failures, reversions to old patterns, discoveries, and small incremental gains. But there is also something else at play that the four-stages model of skill development doesn't pick up: an obsession with perfection.

Gifted and remarkable people, says Malcolm Gladwell in a marvelous article on what he calls "physical geniuses," have great passion for their work and endless inquisitiveness about how to do it better. They are in love with what they do and they do it over and over. They seem to be on a high-level quest for exactness, flawlessness, and precision, and their commitment to the pursuit is recognizable by others. Fighter pilots (the Top Guns) and professional athletes (the Pro Bowlers) are good examples, but so too are many auto mechanics, barbers, and chiropractors I know. Everyday lives are filled with great examples, if we stay alert for them.

High on my personal list is Dr. Harry Ishida, who is able to bring science, craft, and art together in dazzling ways. Harry is my dentist. He understands mouth anatomy, jaw dynamics, and disease. He works with human and synthetic materials with equal dexterity, does extractions and fillings without pain, casts molds, shapes molars, and does all of this and more with a continuing, quiet competence that I have admired for many years. The same is true of Bill Steinhoff, the guy who annually trims our sixty-year-old avocado tree. For all of his 215 pounds of bulk and discomfort in social situations, Bill is agile, graceful, and shrewd when he gets anywhere near a tree. Moving through the branches and limbs, he is constantly surveying the tree, looking at the health of leaves and bark, examining its features, and noting the tree's basic desire to grow over and into my neighbor's window. Like Ishida, Steinhoff translates complex ideas into demanding movements and intentional strategies, in this case, the craft of the arborist (Adler, 1993).

Then there is Charlie Wilson (no relation to psychologist Thomas D. Wilson), who, according to Gladwell, is one of the best brain surgeons in the country. He is a high achiever who works mainly on pituitary tumors. Wilson thrives on complexity. Gladwell reports this reflection from one of Wilson's younger colleagues: "Most people are afraid of aneurysms. He wasn't afraid of them at all. He was like a cat playing with a mouse" (Gladwell, 1999, p. 58). Or listen to Anthony Bourdain, a well-regarded chef who is also a heroin addict; he never wanted to do anything else except work with food. "Line cooking done well," he says, "is a beautiful thing to watch. It's a high-speed collaboration resembling, at its best, ballet or modern dance. A properly organized, full loaded line cook, one who works clean, and has 'moves'—meaning economy of movement, nice technique and, most important, speed—can perform his duties with Nijinsky-like grace" (Bourdain, 2000, p. 55).

Observers of very accomplished people tend to wax metaphoric about the virtuosity of unconscious competence, but it seems to come down to six interlaced elements that I call "gifts," "models," "reps," "chunks," "critiques," and "grace." If these really progressed steplike in a sequential way, life would be neat and predictable. Reality seems otherwise. Think instead of these as layers of a Viennese chocolate-raspberry torte with a mocha sauce and a light slathering of whipped cream. All of the parts nest, blend, and ultimately bind together in ways that could be disaggregated if you preferred to make a mess and eat everything separately but that somehow do much better together. The ingredients create a culinary synergy in which two plus two equals seven on the ten-point Richter scale of desserts.

Let's take gifts and endowment first. Basically, some people (perhaps most people) are blessed with certain raw talents and dispositions. It may be a unique capacity, a special mental acuity, or even some uncommon physical peculiarity. Former U.S. Senator Bill Bradley, for example, was one of the best basketball players Princeton ever produced and a starter with the New York Knickerbockers. A little known fact: Bradley was actually born with extra peripheral vision. Baseball player Tony Gywnn, a superb hitter, says he can see the ball traveling to him. The average speed of a pitched ball is eighty-nine miles per hour. Most of us can't see anything. Harry Ishida, my dentist, has very small hands that can fit into large talkative mouths like mine quite easily. Ludwig Beethoven, Bruce Springsteen, and Madonna all seem blessed with a certain ear for the sounds and cadences of their time.

The concept behind this has been well described by Howard Gardner (1999a, 1999b). Although we tend to think of logical-mathematical aptitude as the key attribute of success, there are, in fact, many other forms of intelligence. Gardner sees physical and kinesthetic abilities as a different but equally useful form of intelligence. So is musical intelligence (think of Yasha Heifetz), spatial intelligence (Frank Lloyd Wright), natural intelligence (Daniel Boone in America or Sir Richard Francis Burton in Africa), linguistic intelligence, or emotional and interpersonal intelligence. Ability comes in many forms, and it is highly differentiated.

By itself, however, talent doesn't guarantee anything. Lots of us have mental, physical, spiritual, or emotional gifts that, for a variety of reasons, are squandered or so unbridled that they never amount to anything. Or perhaps parents and teachers fail to recognize them, or we are told over and over again that they are useless. The second component of mastery, therefore, is a model that arouses our curiosity. To cultivate ability, we need examples that open up prospects. The person on the beach needs to see the surfer surfing before being smitten. A Winton Marsalis gets his jump-start from hearing Louis Armstrong. A young woman with sculptural instincts must see (and more likely feel) an Alexander Calder or Jean Arp before she grasps that the mind's eye can visualize forms that lead to something beautiful and enduring. Models create possibilities. Mediators and facilitators are no different. We require a picture or schematic of that which intrigues us. In effect (and in our case), the model says, "Look, here's someone doing something unusual to help make an agreement, and I want to do that."

In the realm of conflict resolution, there is no lack of models. In fact, most of us in the profession tend to delimit our thinking, settle on one approach, and then put on blinders to others. Finding something that works and getting good results, we tend to forget that biological necessity and social ingenuity have, over forty thousand years, created thousands of interesting and artful ways of mediating disputes. The Big Man tradition in New Guinea is one. Hawaiian *Ho'oponopono* is another. So too are the Leopard Chief traditions of central Africa, the disentangling ceremonies of

Melanesia, the traditional Lok Jirga in Afghanistan, the peace pipe rituals of Native America, and the song duels of certain Eskimo peoples. All of these (including our peculiar obsession with only two forms of mediation: "transformative" and "evaluative") are part of a broad tapestry of ideas, models, and tools for managing controversy. They are models.

The third component is repetition. Said in everyday language, practice helps move us toward better and then pushes us on toward perfect. Cellist Yo-Yo Ma rehearses every piece in his mind. He does this on the plane, in his dreams, and while he's brushing his teeth. Jack Nicklaus never took a swing with his golf clubs that he didn't go over in his mind beforehand. Charlie Wilson, the best pituitary surgeon in the country, does half a dozen operations during the day and then practices on rats and mice before he goes home for dinner. The result is a knack for working smoothly, quickly, and with economy of motion. Repetition is also the breeding ground of innovation. Through repetitive exercise, we can experiment in private and study the failures.

Extended, continuous, and disciplined training is probably the root source of the fourth component of mastery: chunking.[2] Chunking refers to the storing of arrangements and sequences, sometimes exceedingly subtle ones, in long-term memory. Wayne Gretzky, says Malcolm Gladwell, remembers certain positionings and configurations in the hockey rink that the rest of us merely mortal hockey fans may briefly observe and even possibly hold in short-term memory for a moment or two but then quickly let go. Nonhockey players have no reason to remember such stuff. Gretzky does. When he says he "skates to where the puck will be," he is literally calling up a chunk of memory that can keep the coordinates of the puck, the goal, himself, his teammates, and his opponents in mind. To use a different metaphor, chunks are the mental instructions Gretzky uses to triangulate the "X" on the ice where everything converges for a good shot at the goal.

The same idea—chunks of mental instructions that can be called up in complicated situations—is true of Michael Jordan sweeping toward the basket, Julia Child cooking a soufflé, Winton Marsalis taking us to dizzying heights on the horn, a skilled forklift operator laying pipe in a trench, or a gifted mediator holding off on asking people for their positions while he or she sets up the political face-saving move that will break an impasse. In each case, you are intuitively and subconsciously pulling a strand, clump, nugget, or sequence of previous experience out of long-term memory, unconsciously inspecting it to see if it is the right one, holding the image steady, and applying it to the particular circumstance or fact pattern that you face across the table with disputants.

All of this takes place in nanoseconds. Ironically, if we asked Michael Jordan, Julia Child, Winton Marsalis, Ishida the dentist, or Steinhoff the arborist to explain their brilliant moment to us, they will probably say, "I dunno." It is not because they are being modest. Without being aware of it, they are doing something they think is instinctive or intuitive, something the rest of us assume is intentional and strategic. Even though it defies precise description and measurement, their mastery is apparent to people in the know. Colleagues who are watching them and who are also skilled and effective at what they do can pick out the real masters and see their ability.

This kind of internal, possibly subliminal visualization gives rise to a fifth layer of mastery: critique. Real experts—unlike the incompetents Dunning studies at Cornell—are intellectually honest and brutally self-critical with themselves. They examine their mistakes squarely, deconstruct them, and relentlessly search for the impecable. Some professions force this contemplation, even if isn't welcomed or pleasant. Lawyers must be able to argue alternative theories of both sides of their case in depth. Doctors routinely have to bring their failures before scowling panels of colleagues and defend their practices. Scientists are expected to undergo the banging and bruising of peer review for their research. Child welfare workers must do death reviews and confront the failures of their prevention efforts.

Using somewhat different terms, Donald Schön in his book *The Reflective Practitioner* studied engineers, architects, managers, urban

planners, and therapists and showed how high accomplishment in
these professions involves building visceral competencies that are
beyond strictly rational and technical proficiencies (Schön, 1983).
Mental preparation—learning the theories and practices of diag-
nostics, analysis, and intervention—sets the stage for the kind of
unconscious absorption that psychologist Thomas Wilson is discov-
ering through his experiments. When we are data-, fact-, and theory-
"sodden," other things kick in. Critique, appraisal, and criticism,
hard as they may be at times, sharpen our discipline and create mental toughness. But more than building character, they extend and
deepen practice, build intuition and instinct, and set the stage for
building the hunches, anticipations, and premonitions that Schön
finds to be an integral part of professionalism.

Finally, there is something in the realm of mastery and excellence
that happens at apex moments when strategy, impact, problem,
solution, cause and effect, and intervention and result converge.
Think of it as a moment of grace. Although religious people speak
of grace as one or another version of unmerited divine assistance
given to humans, grace has other collateral and derivative meanings.
It is also the effortless beauty of a maneuver or movement, the eye-
pleasing proportions of a form, the favor or gift given by someone
who is under no obligation to do so, a disposition toward kindness,
and the state of being protected.

As they rise to the top of their game, masters of smaller and
larger things—from football playing to flower arranging—develop
a feel that comes to be more important than head knowledge and
that leads to those efficient, clean, and graceful moments. Sometimes we describe this as being in the zone, a time, space, or place
that is beyond conventional notions of success and failure and that
seems to be a complete convergence of knowledge, skill, experience,
intuition, and inspiration. I've heard mountain climbers talk about
it as a kind of autopilot in which you are thinking like chess and
moving like ballet. Other athletes refer to it as raw, basic "muscle
memory." Baseball pitchers talk about "finding the groove," and jazz

musicians try to "get their mojo working." For mediators and facilitators, the perfect golden moment is when substance, process, and relationships all come together in sync, the participants or disputants accomplish their goals, and there is a result that they find salient and valuable. To paraphrase Frank Sander, a professor of ADR (Alternative Dispute Resolution) at Harvard, we get our mojo working right when the forum we created or managed fits perfectly for the fuss at hand and the fuss is tamed, streamlined, or resolved.

One final aspect of mastery is worth noting. The rigors of training, practice, and critique may be the inevitable preparation that is required to exercise ingenuity and judgment, but imagination is the connective tissue. It links the analytic and emotional, the moral and pragmatic, and the cooperative and the competitive aspects of our work. It builds off all the data dots and enables the occasional leap of insight that bridges to a solution. Imagination, says David Brooks, is "amphibious." It constructs both the visionary inspirations as well as the dark forebodings that inform analysis, strategy, and calculation (Brooks, 2002). Einstein was correct when he opined that imagination is more important than knowledge. Unwitting, unintentional, and unconscious excellence is the exercise of both fantasy and reason.

Struggling Upstream . . . Forever

It's the end of the month. I'm shuffling through papers on my desk looking for time sheets and invoice forms to close accounts. Paperwork is part of the yin and yang of being a full-time practitioner. Some days it's the dark side, some days the light. At this particular moment, I'm looking at two files. One contains papers about a water dispute that has two developers and phalanxes of lawyers and technical experts at each other's throats. The other file is my running record of a group of scientists, lawyers, fishermen, and cultural experts who have been meeting for months to break a legislative logjam centering on the creation of new marine protected areas. The cases couldn't be more different from each other. One of them represents a failure. The other is full of magic and light.

With hindsight, I can see my mistakes on the first case and maybe the general contours of some things I did right on the second. After a round of initial meetings on the first, I misjudged the nature of the dispute between the two property owners. In joint session, it was all about "principle." In separate caucuses and in different ways, both of them then assured me their dispute wasn't personal, nor was it about money. It was about contractual duties to purvey water through the pipes on each of their properties.

As it turns out, their conflict was all about the money and their concomitant mutual desires to inflict pain on each other. It is not for personal satisfaction that they were doing this but because of the competition between their respective future business ventures once they each secured the water they need. I missed this entirely. My mistake was accepting at face value their initial representations. It's not fatal, and I suspect we will get to a negotiated conclusion eventually. Yet in the process, I have probably unnecessarily consumed more of their time and stamina than is necessary.

In the second case, things are entirely different. The process of getting people to reveal their fears, hopes, and interests over several meetings, coupled with the infusion of high-quality data into discussions about fish stocks, local community practices, and ocean regenerative capabilities, has brought us very close to a solution. Unlike our previous meetings, this last session turned a corner and created what Malcolm Gladwell calls a tipping point. People were focused, civil, helpful to each other even when they disagreed, and oriented toward finding answers.

Reflections of this kind on personal experience are useful to me as a way of sorting things out, but I am also aware that they may be completely delusional. One of the hard realities doctors face is how little they actually know about cause, effect, prevention, intervention, and healing. In many cases, they can't actually explain why many patients live when they are supposed to die, or die when everyone expected them to live. The logic of their nostrums and therapies gives them the comfort of method, but it doesn't explain what's going on. Similarly, I'm aware of the disconnect between how we mediators and facilitators look at our work and how our work is seen by the mediated and facilitated-upon.

Several years ago, Kem Lowry of the University of Hawaii Department of Urban and Regional Planning did an analysis of some thirty successfully mediated cases that had been in a program I directed. His study drove the point home for me. First Lowry asked the mediators in our cases to explain what they did to bring about success. Then he asked the parties in those same cases what they actually observed the mediators doing. The mediators—myself included—gave elaborate explanations of strategies, timing, and tactics. We identified how we went about conducting our conflict analyses and circumscribing issues to be worked on. We deciphered the breakdowns, breakthroughs, and the windows of opportunity both lost and found. The participants in our cases had a very different view. What they recalled us doing was opening the room, making coffee, and getting everyone introduced.

If our goal is seamlessness and invisibility, Lowry's study suggests we succeeded brilliantly. There may be other explanations, though. Maybe we don't know as much as we think we know. Or maybe we give what we do know too much weight and credence. Or maybe it's all placebo and Hawthorne effect and we are really just setting up a time and place for people to act out their own rituals of making war and peace. In the end, it may really be about room keys and cookies.

For myself, I will keep tussling and fuddling and muddling my way toward the highest perfection I can, whether it be refreshments, door opening, data management, or the politics of face making and face saving. It's my life work and a quest. Meanwhile, I keep taking comfort in the words Gertrude Stein barked at a young Ernest Hemingway while they were hanging out in Paris and living the big life: "There ain't no answer, there's never been an answer, there never will be an answer, and that's the answer."

Reflective Practice Questions

1. In the progression from unconscious incompetence to unconscious competence as a dispute resolver, where would you place yourself? Have you had moments in which you felt a sense of conscious or unconscious mastery?

2. Have you met someone who, like the dentist, arborist, and cook described by the author, inspires you by his or her mastery? If so, what were the qualities that inspired you? Are those qualities that you seek to develop in yourself?

3. Have you found imagination (the "connective tissue" that, the author says, links the various components of mastery) to be important in your work as a dispute resolver? If so, in what ways?

References

Adler, P. *Beyond Paradise: Encounters in Hawaii Where the Tour Bus Never Runs*. Woodbridge, Conn.: Ox Bow Press, 1993.

Begley, S. "The Unconscious You May Be the Wiser Half." *Wall Street Journal*, Aug. 30, 2002. (courtesy of SFGate.com, www.sfgate.com/cgi-bin/article.cgi?file=/news/archive/2002/08/30/financial0919EDT0060.DTL)

Bergreen, L. *Voyage to Mars: NASA's Search for Life Beyond Earth*. New York: Riverhead, 2000.

Bourdain, A. *Kitchen Confidential: Adventures in the Culinary Underbelly*. London: Bloomsbury, 2000.

Brooks, D. "Light Shows of the Mind." *Atlantic Monthly*, Dec. 2002, pp. 30–31.

Gardner, H. *The Disciplined Mind*. New York: Simon & Schuster, 1999a.

Gardner, H. *Intelligence Reframed: Multiple Intelligences for the 21st Century*. New York: Basic Books, 1999b.

Gardner, J. *Excellence: Can We Be Equal and Excellent Too?* New York: Norton, 1995.

Gladwell, M. "The Physical Genius: What Do Wayne Gretzky, Yo-Yo Ma, and a Brain Surgeon Have in Common?" *New Yorker*, Aug. 2, 1999.

Goode, E. "Why the Ignorant Are Blissful: Inept Individuals Ooze Confidence." 1999. [www.zenspider.com/RWD/Thoughts/Inept.html] (Originally published in *New York Times*)

Kanahele, G. *Ku Kanaka Stand Tall: A Search for Hawaiian Values*. Honolulu: University of Hawaii Press, 1993.

Peters, T., and Austin, N. *A Passion for Excellence*. New York: Random House, 1985.

Schön, D. A. *The Reflective Practitioner: How Professionals Think in Action*. New York: Basic Books, 1983.

4

Managing the Natural Energy of Conflict

Mediators, Tricksters, and the Constructive Uses of Deception

Robert D. Benjamin

Conflict is first and foremost about people's passions, desires, and emotions in collision. The friction of conflict generates heat, which, like any form of natural energy, can be squandered or harnessed. The sources could be scarce resources, an inability to communicate or empathize, a moral clash over good or evil, or a power struggle of some variety. Typically, they are inextricably intertwined and sometimes disguised.

The Natural Energy of Conflict

Regardless of the sources, the trick is to separate the core elements of conflict from the less pure, residual, and unnecessary by-products. In especially difficult matters, what is required is the deft and subtle touch of a third party attuned to the rhythms of conflict, with the necessary feel and intuition to be effective. Those qualities are, however, difficult to find in the midst of a Western techno-rational culture that is dedicated to the belief that problems are predominantly solved by rational analysis and reasonable discourse. At least initially, disputes are not susceptible to logic; traditional notions of the dispassionate, above-the-fray, neutral, and objective expert can be not only ineffective but even counterproductive in managing heated, long-standing disputes. A disproportionate amount of attention has been given to rational problem solving. That approach is essential but not sufficient in and of itself. The complexity, chaotic, and dynamic character of events and issues faced personally and as a society require conflict management approaches that meld rational and intuitive aspects.

Developing the requisite qualities is a twofold task. First, we must recognize the importance of moving outside the strict and narrow rational paradigm our culture has defined. We are increasingly coming to the awareness that the idea of rationality necessarily includes not just objective data but the subjective realm as well (Nozick, 1994). Second, we must find models of practice that offer support and give direction.

Ironically, drawing from our past history and folklore offers up a figure that is uniquely suited and especially adept in traversing the intricacies of complex present-day conflicts. The folkloric "trickster" figure appears in virtually every culture, across the entire spectrum of time from prehistory to the present, and in every guise, with remarkable similarity of purpose and approach to that of the mediator, facilitator, or for that matter anyone who encounters and seeks to manage conflict. After all, the stuff of trickster stories and folklore is their insights, antics, and modus operandi—strategies, techniques, and skills—calculated to finesse and survive conflict. Note immediately that the purpose of both the trickster and the mediator is not to defeat or stop, but merely to survive and manage, conflict. Both face the ultimate challenge: to mediate between immovable objects and irresistible forces.

It is the premodern trickster figure that demonstrates, better than any professional expert could, the deft and subtle integration of all the requisite human talents and brings them to bear on the most serious and problematic matters that confront humankind. Tricksters will use both sacred and profane means, sometimes even pushing the limits of moral propriety in pursuit of the ultimate moral end of survival. They demonstrate an uncanny, resourceful, and pragmatic ability that gives glimpses of considerable intellect and wisdom. They strategically decide whether to be straightforward or circuitous and "crazy" in approach.

Although theory and rational analysis are not unimportant, the mediator and the trickster function predominantly by gut instinct (Benjamin, 2001a).

As the conflict management field has developed, and especially in recent years as it has become increasingly institutionalized, the traditional disciplines of law, mental health, or medicine, anchored in a techno-rational tradition and thinking frame, have predominated as a model of practice. Standards of practice, notions of competency, and other professional accoutrements have been imported and in many instances allowed to set the limits for conflict management practice. One glaring example is the use of the term and the concept of *neutrality*. The product of "scientistic" thinking, and culturally linked to a culture that emphasizes objectivity and rationality, the claim of neutrality is the expressed aspiration of most mediators without much reflection or critical examination of the risks. Practiced in the extreme, neutrality can straitjacket and constrain the use of strategies necessary to manage difficult conflicts. Neutrality is only one of many notions that have disinclined mediators, facilitators, and other conflict negotiators to sense and respond to the natural feel of conflict and to overrely on structured protocols and formulaic practice approaches (Benjamin, 1998d).

Similarly, outside the purely rational box of traditional thinking, a mediator, not unlike a trickster figure, is not infrequently called on to use techniques and methods that are frowned upon in polite professional practice settings. Specifically, pursuing the management of conflict sometimes requires resorting to such profane means as constructive use of deception. In difficult conflicts, where rational discussion and logic are insufficient to dislodge disputing parties from their entrenched positions, unorthodox strategies and techniques that do not easily fit within published standards of practice are necessary, although they raise practical, professional, and ethical questions.

What is often dismissed or outright denied in Western cultures, where scientific inquiry and the quest for the truth is held sacred, is the necessary place of deception in our human functioning. Deception is not only a normal activity but an essential one for the survival and propagation of all life-forms, including human beings. Nonetheless, although a factor in every communication, there remains a deeply ingrained antipathy to the use of deception, and it continues to carry a pejorative connotation (Berlin, 1991; Rue, 1994). Highlighting and analogizing the work of a third party in a conflict to the age-old trickster figure is not intended to encourage or justify the abdication of responsible practice standards, but it is a necessary part of conflict management practice that must be addressed and accepted.

Of far greater importance is the trickster figure as a model for the effective management of the natural energy generated by conflict, rather than being merely another expert technocrat trying to solve other people's problems. The trickster motif is a frame for emphasizing and appreciating the full range of strategies available for managing conflict. Importantly, it offers a practice model that can seamlessly incorporate both objective and subjective ways of knowing and the complete spectrum of rationality (Benjamin, 1995b). It escapes the often facile and oversimplified dichotomies drawn between truth and deception, good and evil, and right and wrong (Benjamin, 2002).

Tricksters and Mediators

The trickster figure thrives on change and conflict, alternately causing or resolving it. He serves as a mediator, seeking to reconcile immovable objects and irresistible forces. The trickster of folklore and mythology helps humans cope with the insurmountable and uncontrollable forces in their lives and contain the chaos that always looms and threatens to disintegrate their social fabric. Tricksters in folklore, just as is true of present-day mediators, can never gain full control of the dilemmas presented and can seldom wholly resolve problems. Often the means used by tricksters or mediators to settle conflict are less than noble. But the fundamental purpose of the trickster and the mediator is the same: to help the characters or parties survive (Niditch, 1987).

The trickster figure, as must a sophisticated mediator, might appear to be "crazy like a fox" (Nisker, 2001). The trickster figure is a beguiling contradiction in terms, simultaneously using both natural wit and calculated, practiced skill. Observing the manner of the trickster figure offers a clear view of the necessarily elusive and difficult role of the present-day mediator. Both seek to transform disputing parties' construction of reality and to transform the context of the dispute to allow other perspectives to be considered. This often requires the use of manipulative techniques to unsettle or tweak parties entrenched in set positions not admitting of settlement. However, just as the trickster sometimes resorts to unorthodox, and even profane, methods, so on occasion must a mediator. This goes against the grain of the values of most professional disciplines, not to mention our culture and morality. Paradoxically, the trickster figure, a reassuring motif that is well ingrained and evident throughout human history, directly challenges strongly held beliefs about truth and honesty that are the cornerstone of our modern-day belief system.

The Natural Mediator and the Trickster

Conventional wisdom—encapsulated half-truths, based in equal parts on our own limited experience and conditioned by personal bias—would suggest a mediator should be a humanistic, compassionate, patient, and empathetic sort; slow to anger and frustration; and eternally optimistic that all issues can be resolved with reason. It is, of course, useful to exhibit some of those traits sometimes. For the most part, however, despite the suggestions of career counselors, who, armed with psychological tests, such as the Myers-Briggs Type Indicator, presume only the most genuinely caring among us have the potential to be good mediators, there is some reason to be skeptical.

The personality traits that best serve mediators may not be the most obvious or commonly presented: (1) confused, (2) voyeuristic, (3) compulsive, and (4) marginal. Although some people are born naturals, others can acquire the traits with disciplined effort (Benjamin, 1998c).

Confused

For the mediator and the trickster, the truth, clear rules, and simple answers are troubling. Even though the clarity of predictable results and ultimate final theories offers an allure in a world filled with ambiguity, too often their application leads to greater confusion and unintended consequences (Berlin, 1953). Many have properly been drawn to the work of mediation just because they have found themselves sitting on the fence, seeing the validity of all sides in a dispute, and there are few places for fence-sitters in a culture dedicated to finding the right answer. Western cultures have substituted the quest for the truth for the search for the Holy Grail. In negotiated processes such as mediation or facilitation, the truth of the matter is not and cannot be the primary focus, if for no other reason than there is no machinery available to discover and determine the truth (Benjamin, 1999). The object is a practical and workable agreement. The mediator is relieved of any responsibility to determine who is right or wrong and what is the right answer. In fact, being naturally of a confused state of mind is useful as a third party helping others to manage conflict (Benjamin, 1998c).

Ironically, even though many people caught in the grip of conflict present themselves as certain of their rightness and position, a good measure of conflict can be attributed to their being confused and overwhelmed. Their entrenched positions are seldom more than defensive postures, statements of their fear of being played for a fool. The mediator's confusion about which position is most or least valid can help undermine some of their presumed certainty and inject a measure of doubt and ambiguity into the atmosphere. Those who are most adept at taking on the confused persona are those who have always been ill at ease with presumed clarity or certainty. This confusion serves a mediator well; it allows him or her to naturally understand there are no easy answers and to help confuse parties who presume otherwise. The confused mediator more readily sees the validity of each person's perspective and more naturally resists aligning with a particular side. Experience generally breeds a reluctance to be sure one is right and less willing to venture a guess, let alone presume to give an objective evaluation. Confused mediators recognize the dual nature of all things human— that heroes can be scoundrels and scoundrels heroes, victims can be bullies and bullies victims, and terrorists might be freedom fighters and freedom fighters might be terrorists.

A mediator is not allowed the comfort of certainty in thinking about the right outcome. Such rationalized clarity carries with it the risk of being perceived to be aligned with a particular position or cause. Amidst all the "certainty mongers" and within the strict rules of law, custom, and ritual set down by the righteous, the trickster offers a measure of relief. By cleverness; humor; and reframing, shifting, and reorganizing of issues, tricksters and mediators shake up the situation and cause a certain amount of confusion so that the disputants might have an opportunity to gain a different perspective.

Voyeuristic

Being voyeuristic can be a troubling attribute; in some contexts, voyeurism is viewed as a form of perversion. In managing conflict, however, it is an invaluable attribute, for what is required of a negotiator or mediator is an endless fascination with how other human beings engage each other and construct their realities. As a voyeur, the mediator can more ably resist being judgmental, knowing that "there but for the grace of God go I." A mediator does not so much do disputing parties a favor by helping them settle conflict but is instead honored by being invited to aid in managing some of the most intimate matters of their lives.

Compulsive

The mediator must have a penchant to bring order out of chaos because a good measure of conflict arises from confusion—misinformation or no information that feeds the parties' fear of being played for a fool. Compulsive organization, just short of descent into outright neuroticism—the use of charts, maps, and a clear structure—can fend off a good measure of unnecessary conflict. The mediator is the wilderness tour guide and must be well prepared. The mediator can't just wander along with them but must instead sense and anticipate the parties' fears before they become overwhelmed.

Marginal

Finally, a mediator necessarily must dwell alone in the middle; he or she is and must remain marginal. The mediator cannot be aligned or associated with any cause or purpose other than to help the parties make decisions for themselves. Groucho Marx said it best: "Any group that would have me as a member isn't worth joining." It means letting go of attachments to what life should be in a perfect world—one good for children, women, men, minorities, and other people of every stripe and kind. The mediator has to be on the fringe, an outsider, less concerned about what is right than with what will work to settle a dispute in the present circumstance. Mediation is not about social justice, and the mediator cannot be an advocate for a cause and effectively manage a conflict at the same time. Mediators, like tricksters, hold a marginal social status in the cultures they inhabit. They may garner some measure of respect, but that fund of goodwill is only as valuable as the last dispute and means little in the next one. Credibility must be earned in each dispute separately. The mediator has no authority except that conferred on him or her by disputants who have chosen to invite the mediator into their dispute. In pure form, regardless of social status or prestige, the mediator and the trickster succeed only through cleverness, not by force or external authority. Many mediators who work for courts or in in-house mediation programs have discovered that their presumed authority was, as often as not, unhelpful (Benjamin, 1998b).

Like the folkloric trickster figure, the present-day mediator must be willing to some extent to assume a marginal status (not be the authority), if disputing parties are to be allowed to self-determine the resolution of their own dispute (Niditch, 1987). The mediator operates in the shadow of the law, encouraging disputing parties to adopt a personal standard of fairness that may as likely depart from any perceived or preformulated or normative standard of fairness, legal or otherwise (Mnookin and Kornhauser, 1979). The mediator may even encourage the consideration of options for settlement of disputes that are outside the norms of social convention or the law.

At the same time, this marginality or nonalignment should not be confused with neutrality. The mediator needs to be free to engage or challenge any party in a conflict. Neutrality is a holdover concept from the technical-rational thinking frame of traditional professionals. It carries with it an implicit, if not explicit, responsibility to be objective, distanced, dispassionate, and above the fray. Mediators and tricksters cannot afford that luxury; they are participant-observers to the conflict and must be actively engaged. At best, they strive to be balanced, not neutral (Benjamin, 1995a, 1998d).

The trickster figure is a mentor of sorts for the difficult role of being a conflict mediator working in a culture that has a decided preference for swift action, bold advocacy, and heroes. The slow, careful work of conflict management does not often produce the climactic moments that are the stuff of legends. The trickster figure, if nothing else, exhibits how to harness our basic noble (and sometimes ignoble) attributes as human beings to the management of conflict. Many more of us are naturally confused, voyeuristic, compulsive, and marginal than we are rational, patient, and understanding in the path of conflict. The difference is that a sophisticated natural mediator has learned not to deny his or her basic nature, but rather to harness and use those amply provided attributes or vulnerabilities to our advantage. In other words, we try to be saints when what may serve us best is the recognition that we all are potential or real "sinners."

The Trickster Versus the Hero

The folkloric trickster figure is never a hero; he or she is typically a marginal personage either by reason of social status or force of circumstance. A heroic figure in mythology and literature is a character who develops, symbolizes, or reinforces the cultural norms of the established order of society. Thus King Solomon stood for wisdom and justice, and George Washington stood for honesty. A hero is, by definition, bound up in or associated with a particular cause, position, or purpose. Heroes must remain resolute and passionate in their cause, "the perfect line that never wavers." The trickster figure, by contrast, must be free to flaunt authority and remains forever outside the norm and socially marginal. Thus the trickster figure in most of folklore, whether coyote, leprechaun, court jester, clown, or fool, is a paradoxical character, a spirit of disorder and hater of boundaries who tests the central beliefs and values of the predominant culture (Niditch, 1987).

Not only is a negotiator or mediator not a hero, but he or she runs the risk of being viewed as a pariah merely for suggesting the idea of settlement. For many, negotiation is aligned with evil or immorality (Benjamin, 1998e). Take negotiating with terrorists, for example. Those Jews who negotiated with the Third Reich for the release of Jews from Germany in the years just before the Second World War continue to be hated to this day by many other Jewish people (Bauer, 1994).

Political and social leaders, to obtain their positions, must present themselves as heroic figures. Hero types, or those who aspire to be so viewed, conform to a relatively common mold. Their public relations material will indicate they came from deprived or limited means and have encountered and overcome adversity because of their exceptional virtue. As heroes, they are necessarily constrained by their role to be clear and unambiguous about the righteousness and justness of their partisan cause. If they were to change their mind on an issue, that would likely be viewed as weak—or worse, duplicitous and opportunistic. They are visionaries, certain of their mission and the justness of it. For them, good and evil and right and wrong are clearly delineated (Niditch, 1987).

For trickster figures and mediators, good and evil are not opposites or mutually exclusive; they are overlapping and inseparable qualities of the same whole. Behaviors and events are seen by mediators and trickster figures as confused mixtures of both right and wrong, making available multiple opportunities or possibilities that have both positive and negative ramifications. Tricksters and mediators, unlike heroes, must have a high level of tolerance for ambiguity.

Heroes and leaders must provide the clarified message their followers need to hear to mobilize them. They cannot risk confusing their message with subtlety and nuance; they seek action, not discussion. Mediators, on the other hand, are the house skeptics, obligated to challenge the reigning wisdom and poke holes in the utopian vision.

The Limits of Rationality

A brief rendering of the traditional technical-rational model of thinking and practice that has evolved over the last 150 years is a useful backdrop and offers a good figure-ground perspective as a means of comparison with the trickster model (Schön, 1983). Law, medicine, and counseling are disciplines anchored in a linear, analytical thinking frame. Those disciplines are informed by the universal laws of classical physics first articulated by Newton and incorporated into the scientific method postulated by Francis Bacon in the Age of Enlightenment; ultimately they resulted in the logical positivism of the Industrial Revolution in the late nineteenth century. The operating premises of the Western world are first that there is a truth, second that truth can be known and determined with predictability and certainty, and third that there is only one truth (Berlin, 1991). The notion of "come let us reason together" is rooted in those premises and continues to be practiced by many traditional professionals—and not a few mediators.

The scientific method was quickly imported to the traditional professionals and very soon became their underpinning. The theory, practice, and education in medicine and law changed unalterably. The professionals became technical experts and scientists of sorts. Doctors moved away from the art of healing and adopted an analytical protocol that appeared infallible: diagnosis, prognosis, treatment, cure. Subsequently, psychologists and other mental health professionals would borrow that approach. Nor was law immune from the attraction of becoming, or at least appearing, more scientific. Christopher Columbus Langdell, the founder of the first law school, at Harvard in the late nineteenth century, set as his operating premise that "law is science," and lawyers would do well to study "black letter" universal legal principles that can be deciphered with careful analysis (Schön, 1983). Lawyers, like doctors, need only approximate the scientific method: fact assessment, legal/case analysis, strategy, and predictable outcome.

Traditional professionals have become the high priests of a techno-rational belief system; they presume and are assumed to be experts in their particular disciplines, and deference is given to them accordingly (Lewontin, 1991). Yet in most disputes, the last thing needed is another technical expert. As a result, difficult and complex conflicts such as divorce, business, or environmental disputes are often fragmented or piecemealed into separate parts by the technical experts. Each discipline approaches the matter from a carefully prescribed and conditioned practice focus in accordance with settled principles. Lawyers have a legal dispute resolution paradigm and tend to view disputes as strictly legal matters (Menkel-Meadow, 1985). Mental health professionals view disputes as intrapersonal or interpersonal conflicts, and business professionals view disputes as purely a function of economics. In short, depending on the professional to whom an issue is presented, the problem runs the risk of being overly "legalized," "therapized," or "economized."

Traditional professionals approach a complex conflict as if the matter were an elephant and each of them—the lawyer, counselor, financial analyst, or doctor—is standing one foot away from the beast, each in a particular location, front, back, or side. Each describes a different part—the trunk, the tail, the flank—and each believes he or she knows the whole truth of the beast from the part seen. Many professionals and consumers have gravitated to mediation because the constraints of traditional profession practices have not sufficiently allowed effective problem solving. Professionals do not enjoy practicing within the narrow strictures of their discipline, which often seems as much a hindrance as a help to managing a client's issues; they are given all of the responsibility to solve the problem and little or no authority—a high-stress situation. Clients, likewise, often feel they are running between pillar and post—from counselor to lawyer to accountant—obtaining different advice, with no clear overall sense of how to organize that information.

"Systematic Intuition"

In contrast to the fragmented and often linear approach of most professional disciplines, mediators, not unlike tricksters, rely less on specific protocols and develop a Gestalt, or whole-picture, approach. They look less at the specific parts and concentrate more on the systemic and holistic dimensions. The mediator must be free to borrow information and problem-solving approaches eclectically from a variety of professional disciplines (Schön, 1983). Although some basic protocols are initially helpful, they are no substitute for the need to sense and intuit how to move and manage the conflict. This is much the same as a surfer who feels her balance riding a wave, or a rider who must feel the movements of a horse and respond.

Lawyers, counselors, business advisers, and other professionals all serve a necessary purpose and function. Most complex disputes require consultation with such experts if there is to be substantially informed decision making. But even though there is some overlap, those professionals are not and cannot be the same as the mediator. In the best trickster tradition, the mediator must be free to roam the terrain of the dispute unfettered by prescribed professional protocols. The purposes and functions of mediation are more subtle. How and what a mediator does to resolve a dispute is not easily amenable to prescriptive rules and analysis. Mediation between or among disputing parties, almost by definition, is done in the shadow not only of the law but of other professional disciplines as well (Mnookin and Kornhauser, 1979). The mediated resolution to an issue often does not square with determinations that might be applied by a lawyer, doctor, or therapist. In mediation the right answer to a problem, if there is one, becomes secondary to obtaining some measure of resolution of the dispute by the parties themselves. A mediator, by definition, must have a high tolerance for ambiguity and be capable of operating less formally and often in the middle of great confusion. The typical terrain of a mediator is in the realm of "fuzzy logic," between the extremes of the clearly right or clearly wrong answer (Kosko, 1993). Rational-logical thinking alone is seldom sufficient or effective in resolving difficult conflicts.

The mediator practices by "systematic intuition," an intentional oxymoron designed to convey the ability and necessity of working with subjective and objective information simultaneously (Benjamin, 2001a). Most intractable and protracted conflicts defy simple rational analysis and conceal multiple variables and factors in play, only some of which are expressly stated but all of which must be addressed and managed in some measure. This requires both analytical skill and intuitive ability. In contrast to the linear thinking frame of traditional professionals, mediators of necessity must operate from a systemic or holistic thinking frame.

The folkloric trickster figure dynamically mixes the character traits of wit and reason. Like the mediator, the purpose of the trickster is the management of conflict. This is not to suggest that mediators should operate by wits and intuition alone, but that the mediator requires both intuitive sensibilities as well as analytical skills—systematic intuition.

The Thinking Frame of Tricksters and Mediators

Traditional professionals typically work from a logical positivist operating premise; problems symbolize a state of disorder or disequilibrium. For them, all problems can be solved, and they can be solved so that order or stasis is reestablished. Problems are aberrations to be fixed, remedied, or cured. This is the core of the technical-rational belief system of most traditional professionals (Schön, 1983). Mediators and tricksters have a wholly different thinking frame. For them, problems are an expected and normal part of the real world (Diamond, 1972). They recognize that no matter how necessary, well intended, or well conceived a social order may be, none is foolproof or perfect, and there are always choices. There is no question that rules, laws, and regulations are essential for an ordered society to progress, but at the same time all that rational ordering can easily become oppressive and stultifying. The same rules that afford uniformity, safety, and protection of the norms often constitute the major source of an individual's or community's sense of powerlessness. Some individuals and groups, especially minorities, often feel constrained or locked in by the rules, which ostensibly protect the majority. We often become "prisoners of good government." To the trickster and the mediator, peace and order are not an end in themselves.

In society, mechanisms must be available to allow some wiggle room. Allowing discretion to be exercised is the most potent antidote for the sense of constraint caused by the "myth of rationality." This myth is the operative belief held by many, especially in Western cultures, that all problems or issues have rational solutions and that those issues can be solved by logical thinking and rules (Benjamin, 1990). Governments are premised on the myth of rationality.

A myth is not a lie, nor it is the whole truth. At best, it is a noble lie, a concoction of what people need to believe rather than a provable proposition (Rue, 1994). There are limits to rationality, a point at which being rational alone is, in fact, irrational and where the rote application of a rule or policy becomes absurd and exacerbates the problem (Elster, 1989; Saul, 1992). For societal systems to work, the formal operation of law must be tempered by the exercise of discretion. Negotiation and mediation are the primary modes of "private ordering" that allow parties to retain control over their own lives and avoid the imposition of often unexpected and unwanted determinations by the formal system of law (Mnookin and Kornhauser, 1979).

Traditional professionals are the ministers of the established order (Saul, 1992). Their underlying thinking frame is essentially bivalent: one is either right or wrong, sick or healthy, within the law or not within the law. Most complex issues, however, occur within the ambiguous center, the fuzzy middle, where matters are mostly a question of degree. The variables of a dispute are in most real-life circumstances multivalent, ambiguous, and continuously shifting (Kosko, 1993). Most complex disputes require risk assessment and management. There are seldom clear choices and certainly no guarantees. Mediators, by definition, work in this terrain of ambiguity, which requires a multivalent thinking frame.

The purely rational and ordered society first suggested and envisioned by Aristotle, which serves as a foundation for the thinking of our Western society, is an artifice imposed on reality (McKeon, 1947). Subsequently, much of our history has been taken up with the attempt to find the balance between an ordered society and individual freedom. Trickster figures have been among those personages who have been institutionalized to make day-to-day life more tolerable, perhaps even survivable, in the meantime. They were privileged to explore the nonrational or irrational consequences that resulted from too much rational thinking. Present-day mediators, like trickster figures, continue in that tradition.

Trickster and Mediators as Conflict
Analysts and Managers

Conflict is the natural soil of the trickster figure, as it is of the mediator. Conflict is endemic to human development. Change, by definition, engenders stress and conflict, whether intrapersonally, interpersonally, or both. Whereas for traditional professionals conflict is negative and to be avoided, the trickster-mediator understands that conflict has the potential to be the source of both risk and opportunity. Cholesterol can be of a molecular structure that aids the metabolism of the body chemistry or it can be in a form that constricts arteries and blocks bodily functioning and ultimately causes death. Similarly, conflict can stimulate and alert individuals undergoing change or it can immobilize and block the problem-solving process. Thus some conflict is very real and substantive, as with disputes involving scarce resources (land use or the future financial security of a divorcing couple). Other conflicts are essentially avoidable or peripheral, as with relationship or communication disputes (misunderstandings, accumulated slights, both real and perceived). Tricksters and mediators need to understand conflict in all of its forms in order to manage it effectively.

Human beings, especially in Western cultures, tend to think in a linear chain of thought, even though the nature of things is decidedly more complex (Bateson, 1972). Thus conflicts are often presented in dichotomous and dualistic terms, such as good versus evil, life versus death, rational versus irrational, right versus wrong, love versus hate, enemy versus friend, health versus sickness, objective versus subjective knowledge, mind versus body. Problems so framed are essentially unresolvable. To cope with or manage the conflict, the trickster-mediator works to develop a third perspective that shares traits of both sides of the dichotomy, thereby transforming a conflicted dyad into a more harmonious triad (Levi-Strauss, 1963). For the trickster-mediator, conflicts are never resolved; there is seldom a final or ultimate right answer, but the conflict can often be managed or finessed so that the parties can survive and move on in their lives.

Trickster figures thrive on conflict, and sometimes they are even the source of the conflict. Their machinations and trickery cause stress and confusion for the unwitting plot protagonist. Yet they do not play tricks or cause conflict for personal gain and without purpose. Out of the confusion, participants can reconsider their purposes and the dilemma, and perhaps reformulate their perspectives. Mediators, in like fashion, cannot afford to shy away from conflict. They are not so much peacemakers or conflict resolvers as they are conflict managers. They analyze and use conflict in much the same way as tricksters. The mediator's duty is often to present hard, necessary questions to the parties—to constructively create confusion—and then, in relief, to reframe the issues with greater focus on the essential substantive conflict, as opposed to peripheral matters. The mediator uses the stress of the circumstances or events as an opportunity to forge a shift in perspectives.

Both mediators and tricksters pay less attention to the logic of the situation than to the nature and source of the conflict. Both tricksters and mediators understand that for every logic A there is an equal and opposite logic B; confronting one force of logic with an opposing force of logic is often ineffectual. If the mediator enters a dispute from a logical thinking frame to determine who is right or wrong, he or she will surely lose balance with the other party. The mediator will become merely another antagonist to one or both parties.

Neither the mediator nor the trickster can avoid conflict, and confrontation is of limited value. Both the mediator and the trickster have learned how to use conflict to their advantage: to harness the energy of the dispute and to redirect it toward a constructive settlement.

Varieties of Trickster Figures and Themes in Folklore, Literature, and Theater

The trickster figures are the products of myth, folklore, and literature. Many people limit their understanding and awareness of mythology to ancient Greek and Roman history, a topic studied in high school and no longer relevant to the present-day world. But mythology is as relevant now as ever. Myths are stories of significance that have been repeated and ritualized by a culture to help people understand and make sense of their experience and the world around them (LeBaron, 2003). Myths organize our thinking and approach to the world as much as, and sometimes even more than, logic does; few important life decisions are made by rational analysis alone. Nowhere is the presence of myth more strongly felt than in the middle of a conflict—that is, when people are most likely to fall back into a primal level of understanding about what is happening to them. Myths are stories of people's search for meaning in their lives in order for them to understand life changes (Campbell and Moyers, 1988).

As people form attachments (marriage, employment) or undergo separations (illness, death, divorce), each life event requires a story or myth that gives meaning to the experience (Bowlby, 1973, 1982). Without mythology, there is no way to relate to or harmonize one's life with the world beyond what is seen. Truth, as it is defined by a culture, is given through stories. Myths and parables are those truths "dressed up" in acceptable clothes; a truth paraded around naked is likely to be resisted or avoided. Thus death as a cold fact is an ominous and fearful event, but given meaning through myth this life-cycle event can be understood and more easily accepted. Religious stories most obviously serve that purpose. In trickster tales, especially in the biblical context, the story is taken to be the truth itself as actual facts are fused with stories about the facts. Ultimately, factual history is often revised to serve other purposes (Popper, 1961).

Mediation of Conflict as Theater and Negotiation as Performance Art

Human beings need stories and myths for life to be palatable; they hold a healing power. Not just stories, but theater as well. Most conflicts approximate in some form a passion play.

Conflicts are generally about circumstances or situations that happened in the past: a doctor's errant treatment, a spouse's thoughtless behavior, an automobile accident, a hostile workplace. The event sparks feelings that solidify into the emotions of frustration, anger, or righteous indignation. By the time those conflicts are addressed in a court or mediation session, the stories of what happened have been spun, revised, and redacted in a way that supports and justifies each party's emotions, and each prepares a script, casting himself or herself as the hero (protagonist, good person) and ascribe to the other party or parties the role of villain (antagonist, bad guy).

The original passion play of the death and resurrection of Jesus forms the backdrop for most conflict scenarios. There is a wrongful act alleged, a suffering endured, and the denouement in justice being served, by either righteous revenge or an act of God. For centuries, the passion play has been part of the oral tradition and dramaturgy of the Christian church to reenergize the emotional base for religious faith and belief. As with any play, the accuracy of the historical facts is immaterial; the drama serves an altogether different purpose (think of an Oliver Stone movie). In similar fashion, the mediation of a dispute is about a present reality—the dramatic re-creation of the conflict—not really about what actually took place. It is not just metaphorically a theater, but a theater in fact. It cannot be about the truth of the matter because there is no way to ascertain truth in the mediation process, and that is not the purpose of the process. The visceral level at which most conflicts are played out cannot be reached by talk; theater and storytelling are two of the most potent methods of reaching that level (Benjamin, 2001b).

Conflict arises out of the collision of passionate beliefs and thus cannot be managed dispassionately. By definition, for a matter to be a conflict there must be an element of passion—even in a seemingly sterile business dispute that presumes to be "just a matter of money." The parties must believe in their role and the justness of their cause.

All conflict is personal; therefore, efforts to separate people from problems is not plausible even in theory, let alone practice (Fisher, Ury, and Patton, 1991).

The duality of mind/reason and body/emotion underpins most of Western thought and is an article of faith in techno-rational cultures. The operating presumption, which is rooted deeply in our philosophical beliefs, is that reason can be separated and consciously willed to control, suppress, and supersede emotion. "Coolheaded" reasoning is popularly encouraged over hot emotion. This is the foundational premise of the so-called Age of Reason ushered in by Descartes four hundred years ago. Some of the most common refrains heard are "calm down," "relax," "get ahold of yourself." Would that saying one of those phrases to someone upset, hurt, or angry actually worked; as likely as not, hearing comments such as these will actually intensify the emotion.

What is especially ironic is that neurobiologists—the ultimate representatives of the scientific establishment—are themselves beginning to understand that our ability to reason is inseparable from emotion; they function in tandem in the neocortex. This directly challenges centuries of Western thought, and more directly the fundamental operating premises of many mediators and facilitators about the management of emotion in general and conflict in particular. Strategies, techniques, and skills all need to be reconsidered in light of the understanding that people's reasoning processes, especially in conflict, may be hindered by precluding or minimizing emotion, as much as or more so than when there is an excess of emotion (D'Amasio, 1994, 1999).

The implications for the mediation or facilitation of conflict should be clear. For parties in conflict, it is more of a visceral, gut-wrenching experience that is felt physically and emotionally than an intellectual exercise. Conflict is experienced, not just coldly and dispassionately discussed in terms of interests and needs. The full measure of the story behind the conflict must be taken in any management option to be considered. Mediators and negotiators are at risk of being overly rational in approaching conflict. If their approach is predominantly cognitive, and essentially limited to talking rationally, they may miss the real source of the conflict drama being played out before them. Of course, missing the core elements of the conflict likely means missing the clues that could lead to settlement.

Tricksters have never presumed to be rational; they are, by definition, actors in the human dramas of conflict. They operate more by wit, intuition, and gut instinct, as do the best mediators. Note as well that in the theater of conflict, the mediator in fact has a number of roles in the staging of the mediation process. He or she is at once a director, set designer, script editor, narrator, and sometimes a character actor playing a supporting role. The drama is not hers or his, but the mediator must conjure up sufficient inspiration and passion to play the roles convincingly and authentically.

Constantin Stanislavski, the great Russian actor and director, in his 1936 book *An Actor Prepares* (1970), offers important suggestions that could easily be drawn from a trickster's or mediator's playbook and are as useful to them as they have ever been to actors. The best actors are so studied in their technique that they can be carried away by the play without losing themselves in it; they live their parts inwardly and rely on their intuition and subconscious—their practiced instincts. Novices, by contrast, resort to mechanical acting and rely on words and scripts. They tend to overact in compensation for a lack of experience or training.

Even though the mediator is acting, this does not mean she is less authentic, if she is genuinely engaged and involved in the reality of the present drama and committed to the resolution of the conflict (Benjamin, 2003). Although it is true that the mediator does not go home with the parties or have to live with the outcome, she does need to live with the quality of preparation and effectiveness of her performance. Just as the best actor must be able to transport an audience to a different reality, so must a mediator be able to tweak and reconstruct reality so that people in conflict are afforded the opportunity to find some measure of resolution for themselves (Benjamin, 2001b).

All negotiators, and especially mediators, like tricksters, are performance artists. Against the backdrop of a carefully analyzed strategy, with practiced and disciplined technique and skill, they are able to improvise. The mediator, like the accomplished actor, is totally involved with the dramatic environment—intellectually, physically, and emotionally or intuitively. Too often the intellectual side of mediation is stressed and the physical and intuitive dimensions are lost. The mediator needs a great comedian's sense of timing (think Lily Tomlin in *The Search for Intelligent Life in the Universe*) and stage presence to create and congeal dramatic moments that shift the focus of the parties in conflict (think John Gielgud in *Hamlet*). But timing and presence cannot be taught; the mediator must choose to learn that intuitive sense of saying just the right words at the right time, without thinking.

Improvisational techniques and exercises are the way an actor learns intuition—to feel the role—and that preparation is directly useful to mediators. Virginia Spolin, in *Improvisation for the Theater* (1969), helps actors tap their ability to be spontaneous and intuitive, to work with the present moment. Much of her focus was more on "untraining" ourselves from an unwarranted overreliance on rational analysis, and how instead to reach and develop our intuition. She discouraged dependence on mechanistic and formulaic techniques. The difference between the good actor or mediator and the great one is the ability to feel the rhythms of the unfolding drama/conflict.

When people tell stories to one another there is a measure of intimacy developed between the teller and listener. Storytelling is essential for a relationship to develop, whether personal or professional. Classic stories of literature have a reality all their own and can often serve as effective therapeutic agents (Coles, 1989). Stories convey metaphors that allow experiences to be understood in a context that makes sense and becomes more real. Literature and poetry are stories that have no value except for the meaning they provide to the readers, which in the proper circumstance can be considerable (Nemerov, 1978). Some stories of birth, death, and transcendence are ritualized, and their retelling becomes the basis for religious and spiritual experiences (Eliade, 1964). Folklore is composed of stories with a patterned repetition that perpetuates a culture's mythology. Trickster myths and stories especially are pervasive in virtually every culture, traceable across cultures, throughout history, even into the present day. They are so common that the fictional stories have in some sense become reality (Niditch, 1987).

In mediation, as in the trickster folklore, the drama and storytelling are as important as the point of the story itself. The script is the blood plasma of reality; it carries and conveys the metaphors of meaning and hints for possible resolutions. The story that a party chooses to tell the mediator and how it is told affords a glimpse of that person's construction of reality (Folberg and Milne, 1988). At the same time, the mediator's use of stories brings substance to the mediation process. The use of stories and metaphors in the mediation process often serves to shape and shift the context of a dispute just enough to allow admission of a variant construction of reality. Although disputing parties cannot even envision themselves on the same stage together, the mediator, as master storyteller, must be able to edit the script of each disputant's story of the conflict and concoct another scenario in which all participants can play a part in the drama. Thus, like the trickster figure, the understanding and manipulation of the story is the primary technique by which a mediator dislodges disputing parties from their entrenched positions. The close comparison between the purpose, approach, and technique of the trickster figure and those of a practicing mediator becomes readily apparent in the stories.

Trickster figures hold particular fascination because they are by intention and design ambiguous and contradictory personages, at once a joker, prankster, or fool and at the same time clever, compassionate, and wise. The classical trickster is both evil and good, wise and stupid, heroic and cowardly, spiritual and profane, culture adherent and culture violator. The trickster figure, like life itself, is confused and imperfect (Welch, 1990). Trickster stories are clearly intended to be entertaining but also carry within them the learning and values that characterize the culture. A consistent and characteristic theme in trickster stories, as the trickster figure interacts with humans, is the insistence that each person take responsibility for his or her decisions and bear the consequences of his or her actions (Welch, 1990). This theme bears strong resemblance to the fundamental premises of mediation practice.

Trickster figures come in a variety of forms. The joker or comedian, the wise fool, or the shocker are among the most common typecasts. The wily coyote of the Native American Indian tradition is well known. Charlie Chaplin brought the wise fool brilliantly into focus in the classic movie *The Great Dictator,* where he plays a seemingly stupid character ridiculing a Hitleresque tyrant while all around him are captivated by his power. The tradition is long and deep, from the Holy Fools of the Catholic Church to the court jesters of the early monarchies. All of them were given informal permission to poke fun at the pretensions of the controlling authority. In the current age, television and movie characters serve in the role of court jesters. The police detective Columbo, played by Peter Falk on television, updates the "wise fool" personage. No matter how disparate the cultures or distant in time, the trickster's role and purpose remains fundamentally the same: to manage conflict, to reconcile immovable objects and irresistible forces in such a way that mere mortals caught in between might survive another day. Though their methods and means borrow from the magician's trade of successfully creating illusion, it is not magic, but more about finding and using the natural energy of the conflict (Cooley, 1997). They can sense how and when to twist, modify, adjust, and moderate the desires and fears of the antagonists to keep conflict at bay. This is also the essence of a mediator's role: to be in the middle of a heated controversy and manipulate and tweak the parties' perspectives just enough to allow a settlement to emerge.

Tricksters in Biblical Folklore

Trickster figures and the use of trickery are evident throughout the Old Testament, and the stories or themes have parallels in the folklore traditions of many other, non-Judeo-Christian cultures. There are a number of examples. In Genesis, explaining the creation, the serpent tricks Eve into eating the apple of the tree of knowledge against God's law, suggesting that human wisdom arises from transgression (Pagels, 1988). Abraham appears willing to break the law of this world by the sacrificial killing of his own son, Isaac, to protect the law of God. God, in fact, is himself or herself a trickster figure in his or her own right, appearing to test Abraham's loyalty through unreasonable demands. In other scenes, Joseph and Jacob, who are both youngest sons, use trickery to gain their "rightful" birthrights at the expense of their older siblings. Jacob outwits (or outnegotiates) his brother Esau by trading him a good meal for his birthright in a style reminiscent of a true con artist. Similarly, Joseph intentionally insults his brothers through his dream reports in a scheme calculated to subvert the birth order of his family. Again, in the Book of Esther, the heroine is a trickster of a particularly troubling sort in light of modern feminist thought. She uses her feminine wiles to displace and supplant the king's wife and become queen herself. The justification for this ruse is given as the necessity of saving the Jewish people from destruction.

In the biblical stories, as in most of the trickster literature, deception is an acceptable means to obtain a justifiable end. The actions are often legitimized as necessary for the survival of a minority, subjugated person, or group in the face of an oppressive majority or force. Survival of the immediate conflict competes, as it always does in daily life, with ultimate values and principles. This is a common question in mediation: How tenaciously does one hold to principle in light of practical realities? Said another way, a reflective question often asked by a mediator in a conflict is, "Which is more important, being right or being settled?" Trickster tales compel us to consider when the rule of law must give way or be sidestepped in the face of necessity or to obtain justice.

The most classic Old Testament story, one that takes no stretch of the imagination to apply to mediation, is that of King Solomon and the two women claiming the same infant child as their own (1 Kings 3:16–28). By proposing to cut the child in half with his sword, the story compels reflection on an important rhetorical question: Would the great king have, in fact, hurt the child or was he bluffing? The answer is less important than the recognition that King Solomon, the paragon of judicious wisdom, did not know the right answer but did have an effective technique or trick to clarify the dispute. Solomon was not formally a mediator, but he clearly employed a mediation strategy worthy of any trickster figure. The story has been recounted and the technique employed in countless variant forms throughout history and has even been used by judges in the present day.

The New Testament is also a rich source of trickster lore. Jesus is the consummate storyteller who spawns parables that seek to entice humankind into reflection on their circumstance. For instance, the lines "Render unto Caesar what is Caesar's and unto God what is God's" (Matt. 22:21) or "Cast not the first stone" (John 8:7) are examples of an elliptical, not directly confrontative, technique by which Christ sought to frame issues and not give answers. This is a purposeful use of ambiguity worthy of any trickster or mediator.

Each of these biblical stories reflects either a personal, social, and moral dilemma for people living under strained conditions resulting from an imposed political or social order or a serious conflict. The protagonists are figures looking for ways to stave off an impending crisis, manage the conflict, and survive (Niditch, 1987). Most trickster tales reflect variations of those circumstances; trickery is allowed to redress or mitigate extreme or difficult circumstances. Mediators work the same territory.

Some biblical scholars have discerned in the early literary traditions of the Bible the notion even of God as a trickster, wreaking havoc in the form of floods, plagues, and other natural disasters for the perceived wrongdoing of humankind, ostensibly as a motivator to modify human behavior (Bloom, 1990). The ideas and roles for God have changed over time to correspond to human needs (Miles, 1995). God as a trickster reflects the depth of our human need for such a figure in our thinking as mortals.

Tricksters in American Indian Folklore

The trickster tales of the Native American Indians, like those in the Bible, confront the same fundamental dilemmas of humankind. They seek to provide understanding of our creation, fall from grace, death, and redemption. The tales remind us, as any mediator must, that life is not necessarily fair and that nothing lasts forever. The trickster, at the same time he or she saves the world, makes it more uncertain and difficult, filled with traps and contradictions. There are countless examples, many of which center on the coyote, a traditional American Indian trickster figure. A Caddo Indian tale, for instance, helps listeners understand death. It recounts how the coyote tricked humans into accepting death and thereby saved the world from overpopulation. A Kiowa Indian trickster story reflects the tension and struggle of the minority Indian culture to survive in the midst of an overbearing, dominant white culture (Sherman, 1990). By shape-shifting and other maneuvers, the coyote outsmarts a white man who is bent on taking advantage of the Indians (Radin, 1972).

The purpose of the American Indian storytelling tradition, as with the biblical tales, goes beyond merely entertaining others or passing on useful information. Both narrator and audience partici-pate in a minidrama of sorts that allows the listeners to obtain a moral useful in considering their present circumstance. A mediator operates in a similar manner. A mediator might tell two disputing parents the story of a judge who asks parties in court if they each love their child, and then after hearing they do, comments to them that he does not love their child and cannot understand why they would want him to make decisions for their child. As the story unfolds, the parties become active participants in the story and thereby compelled to take responsibility for their own actions. In the trickster stories, as in mediation, parties are given direct responsibility for their own decisions (Toelken, 1990).

Tricksters in Modern Culture

Though perhaps not of the same mythic or sacred dimensions as in the Bible or in Native American Indian oral tradition, the trickster figure is still very much a part of our present-day modern culture. The entertainment industry, television, movies, and literature are replete with trickster tales and figures (Santino, 1990). In movies, Charlie Chaplin played a wise fool, whose antics mocked the policies and politics in the society of his day. In television, the police detective Columbo continually asks obsequious questions of suspects in a charming and disarming manner until the culprit is hopelessly trapped by his or her own deceit. The wise fool is a frequent literary character in every culture. For example, Isaac Bashevis Singer (1953) offered Gimpel the Fool and the Czech writer Jaroslav Hašek (1974) presented the Good Soldier Švejk. Some trickster prototypes operate in a more shocking and sacrilegious manner. The character of Hawkeye in the movie *MASH*, like his precursor Yossarian in Joseph Heller's *Catch-22* (1961), is a conniver who subverts the military order at every turn to reveal the absurdity of war.

Many entertainers (for example, Michael Jackson, David Bowie, and Mick Jagger, and of course, Liberace) perform as androgynous, shamanlike figures who challenge cultural norms of accepted behavior and even sexual role stereotypes. Curiously, there is precedent for such personages in many traditional cultures. Among the Zuni Indians, those persons who were sexually ambiguous were easily accepted and sometimes thought to be imbued with special spiritual powers (Roscoe, 1991). These personalities demonstrate the trickster figure's qualities of elusiveness and ambiguity. They combine masculine and feminine attributes, wisdom and foolish-ness, meanness and kindness, deceit and honesty. They transcend cultural, legal, and sometimes moral norms that apply to the rest of society. Yet, through it all, their cleverness is a source of amusement and sometimes admiration.

Blues, jazz, and rap are all musical manifestations of the trick-ster tradition. The original intent and enduring appeal of those styles are drawn from their iconoclastic appeal. Improvisational, unstructured, sometimes shocking, and even sacrilegious, those forms of music require at the very least that we consider alternative realities and cultures. In particular, the blues grew out of African Americans' need to have a model of behavior to cope with oppres-sion. Both blues singers and songs incorporate and exhibit the trick-ster persona of "synchronous duplicity"—unifying good and evil, the sacred and profane. The music gives many African Americans a reason and means to endure and survive (Spencer, 1993). Beyond music, in African and African American cultures there is a strong trickster folklore tradition.

Every culture has similar trickster stories. The trickster character has been so important throughout history that such figures have invariably been made part of the institutionalized order. Thus the Catholic Church had Holy Fools, and in the Middle Ages ruling monarchs had court jesters. It is as if the established order of a soci-ety senses the necessity for a certain measure of built-in chaos in order to persist (Dooling, 1979). Mardi Gras is an outgrowth of that tradition.

Variety of Trickster Prototypes

Trickster figures, and the mediators who wittingly or unwittingly imitate them, demonstrate a variety of styles and forms. Some play the wise fool, who challenges the accepted reality or established order by seemingly innocuous or naïve action or questioning. Others play the clown or joker, using humor to tease out our human pen-chant for inconsistency. Still others use outlandish behavior to shock actors or parties toward a new perspective. Finally, some tricksters use outright deceit to con targeted parties into reconsidering their actions despite themselves. Regardless of technique, however, most tricksters and mediators have two primary purposes in mind: first, to create sufficient dissonance in the thinking of the parties in conflict (doubt about their rightness) so that they might consider other views or alternatives of actions, and second, to press the parties to take responsibility for their behavior and the resolution of the immediate conflict.

Strategies, Techniques, and Skills of Tricksters—and Mediators

The trickster figure offers a two-part strategic approach to shift people from their accepted reality or entrenched position to another perspective. First, the trickster figure is a shape-shifter, who transforms himself or herself into a less threatening form. In a similar manner, an effective mediator transforms himself or herself to enter the construction of reality of each party or to be on the same stage with each of them. At the same time, the mediator must project a sense of authenticity that can allow for trust to develop.

Second, the trickster seeks to transform the context of the dispute. This might be done either by confusing or by creating dissonance in the party's thinking and then reframing the issues in a manner more susceptible to resolution. These two stratagems operate together to finesse the problem at hand and to allow it to be approached from a new angle.

There is a close parallel between the strategies of a trickster, an effective mediator, and a guerrilla fighter. Neither mediators nor tricksters can afford the luxury of believing that people in conflict will start out being trusting, cooperative, and reasonable. Among other techniques, the trickster/mediator learns how to camouflage herself so that she blends into the scenery and at the same time, when and how to use hit-and-run tactics to plant notions that alternatively disturb, unsettle, and undermine entrenched thinking, and at the right time consider other options that might lead to settlement. There is little difference in the strategic planning for war or for settlement; only the purpose differs. The gist of Sun Tzu's message in the *Art of War,* written centuries ago, is relevant in conflict management today: "If one wants peace, study war" (Benjamin, 1998a).

What should be clear is that negotiators, mediators, facilitators, or anyone who engages in conflict is necessarily strategic. The etymology of *strategy* is the Greek word *strategema,* which is translated as a trick or a ruse—a maneuver to deceive or surprise an enemy (Benjamin, 1998a, p. 8). This is troublesome to some—the idea that a mediator would be manipulative and deceptive, and likened to a trickster figure—but effectively an inescapable reality in dealing with difficult conflicts. There is no question but that being strategic in general and deceptive in particular goes against the cultural grain and even assaults deeply held precepts of truth and honesty. Yet, notwithstanding the pejorative connotations, the practice of deception often serves a necessary, constructive, and essential purpose. This is the profane aspect of the trickster and the reality of the mediator. Thus careful thought must be given to the ethical considerations and ramifications about how and when deceptive or manipulative techniques are used and the limits of their use (Cooley, 1997).

Mediator's Transformation of Self: Shape-shifting

In many American Indian stories, the trickster coyote figure shape-shifts into human form. He knows that to approach the white man directly as a coyote would only serve to alert his mark to put up his guard (Radin, 1972). Likewise, the mediator needs to adopt the perspective or take the shape of (validate and acknowledge) each party and connect with them. To say directly, "I am here to change your mind and to convince you that what you think is a reasonable position is wrong" is likely to elicit resistance.

For a mediator to transform himself or herself into a party's construction of reality requires the mediator to initially suppress rational modes of analysis about the party's motives and interests and to exorcise from himself or herself preconceived notions about appropriate outcomes for the dispute. The mediator's sense of self as a separate person needs to be subsumed or melded into each party's perspective. The mediator must be able to see events from the view of each party to the dispute. Individuals' worldviews or constructions of reality are an amalgam of their hopes, desires, fears, needs, operative myths, and (perhaps only last) rational interests. The mediator must connect or get in sync with each party. The mediator must be able to identify with the perspective of each party sufficiently so that the party feels joined and accommodated. This identification works to establish the bond and credibility necessary for trust to develop between the mediator and each party. This reservoir of trust is traded on later in the process, especially in difficult cases. It is often a tricky business (pun intended) because the mediator must be able to synchronize with each party's construction of reality in a manner that does not appear to invalidate any other party to the dispute. To do so, the mediator needs to distinguish between validation of a party's construction of reality and agreement with that position. Validation, an intuitive or subjective concept, must not be confused with agreement, a logical or rationalist concept. If the mediator appears to be agreeing with one party or the other, he or she may well lose balance, risk offending one or both of the parties, and become ineffectual. The validation of one party, done skillfully, need not be at the expense of another party.

The mediator's self-transformation requires an explicit acknowledgment that virtually every conflict (whether a business or family dispute) has subjective, nonrational (not irrational) aspects that must be addressed. Even business conflicts are in essence personal disputes in disguise. A disputing party almost always has a personal and emotional stake in the outcome. The mediator loses an important edge by hesitating to take account of the subjective undercurrents of a dispute. Difficult conflicts are seldom resolved by the use of logic or reason alone, as Fisher, Ury, and Patton (1991) may be taken to suggest.

The mediator uses several techniques to transform himself or herself and gain entry into each disputing party's construction of reality. Communication theorists have observed that people construct reality by the symbolic representation of their worlds in their language, stories, metaphors, operative mythologies, and methods of communication (Bateson, 1972; Watzlawick, 1976; Bandler and Grinder, 1975). The central premise of neurolinguistic programming techniques, drawn from that theory, is that a party's speech and language patterns can be analyzed and imitated or approximated, and that by so doing one can enter that person's construction of reality. Once the intervenor mediator is synchronized—essentially in the same emotional "gear ratio"—he or she can then change the ratio, slow the intensity, and allow the parties to shift to another emotional state. The necessary rapport is developed by pacing or gently mirroring the party's style, gestures, body language, voice tone, timbre and volume, and the use of similar words and metaphors (Bandler and Grinder, 1975). This is the skill behind the technique of strategic empathy. The mediator deftly shifts his or her shape to take on the appearance of a party; the mediator chooses when and with which party to be strategically empathic. The technique, however, requires practice. Gaining access to a party's construction of reality cannot be done mechanically. As any actor knows, the hundredth performance must be as convincing and sincere as the first. In difficult conflicts, with entrenched parties, finding ways to enter their constructions of reality is an essential ongoing activity throughout the mediation process (Benjamin, 2002).

Transforming the Context of the Dispute

Once some level of entry to a party's construction of reality has been obtained, then the task is to pierce the party's operative mythology and alter, shift, or transform the context of a dispute so that it is susceptible to resolution. The context is the framing or understanding of the dispute, how a party views what the fight is about and presents it. Disputing parties cannot be allowed to remain settled or sanguine in their established thinking frames; they must be unsettled sufficiently to accept other alternatives. Most people approach problem solving in dichotomous, dualistic terms; something is either right or wrong, healthy or unhealthy, a personal issue or business issue, and so on. The categories are, by the logic of dichotomous thinking, taken to be mutually exclusive. Mediators, like trickster figures, must blur or confuse false dichotomies or polarities if settlement is to occur or even to be considered. There are a number of techniques and strategies that can be used to shift the context of a dispute: creation of dissonance in thinking, use of words and language, use of metaphors and stories, use of reframing techniques, use of resistance and paradox, manner of questioning, use of mistakes, understanding of negotiation as ritual and drama, and use of metastrategic thinking. Some of the techniques are common and have been discussed or merely noted elsewhere in the literature; others are uniquely illustrative of the trickster aspects of mediation.

Creation of Dissonance

One of the first steps in transforming the context of a dispute is to create dissonance in the thinking of each party. If parties believe they are right ("the myth of justice") and that a court will predictably determine they are right ("the myth of rationality"), then there is little motivation to mediate. For parties who are entrenched in their positions, the mediator needs to raise sufficient question and cast enough doubt over the parties' presumed expectations about the outcome of the dispute to generate the necessary motivation to mediate. In other words, "Pull the rug out from under them" (Benjamin, 2002).

Tricksters have traditionally used shock and humor to create dissonance. Among the Pueblo Indians, the trickster would become a clown, doing acts that were otherwise viewed as taboo to cause a rupture with the normal and ordinary patterns of thinking (Dooling,

1979). Breaking up established thinking frames allows people the opportunity to see matters differently and yields a greater openness to new ideas and options. In the same way, a mediator creates dissonance in thinking. For instance, to pierce the myth of justice—the notion that a court will determine a matter clearly and definitively in the way the party expects—the mediator might suggest, "I've heard judges say that they typically try to dissatisfy both parties because they don't know the right answer and don't want to make a big winner and big loser," or "Some attorneys say there is no case so good it can't be lost or so bad it can't be won; you can't trust those judges." The lines are calculated to create doubt and cause a disputant to be less sure of his or her position, and a little bit more reflective, and then followed by a dose of humor to diffuse the shock. Statements of that ilk can disrupt parties' myopic focus on who will win and the complacent belief that the court will give them what they want. As a result, the disputants are pressed to take responsibility for their own decisions without being directly confronted.

Words and Language

From the earliest times in many traditional cultures, words and language were understood to have a certain magic. The use of a word could have a strange consequence that allowed what people wanted to happen (Rothenberg, 1986). In a similar way, the particular words and language used by a mediator to frame a dispute can alter or shift the context of a dispute. For instance, the word *custody* is an exclusive term that can intensify conflict; the term implies, like the ownership of property, that one party wins and the other must necessarily lose. Substitution of a more inclusive term, such as *parenting responsibility* instead of custody, allows both parties to participate. In other contexts, medical malpractice disputes are more accurately termed medical treatment disputes. In matters where child sexual abuse is alleged, labels such as *victim* and *perpetrator* make difficult conflicts all but impossible to resolve. Instead, terms such as *child* and *responsible adult* focus attention on the behavior, not on the labeling or moral judgment of a party (Benjamin, 1991). The careful choice of words and language is critical and cannot be underestimated or discounted as mere semantics.

Metaphors and Stories

Stories carry metaphors. Metaphors help people understand what is happening to them. Metaphors can make reality if not appealing then at least endurable. The naked truth is that separation and loss are painful and harsh events in people's lives. Stories and metaphors dress up the truth so that, though not painless, it is at least less painful. The metaphor offers a sense of an actual experience by the use of imagery that resembles the event. It is a compressed story that highlights the critical pieces of the experience in a different and more graspable way. The poet Howard Nemerov (1978, p. 229) likens a metaphor to "the sudden bursting of a flare, so that you see for an instant not only the road ahead but also its situation in the terrain around." The trickster stories are themselves metaphors. The telling of stories about other people's circumstances normalizes a difficult experience. Hearing a metaphor conjures up in the listener's mind a picture of his or her own situation. To be effective, the metaphor needs to be drawn from the listeners' life experiences and offer them some measure of choice or control in their situation. For instance, divorce can be compared to a serious illness that may not be curable but is manageable. The mediator can present himself or herself as an oncologist aiding in the treatment of the cancer. To follow the metaphor, the doctor (mediator) may not be able to cure the cancer (stop the divorce), but he or she can help the patient (party) actively participate in the treatment (have some measure of choice and control over his or her life). Physical health is a good source of material for metaphors, especially in family conflicts. Most people have either dealt with serious illness or disability personally, through a close friend or relative, or know someone who has. Divorce, disease, and death are often closely linked in people's minds, and usually illness is not viewed as a person's fault. Yet the mediator must be careful not to allow the traditional dualistic construct of healthy versus sick to seep into the metaphor. Some serious illnesses, such as cancer, epilepsy, or AIDS, have become metaphors that confuse the person with the malady. If the disease is bad and to be aggressively combated, then so too must the person be bad to deserve the affliction (Sontag, 1977, 1989). Careful construction of metaphors is critical; however, their power and value in transforming the context of a dispute are incalculable.

Reframing

Reframing is one of the most fundamental techniques used by mediators to transform the context of a dispute. The mediator, like the trickster, takes the communication of a party and, without abrogating his or her meaning entirely, alters and redirects that meaning to allow more constructive use in the settlement process. Thus when parties are actively fighting, the mediator might compliment the parties on how well they fight and then go on to reframe their negative statements into positive meanings by noting that "people who fight well can negotiate well." The mediator, like a trickster, twists their words and shifts the context of the discussion. Reframing is a technique by which resistance can be surreptitiously bypassed (Fong and Haynes, 1990). When an issue is reframed, more ways of looking at the dispute emerge, and the parameters of the conflict become more fluid. In reframing, the mediator operates to reposition each antagonist so that the dispute is amenable to a resolution.

Resistance and Paradox

When the level of entrenchment in a position of one or more disputants is especially acute and the resistance to change pronounced, the use of paradox can be an effective technique to transform the context of the dispute. The paradox is a means of changing the rules of the game. When a party frames issues in an either-or or a right-wrong dualism, traditional logic typically fails to loosen his or her hold on the position seized. The use of logic is a form of confrontation or challenge. A particular line of logic is always susceptible to contradiction by another equal and opposite line of logic, and a pitched battle ensues between the competing logics. "Why don't you try this . . . ?" is met with "Yes, but . . ." as the entrenched party thwarts any perceived challenge to his or her position. For the mediator, as for the trickster, logic is the least-effective means of convincing or persuading anyone of anything. Grounded in communications and linguistics theory, paradox, in contrast to logic, co-opts and uses the force of a party's resistance to enact a shift in his or her thinking. Thus a party convinced of the justness of his or her position is encouraged to consider the pursuit of that course of action and to do everything necessary to obtain the result on which he or she is fixed. Only by first exploring and supporting the parties' thinking and encouraging them to hold on to their entrenched positions can the mediator move them to consider other options. Thus is the paradox: intensifying the commitment to a stated course of action lessens the commitment. Conversely, challenging resistance to a suggestion only serves to bolster the resistance, whereas recognizing the resistance may permit it to dissipate (Palazzoli, Boscolo, Cecchin, and Prata, 1985). In short, giving the parties permission to do what they say they must or want to do may let them not feel as compelled to pursue their stated courses of action.

In mediation, there are frequent opportunities for use of paradoxical injunction. For instance, a party skeptical of the mediation process and drawn to traditional legal action might be encouraged to go to court: "You always have the option to go to court. I don't want to make you stay in mediation or try to convince you." By contrast, the use of logic ("Going to court makes no sense because . . .") is not likely to dissuade a determined party and may be counterproductive. Paradox is not merely reverse psychology. To be effective in using the paradox technique, mediators must on some level believe that the parties have to exhaust their preferred courses of action before they can consider other alternatives.

Other mediation techniques are variations of the paradox. Suggesting extreme, unrealistic options that both parties consent to dismiss out of hand fosters a clearer focus on the options that might work. King Solomon's threat to cut the infant in half was such a paradoxical device used to clarify the dispute. Judges also use a variation of the paradox, probably more out of frustration than by design, when they threaten "to sell everything" if the parties cannot come to agreement themselves.

The mediator's use of a party's resistance in this manner is not unlike the use of an opponent's own force to throw him or her off balance in the martial art of aikido (Crum, 1987). Using logic head-on to confront an entrenched party results only in a test of wills. But approaching and acknowledging the resistance and blending with it allows an intransigent party's energy to be redirected constructively.

Questioning Process

The real magic of mediation in transforming the context of a dispute is most evident in the sophistication and style of questioning a mediator adopts (Fong and Haynes, 1990). A working premise of mediation is that disputing parties have a connection with each other on some level. Most conflicts have both distributive and integrative aspects; the former concerns who gets what, and the latter relates to the parties' future or ongoing relationship. Few disputes are purely integrative or distributive in character. In business or personal injury disputes, where the issues are seemingly only a question of money and the parties are not likely to have further dealings, there is still an integrative aspect. The injured party wants some acknowledgment of his or her suffering, and both parties typically want to feel that they have been reasonable and fair-minded. The particular connections or reciprocal relationships of the parties characterize and differentiate each dispute. These connections create circularity in the relationship ("I need you and you need me").

Questions that bring to the fore those interrelationships are "questions of a difference" that can allow a framework for settlement to emerge (Fong and Haynes, 1990), for instance, "What kind of relationship do you both hope to have in the future, after this dispute is resolved?"

On an obvious level, asking questions is considerably less threatening to parties than making declarative statements. Questions tend to elicit further information and reflective responses; declarative statements tend to challenge positions and call for defensive responses. Thus the question "What are your thoughts about these other options?" encourages reflective thinking. By contrast, the statement "This option seems to be the best one, because . . ." is likely to draw a rebuttal, "Maybe, but. . . ."

The best illustration of trickery-at-work in the questioning process is offered by Columbo, the television police detective. He is amusing and self-effacing; with outstretched arm and hand to forehead, precariously balancing his ever-present cigar and sporting a disheveled raincoat, he persists in asking obsequious questions of his suspect out of a seeming state of befuddlement. He is the embodiment of the wise fool; his seemingly simpleminded questions actually spin a web of intriguing complexity (Santino, 1990). Likewise, a mediator might ponderously ask, "I'm a bit confused, help me to understand, how will this work for you?" Solving a crime or catching a witness off-guard is, of course, not the mediator's purpose. However, although the purpose differs, effective questioning is the primary means by which a mediator transforms the context of a dispute. Keeping disputants "on the move" by questioning them, gently but persistently, encourages them to consider the situation from another perspective. This can eventually yield a workable agreement between even the most intransigent parties.

The Power of "Mistakes"—Intentional or Unintentional

The mediator's use of his or her own mistakes, both unintended and intended, can be an effective technique to shift the context of the dispute. Reminiscent of the wise fool trickster, the mediator uses his or her own vulnerability to normalize and relax the atmosphere in the discussion of the problem and to help the parties take responsibility for the problem solving. For instance, if a male mediator is accused by a female party of making a sexist or insensitive statement, whether real or imagined, a defensive response that denies the assertion is likely to intensify the conflict. On the other hand, if the response of the mediator is to listen effectively and give credence to her reality, acknowledge his vulnerability, and encourage her to bring any future "error" to his attention, then the result can be the bolstering of the mediator's credibility. The truth of the accusation is not determinable or relevant; the only consideration for the mediator is how to use the "mistake" constructively to further the mediation process.

There are some circumstances when the mediator might intentionally make a mistake for the parties to catch. This antic can work to foster the parties' joint cooperation in checking the mediator. For example, purposeful miscalculation of numbers, or a request by the mediator for help in tabulating numbers, presses the parties into responsibility for their agreement. Mistakes allow the mediator to use his or her own vulnerability constructively to turn what appears to be a disadvantage into an advantage.

Negotiation as Ritual and Drama

The ultimate transformation of the context of a dispute is accomplished by the structuring and managing of the negotiation process. At core, formal mediation is nothing more than a three-party or multiple-party negotiation. The mediator negotiates his or her authority with each participant and facilitates their negotiation with each other. Negotiation is the primary operative activity of mediation; the mediation process is merely a particular format for structured negotiation that employs the services of a third party. Therefore, how the mediator understands and presents negotiation and, in some instances, actually teaches the parties the ways of negotiation is critical to the success of the mediation process.

Negotiation is often thought of in a rudimentary and simplistic form: offer and counteroffer. Some view negotiation as a practical necessity, others as a form of evil. Most people in Western cultures view negotiation as a practical, rational, and utilitarian activity wherein parties seek to maximize gains and minimize losses in allocating and exchanging basic resources: time, money, product, or energy (physical or psychological). In this perspective, the focus is limited to "get as much as you can or give as little as you have to." In the legal context, attorneys do their calculations in negotiating for their client on the basis of their guesses about what a court might do (Menkel-Meadow, 1985). Styles of negotiation are often presented in dualistic terms; one is either a "hard" negotiator concerned only with the result or a "soft" negotiator concerned only with relationships and willing to settle at all costs (Williams, 1983). The predominant model of negotiation taught in law and business schools emphasizes the outcome; a win or loss is objectively determined by the result.

The negotiation process is far more complex. In most cultures, negotiation is a form of ritual and drama. The deal and its result are important, but the relationship dynamics between the parties is equally important. Negotiation is simultaneously a social and psychological interaction, as well as an economic event (Leff, 1976). Contrary to the conventional wisdom that everybody wants something for nothing, few people actually operate under that assumption. Most expect to contribute something. Thus even con games are premised on allowing the dupe or mark to give the deceiver or con artist something that is needed. Successful negotiation requires creating a drama in which the parties to the negotiation need each other. Curiously, the deal that is made as a result of negotiation can be viewed as a good deal or a fraudulent swindle, depending on who is judging the result. Still, whatever deal is determined, the structure, process, and execution are substantially the same: "Every selling situation, 'lawful' or not, involves the creation of a drama and of roles in that drama designed to move toward the same denouement, a completed sale" (Leff, 1976, p. 183). A swindle, ironically, is at least for some period of time a consensual crime. Deciding when selling becomes swindling often requires determining if a sales pitch that merely uses "fluff and bluff" has crossed some unwritten line of propriety and become an intentional bait-and-switch routine. This judgment is largely a matter of social policy and legal control. However, an understanding of the negotiation process as essentially a social interaction ritual is important for the effective mediation of a dispute.

Understanding negotiation as substantially ritual and drama offers a natural backdrop for the view of the mediator as a trickster. The trickster of folklore is clearly a master actor and negotiator, if not a con artist of sorts (as must be a good mediator). This is not to suggest that the mediator should be a swindler or allow either party to be conned. However, if disputing parties are to resolve conflict, then the mediator must recognize the importance of developing a settlement scenario or drama in which both parties play a role. Disputing parties usually enter a conflict with scripts written in their own mind where one is the hero and the other person is the villain. The mediator needs to rewrite the scripts so that the disputants can see themselves as characters who exchange lines onstage and complete the play constructively. The mediator must necessarily be producer, director, script editor, actor, and narrator in the conflict management performance (Benjamin, 2001b). If the mediator allows the parties to move to the final scene—who gets what—before the plot has developed, the actors may feel that they have not had the opportunity to tell their stories and that the play is a sham. People who remark that they want their day in court do not necessarily literally mean a courtroom; they often mean a stage or forum to tell their stories. Time must be taken to properly set the scene and prepare the participants so that the resolution obtained appears to be of their own design. An effective mediator-trickster knows how to evade discussion of ultimate issues until he or she has ensured that the parties know what the conflict is really about. The mediator stalls the parties so that actual negotiation does not begin until they are ready. Like wine needing to ferment, "no conflict should be approached before its time" (Benjamin, 2002).

The mediator may need to give one or both of the parties stage directions, that is, teach negotiation. The parties need to learn the tricks of the trade. Thus, for instance, as every good poker player knows, it may be better to lose early in the game with a winning hand so that one can win later on with a losing hand. Applied to negotiation, this means to teach the art of trade-offs, how to think strategically, and how to develop both preferred and fallback perspectives. As the mediator imparts some of his or her own negotiation skills, the parties' style of negotiation is modified from a simplistic offer-counteroffer format into a more sophisticated interactive negotiation format. The parties are shifted from thinking in terms of static, hard-and-fast positions to thinking dynamically in terms of multiple options. The parties learn to question and consider what pieces of each other's interests they might accommodate to obtain what they themselves need (Benjamin, 2002).

Metastrategies

Finally, the techniques available to the mediator to transform the context of a dispute include metastrategic thinking, whereby the mediator determines when and under what circumstances to disclose or not disclose his or her strategy. For example, when mediators explain to the parties how the mediation process is structured in the agenda-setting task, they are showing their strategy for effective problem solving. By so doing, the mediators enlist the parties' commitment to the process and responsibility for the decisions. At other times, however, mediators may choose to avoid the discussion of an action or intervention and in fact cloak their purpose. For instance, if a mediator becomes aware that one party is having significant difficulty in negotiating, to call direct attention to the impaired party may make matters worse. A caucus, first with the party with no difficulty and then with the person in difficulty, may help to mask the mediator's purpose of talking privately with the person in need of support without drawing undue attention. Any good mediator, like any good trickster, must appreciate the value of stealth as a device to further the negotiation process (Benjamin, 1998a, 2002).

Deception and Manipulation

The intention behind likening the professional role and practice of a mediator to those of the folkloric trickster figure is not in any way intended to condone destructive, deceitful, or unethical behavior or to endorse the pursuit of agreement between disputing parties at all costs. At the same time, the comparison highlights and emphasizes the importance of the distinctive kind of thinking a mediator must do to effectively manage conflict. It is also worthy of note to draw a distinction between constructive and destructive deceptions. A constructive deception is done to aid disputing parties in their self-determination of informed decisions, whereas a destructive deception is done for the gain of one at the expense of another. Not all deceptions are the same. Forms of deception have been practiced as a means of survival and the propagation of humankind (and every other form of life) since the beginning of time (Rue, 1994; Wright, 1994).

Natural History of Deception in Human Affairs

The dynamics of deception have not only played a decisive role in the cultural history of humankind but they are also deeply embedded in the process of biological evolution. Deceptive traits, and traits for detecting deception, are a fundamental part of the functioning of not only humans but also animals, insects, plants, and other forms of life. Still, humans in general, and those from Western cultures in particular, fear deception perhaps even more than death. This preoccupation with deception has been a primary organizing principle in the formulation of religions (false teachings and doctrines of sin and salvation), the approach to philosophical inquiry, the pursuit and methodology of scientific inquiry, and our conceptions of health (both mental and physical). Rue (1994) suggested that Western tradition has developed as much as a result of flight from deception and false-hood as a quest for certainty and truth, if not more so. Western cultures' rationalist tradition, in which the traditional professions are anchored, advances the notion that problems of deception can be avoided, or at least minimized, by the analysis and articulation of knowledge. In the rationalist scheme only reason is trusted and the senses are viewed as inherently deceptive and untrustworthy.

Trickster figures and mediators, who are their progeny, work sub-stantially by their senses (intuitive wit). Thus, although the pure rationalist struggles to avoid or suppress delusion (both internally and externally), the mediator and the trickster figure accept the necessary purpose and function of delusional thinking in the con-duct of human affairs and especially in the management of conflict.

Ethics of Deception

The notion of a trickster as a professional role model may be dis-concerting since the term *trickster* typically has negative connota-tions, especially in Western cultures. The primary purpose of the trickster figure in myth and folklore is to instruct, but trickery and deception are nevertheless actively employed in that pursuit. Most people associate such manipulative behavior with deceit and dis-honesty. Yet human behavior, almost by definition, includes and sometimes even requires the manipulation of circumstances or other people. Deception, in fact, may be essential for our survival and propagation as a species. Manipulation is the stuff of politics and the political maneuvering that goes on in every human social orga-nization. Implicit in that realization, therefore, is the differentia-tion between appropriate, socially acceptable manipulations and unacceptable ones. Being clever in our society is in fact often valued, even if it is at someone else's expense, as in a successful business deal (another person may be labeled a criminal for similar behavior in a different circumstance). Depending on the context and who is judging, manipulative behaviors may be construed as clever and constructive (a politician), criminal or socially maladjusted (a juvenile delinquent), or sick or pathological (a sociopath). In any event, all manipulative acts are not bad per se. As a clinical definition, deception occurs when a discrepancy between appearance and reality can be attributed in part to the causal influence of another organism (Rue, 1994). Only if the behavior is judged in hindsight to be harmful to others is it disdained.

Many professionals, including doctors, lawyers, and clergy, regularly practice varieties of deception that are formally sanctioned and even encouraged. For a priest, rabbi, or minister, silence regarding a penitent's confidences is a moral, if not a sacred, obligation that has been embodied as a privilege in law (Bok, 1978). Doctors sometimes lie to patients about the severity or nature of their illnesses under the guise of good medical practice for the patients' welfare (Veatch, 1991). Some lawyers believe that it is valid and necessary to embellish the facts of their cases, if not outright lie, in the representation or protection of their clients' interests (Freedman, 1975). In fact, our whole capitalistic culture is based on principles of marketing and negotiation that include elements of acceptable deception; selling and swindling are often a hair's breadth apart (Leff, 1976). Attaching a pejorative connotation to a manipulative or deceptive strategy per se is unwarranted. It is far too facile and simplistic to judge actions as right or wrong out of context. Heroes and scoundrels often inhabit the same body. In the same way, a mediator-trickster may alternately play the role of dupe or deceiver, or be so viewed by those outside the conflict.

If the premise is accepted that the whole or exact truth is not knowable, or is at least out of reach at a given moment, then we are left with only the degree to which we misrepresent, wittingly or unwittingly, the truth. Some may reject this premise as too relative, but the rest of us are left with a conceptual muddle that requires a distinction between truth and truthfulness. Truth is a matter of epistemology and addresses what is known and knowable; truthfulness is an ethical issue and deals with the use and manipulation of information (Bok, 1978). Mediators are less concerned with the truth than with truthfulness.

Truthfulness, as an ethical concern, is more troublesome. The nature of the intention and purpose underlying the manipulation of information is often difficult to ascertain. For instance, the degree of intention to deceive may vary and be colored by both the speaker's own self-deception or misunderstanding as well as the listener's desire to be deceived or simple lack of understanding (Watzlawick, 1976). The purpose of the deception is also germane. A speaker's deception to obtain a specific outcome or advantage must be differentiated from a manipulation that merely attempts to allow other outcomes to be considered (Bok, 1978). The use of deception is not per se negative or unethical. In mediation, effective practice requires the manipulation of information to facilitate the parties' ability to review all available options and to make informed choices. For that reason, many of a mediator's skills, strategies, and techniques are founded on varieties of deception. It is not the least bit inconsistent to suggest that deception is necessarily employed by a mediator to ensure informed, consensual decision making. Deception, as operationally defined for use in mediation, is any manipulation or intervention designed or calculated to encourage a disputing party to reevaluate or reconsider his or her position. Paradoxically, deception is a necessary tool for a mediator to obtain a quality agreement between disputing parties.

The professional and ethical practice of mediation, however, does not condone unbridled use of deception. The check and balance on the mediator's use of trickery is not the achievement of an outcome but rather the achievement of an informed and consensual outcome between the parties (Cooley, 1997).

Conclusion: Pursuit of the "Noble Lie"

Most mediators would be quick to disassociate themselves from mediation as pandering through trickery or deception. However, an effective mediator uses strategies and techniques similar to those of the folkloric trickster figure to help people in conflict view and understand the world around them differently and to help release disputing parties from their self-imposed constraints of limited options. Those are no small feats. An understanding of the necessity and purposes of deception is rooted in the intuitive sensibility of the trickster and the mediator. They both appreciate that conflicts are seldom rational in origin and cannot be settled by logic or analysis alone.

The successful mediation of a dispute sometimes even appears to be like magic. It is not, of course, and the structure and skills of mediation are learnable (Bandler and Grinder, 1975). A mediator must, however, intuitively sense the varying constructions of reality of the disputing parties so that the threads of their respective realities can be woven into the fabric of an agreement. As well, the mediator may also borrow from the shamans of traditional cultures their knowledge of ritual and ceremony (Eliade, 1964). This does not mean mediation should become therapy, even though it may be residually therapeutic. However, there should be a clear recognition that when conflicts occur between people, whether in families or in business, the first casualty is the loss of familiar patterns, habits, or traditions. If the mediator can provide new and different rituals and gain the parties' commitment to the mediation process, then the final agreement is likely to be more resilient and durable.

The role of the mediator is fundamentally different from that of other professionals as they have traditionally functioned. Doctors, lawyers, judges, therapists, accountants, and most other professionals have been given—and have assumed—the mantle of experts in our culture. As such, they are responsible for solving problems or conflicts of clients or patients and for taking the blame if they fail.

In the view of many, the professional's role is to give people answers. Too often, that leads to imposition of their preconceived ideas about reality on their clients. The client is told "the way it is or ought to be" and bent accordingly to fit into the right agreement. This model of professional practice is of little help to a mediator, whose source of authority is not anchored in a specialized knowledge base but rather derived from trust developed between the mediator and the parties.

The mythological trickster figure offers a metaphor and a better model of mediation practice. Tricksters are not experts; they are collaborators and sometimes coconspirators with the parties in effecting settlement of conflict. This is perhaps why the institutionalization of mediation can be so problematic. Mediators working within an agency or organization may be constrained and stifled (Benjamin, 1998b).

Instead of imposing an answer, the mediator helps disputing parties shift their constructions of reality enough for them to develop their own resolution of the conflict. Traditional professionals are grounded in a knowledge base from which to give advice; mediators have no such firm ground. Instead, the mediator, like the trickster, is left to constantly dodge, bob, weave, and maneuver between disputants' entrenched positions, which have been built on all that good advice of traditional professionals. By hook or crook, the mediator concocts with the parties a scheme that can work for all of them. The mediator's conceptual home, like the tricksters of folklore, is in the ever-changing and ambiguous space between irresistible forces and immovable objects.

Mediators, like trickster figures, are in some measure illusionists; both confront the harsh, jagged reality of conflict and seek to shift the appearance of that reality just enough to help those caught in conflict endure. Their use of deception and strategic intervention is calculated not for self-gain at the expense of the conflicting parties but rather for the parties' benefit. As a result, ideally the parties learn, but at the very least they survive the conflict.

All human beings, and especially mediators, must sometimes deceive, manipulate, and even lie as a means of survival. Conflict is about survival. It is the purpose of the deceit that must be examined. If the purpose is solely to trick or force the parties to settlement at all costs or to serve the purposes of the mediator, the ethics of such behavior are dubious. If, however, the deception is designed to shift and reconfigure the thinking of disputing parties and to foster their cooperation, then the deception may well be a "noble lie" (Rue, 1994; Benjamin, 1995a).

Reflective Practice Questions

1. Do you agree with the author's description of confusion, voyeurism, compulsiveness, and marginality as important qualities for mediators?

2. Have you played the role of trickster in your work as a mediator? To what extent are you comfortable or uncomfortable with playing that role? Have you experienced what the author refers to as the trickster's "systematic intuition" as a quality that enhances your ability to bring peace into the room?

3. In what ways do you, like the author, experience mediation as theater? What implications does that analogy—and the author's discussion of deception and manipulation—have for the ethics of mediation practice?

References

Bandler, R., and Grinder, J. *The Structure of Magic*. Palo Alto, Calif.: Science and Behavior Books, 1975.

Bateson, G. *Steps to an Ecology of Mind*. New York: Ballantine, 1972.

Bauer, Y. *Jews for Sale? Nazi-Jewish Negotiations, 1933–1945*. New Haven: Yale University Press, 1994.

Benjamin, R. D. "The Physics of Mediation: Reflections of Scientific Theory in Professional Mediation Practice." *Mediation Quarterly*, 1990, 8(2), 91–113.

Benjamin, R. D. "The Use of Mediative Strategies in Child Sexual Abuse Matters." *Family and Conciliation Courts Review*, 1991, *2*(2), 221–245.

Benjamin, R. D. "The Constructive Uses of Deception: Skills, Strategies, and Techniques of the Folkloric Trickster Figure and Their Application by Mediators." *Mediation Quarterly*, Fall 1995a, *13*(1), 3–18.

Benjamin, R. D. "The Mediator as Trickster: The Folkloric Figure as Professional Role Model." *Mediation Quarterly*, Winter 1995b, *13*(2), 131–149.

Benjamin, R. D. "Guerilla Mediation: The Use of Warfare Strategies in the Management of Conflict." [http://www.mediate.com]. 1998a.

Benjamin, R. D. "Mediation as a Subversive Activity." [www.mediate.com]. 1998b.

Benjamin, R. D. "The Natural Mediator." *Mediation News* (Academy of Family Mediators), 1998c, *18*(1), 8–9.

Benjamin, R. D. "The Risks of Neutrality." *Mediation News* (Academy of Family Mediators), 1998d, *17*(3), 8–9.

Benjamin, R. D. "Negotiation and Evil: The Sources of Religious and Moral Resistance to the Settlement of Conflict." *Mediation Quarterly*, 1998e, *15*(3), 245–266.

Benjamin, R. D. "The Quest for Truth and the Truth of Lies." *Mediation News* (Academy of Family Mediators), 1999, *18*(4), 11–12.

Benjamin, R. D. "Gut Instinct: A Mediator Prepares." *Mediation News* (Academy of Family Mediators), Summer 2001a, 6–7.

Benjamin, R. D. "Mediation as Theatre and Negotiation as Performance Art." *ACR Family Sector Newsletter*, Fall 2001b, 7–8.

Benjamin, R. D. *The Negotiation and Mediation of Conflict: Applied Theory and Practice Handbook* (9th ed.). Portland, Oreg.: Mediation and Conflict Management Services, 2002.

Benjamin, R. D. "Terry Waite: A Study in Authenticity." *Resolutions* (Straus Institute for Dispute Resolution, Pepperdine University School of Law), 2003, *5*(1), 8–9.

Berlin, I. *The Hedgehog and the Fox: An Essay on Tolstoy's View of History.* New York: Simon & Schuster, 1953.

Berlin, I. *The Crooked Timber of Humanity: Chapters in the History of Ideas* (H. Hardy, ed.). New York: Knopf, 1991.

Bloom, H. *The Book of J.* (D. Rosenberg, trans.). New York: Grove Weidenfeld, 1990.

Bok, S. *Lying: Moral Choice in Public and Private Life.* New York: Random House, 1978.

Bowlby, J. *Attachment and Loss.* Vol. 2: *Separation.* New York: Basic Books, 1973.

Bowlby, J. *Attachment and Loss*. Vol. 1: *Attachment* (Rev. ed.). New York: Basic Books, 1982.

Campbell, J., and Moyers, B. In B. S. Flowers (ed.), *The Power of Myth*. New York: Doubleday, 1988.

Coles, R. *The Call of Stories: Teaching and the Moral Imagination*. Boston: Houghton Mifflin, 1989.

Cooley, J. "Mediation Magic: Its Use and Abuse." *Loyola University of Chicago Law Review*, 1997, 29(1), 1–107.

Crum, T. F. *The Magic of Conflict*. New York: Simon & Schuster, 1987.

D'Amasio, A. R. *Descartes' Error: Emotion, Reasons, and the Human Brain*. New York: Putnam, 1994.

D'Amasio, A. R. The Feeling of What Happens: Body and Emotions in the Making of Consciousness. Orlando: Harcourt Brace, 1999.

Diamond, S. "Introductory Essay: Job and the Trickster." In P. Radin, *The Trickster: A Study in American Indian Mythology*. New York: Schocken Books, 1972.

Dooling, D. M. "The Wisdom of the Contrary: A Conversation with Joseph Eppes Brown." *Parabola: Myth and the Quest for Meaning*, 1979, 4(1), 54–65.

Eliade, M. *Shamanism: Archaic Techniques of Ecstasy*. Princeton, N.J.: Princeton University Press, 1964.

Elster, J. *Solomonic Judgements: Studies in the Limitations of Rationality*. Cambridge, England: Cambridge University Press, 1989.

Fisher, R., Ury, W., and Patton, B. *Getting to YES: Negotiating Agreement Without Giving In* (2nd ed.). Penguin Books, 1991.

Folberg, J., and Milne, A. (eds.). *Divorce Mediation: Theory and Practice*. New York: Guilford Press, 1988.

Fong, L., and Haynes, J. "Milan Techniques in Questioning." Paper presented at the annual meeting of the Academy of Family Mediators, Advanced Training Institute, Boston, July 1990.

Freedman, M. H. *Lawyers' Ethics in an Adversary System*. New York: Bobbs-Merrill, 1975.

Hašek, J. *The Good Soldier Švejk*. New York: Penguin Books, 1974.

Heller, J. *Catch-22*. New York: Ballantine, 1961.

Kosko, B. *Fuzzy Thinking: The New Science of Fuzzy Logic*. New York: Hyperion, 1993.

LeBaron, M. "Trickster, Mediator's Friend." In D. Bowling and D. Hoffman (eds.), *Qualities of a Mediator*. San Francisco: Jossey-Bass, 2003.

Leff, A. A. *Swindling and Selling*. New York: Free Press, 1976.

Levi-Strauss, C. *Structural Anthropology*. New York: Basic Books, 1963.

Lewontin, R. C. *Biology as Ideology*. New York: HarperCollins, 1991.

McKeon, R. "Nicomachean Ethics." In R. McKeon (ed.), *Introduction to Aristotle*. New York: Modern Library, 1947.

Menkel-Meadow, C. "The Transformation of Disputes by Lawyers: What the Dispute Paradigm Does and Does Not Tell Us." *Journal of Dispute Resolution*, 1985, 25–44.

Miles, J. *God: A Biography*. New York: Knopf, 1995.

Mnookin, R., and Kornhauser, L. "Bargaining in the Shadow of the Law: The Case of Divorce." *Yale Law Journal*, 1979, 88, 950–997.

Nemerov, H. *Figures of Thought: Speculations on the Meaning of Poetry and Other Essays*. Boston: Godine, 1978.

Niditch, S. *Underdogs and Tricksters: A Prelude to Biblical Folklore*. New York: HarperCollins, 1987.

Nisker, W. *The Essential Crazy Wisdom*. Berkeley, Calif.: Ten Speed Press, 2001.

Nozick, R. *The Nature of Rationality*. Princeton, N.J.: Princeton University Press, 1994.

Pagels, E. *Adam, Eve, and the Serpent*. New York: Random House, 1988.

Palazzoli, M. S., Boscolo, L., Cecchin, G., and Prata, G. *Paradox and Counter Paradox* (8th ed.). New York: Aronson, 1985.

Popper, K. *The Poverty of Historicism*. New York: HarperCollins, 1961.

Radin, P. *The Trickster: A Study in American Indian Mythology*. New York: Schocken Books, 1972.

Roscoe, W. *Zuni Man-Woman*. Albuquerque: University of New Mexico Press, 1991.

Rothenberg, J. *Shaking the Pumpkin: Traditional Poetry of the Indian North Americas* (Rev. ed.). New York: Van Der Marck, 1986.

Rue, L. D. *By the Grace of Guile: The Role of Deception in Natural History and Human Affairs*. New York: Oxford University Press, 1994.

Santino, J. "Fitting the Bill: The Trickster in American Popular Culture." *The World & I*, Apr. 1990, pp. 661–669.

Saul, J. R. *Voltaire's Bastards*. New York: Vintage Books, 1992.

Schön, D. A. *The Reflective Practitioner: How Professionals Think in Action*. New York: Basic Books, 1983.

Sherman, J. "Child of Chaos: Coyote, a Folkloric Triad." *The World & I*, Apr. 1990, pp. 648–650.

Singer, I. B. *Gimpel the Fool*. New York: Farrar, Straus & Giroux, 1953.

Sontag, S. *Illness as Metaphor*. New York: Farrar, Straus & Giroux, 1977.

Sontag, S. *AIDS and Its Metaphors*. New York: Farrar, Straus & Giroux, 1989.

Spencer, J. M. *Blues and Evil*. Knoxville: University of Tennessee Press, 1993.

Spolin, V. *Improvisation for the Theater*. Chicago: Northwestern University Press, 1969.

Stanislavski, C. *An Actor Prepares*. New York: Theatre Arts Books, 1970. (Originally published 1936)

Toelken, B. "Ma'ii Joldlooshi la' Eeya' . . . The Several Lives of a Navajo Coyote." *The World & I*, Apr. 1990, pp. 651–660.

Veatch, R. M. *The Patient-Physician Relation*. Bloomington: Indiana University Press, 1991.

Watzlawick, P. *How Real Is Real? Confusion, Disinformation, Communication—An Anecdotal Introduction to Communications Theory*. New York: Random House, 1976.

Welch, R. L. "The Laughing Gods: An Introduction to the Trickster Essays." *The World & I*, Apr. 1990, pp. 614–624.

Williams, G. R. *Legal Negotiation and Settlement*. St. Paul, Minn.: West, 1983.

Wright, R. *The Moral Animal: Evolutionary Psychology and Everyday Life*. New York: Pantheon Books, 1994.

5

Trickster, Mediator's Friend

Michelle LeBaron

Conflict is a confounding process. It happens inside us, between us, arising out of the cracks between our coming together. It draws our attention to the pieces that don't quite fit our pictures, giving us a chance to smooth the edges or redraw the designs as we seek to address it. Conflict touches us in our innermost selves; if it did not, we would not be so engaged and troubled by it. Sometimes conflict feels as though it grabs a part of our inner selves and yanks it out of place when we least welcome the intrusion.

We are not always sure where conflict comes from, and its course can be unpredictable. Recently, I was with a group of very smart people who have been studying, teaching, and writing about conflict for decades. We were talking about cutting-edge issues for the field, when one of them threw up his hands in frustration, reminding us that "we still have precious little understanding of what causes conflict." Given that we haven't understood this, he wondered, how can we proceed further into analysis, resolution, or transformation?

And yet we do proceed, trusting our intuition that tells us conflict is a circle, not a line. It is a process that we sometimes find ourselves in the middle of before we are aware of beginning. It is a spiral that can take us into insight and growth, but not before it unwinds some of the things we took as givens. Because of the way conflict can tie us in knots, confounding our plans and stimulating our resistance, we sometimes seek the help of a mediator, a mediator who we trust to bring perspective and fluidity to our stuck, con-stricted situations.

Mediators as Boundary Crossers

As mediators, we come with experience. All of us have been engaged in conflicts of our own. We do well to remember these, bringing empathy and understanding in place of the objectivity and scientific detachment we once thought necessary to be effective. Bringing this awareness, we recognize the familiar voice of conflict, jarring and disturbing. But we know also that there are subtler voices to be heard, voices that sing us into places we might not have chosen to go, places where we see views that stir us, quickening our sense of connection. In rare moments, we may be deeply privileged to witness, with parties, the shifting of boundaries between self and other. With them, we glimpse understanding that encompasses and transcends the way we have drawn lines around ourselves and our realities. These moments breathe hope into us, affirming our faith in humankind's capacity to knit itself back together even after dam-age and destruction has torn the fabric of our communities.

At many points during mediations, boundaries shift and realign in small ways. People cross over, not betraying their side but seeing a place previously unrecognized where their sides may overlap. As they do this, parties' sense of self and other shifts as well. No longer is the world divided as neatly into *us* and *them*; a new *we* emerges as the mediator holds open the possibility of change and transfor-mation. This happens in a variety of matters, from commercial issues to zoning disputes, from family conflicts to victim-offender mediations. I remember a commercial mediation where the expres-sion of genuine empathy by an insurance company adjuster to a plaintiff had the effect of breaking an impasse. Neither side aban-doned its views, but they related from their common humanity for a few moments and it changed the course of the session.

Mediators not only help parties cross and redraw boundaries. We are boundary crossers ourselves. We step into the private domain of other people's conflicts, involving ourselves as resources in all that those conflicts evoke and deliver, the inner turmoil and the outer bravado. Mediators challenge the boundaries others have erected, inviting parties to imagine new ways of sharing resources while expanding their repertoires of constructive ways to relate. As mindful mediators, we also challenge boundaries within ourselves, noticing when our assumptions and beliefs get in the way of parties' progress.

As we are boundary crossers, mediators need facility in stepping over fences and deep trenches that would otherwise discourage or impede progress. Little in mediation training addresses this capacity, yet it is an essential quality of effective mediators. To cultivate it is not to take a course nor assimilate a module, but to enter the realm of stories and the wisdom they convey. Particular kinds of stories are especially helpful because they contain time-tested wisdom, wisdom that comes to us from peoples who saw the permeability between worlds, who knew ways of crossing boundaries before the word *mediation* was ever invented. We call these stories myths.

Trickster Myths

Myths are things that never were, yet are always happening. Myths carry the shapes and the whisperings of old ways, posing questions to us and offering diamonds that glint with answers to those who read between the lines. One of the richest resources for mediators is the group of myths about the trickster. Trickster myths are useful because they show ways of transiting boundaries and balancing needs that wind circuitously through conflicts, matching the dodges and defenses of parties with windows and possibilities. Robert Benjamin, a mediator from St. Louis, identified the wealth that trickster tales offer us in two articles published in *Mediation Quarterly* in the mid-1990s (Benjamin, 1995; see also Chapter Four of this volume).

Trickster stories come to us from many cultural traditions. They speak to us of the art of mediation practice, of the flexibility and shape-shifting so essential to our work. Trickster myths speak to conflict and harmony, order and disorder. Most trickster figures are male, but there are also female tricksters, legendary for their cleverness and subtlety. Native American cultures are rich with trickster tales, featuring Coyote from the Plains and California, and Mink, Bluejay, and Raven from the north Pacific. From the Southeast, trickster stories intermingle with Brer Rabbit stories with their African origins. Trickster is Susa-no-o in Japan, and Hare, Tortoise, and Spider in West Africa.

Trickster stories come to us from ancient texts via oral traditions; from whispered words in jungles, around firesides, and in longhouses. They show us aspects of conflict unplumbed by our scientific and fragmenting analyses: the whole of it, the dance of it, the paradox of it. They show us that the route to resolution is seldom direct, for people are complex beings and situations have more than one truth associated with them. They show us about connection, bridging differences, and the importance of boundaries. They show us about imagination as a resource, and they remind us of the physical realities that govern our experience, ignored at our peril.

Trickster is wily and wise, capable and helpful, yet prone to being caught in his own cleverness. Trickster cautions that our experience and learning may not help parties reach their potential if we do not also cultivate resilience, flexibility, creativity, and a sense of our own fallibility.

Trickster's name may elicit uncomfortable feelings for mediators, as Benjamin reminds us in his articles. We seek to stop parties from playing tricks on each other or on us. We work to block deception. We advocate transparency, authenticity, and information sharing in our interventions. Benjamin maintains that we all play tricks, and he prods us to consider our techniques of reframing, process structuring, and using paradoxical interventions as constructive deceptions.

But trickster does not only symbolize deception. Trickster pushes the boundaries between what we know and what we think we know; between facts and perceptions. Trickster playfully reminds us that we cannot know all the truth all the time. Mediations, distinct from courts, are not processes designed to elicit the truth. They are processes designed to create space for individual stories from which new, joint stories may be devised. Hearing stories, we listen for perspectives rather than absolute facts; we watch for how our own perspectives may get in the way of listening openly, just as we are vigilant about bad-faith actions by others. As mediators, we seek to convene processes that have integrity yet provide ample room for a range of ideas and views.

If the tricks implied in trickster's name disturb you, will you stay with the stories a little longer to see what they reveal? Will you remember that conflicts and relationships seldom have clear good and bad characters? Trickster reminds us to be humble since we cannot see very far ahead and we don't always see the complete picture. What appears circuitous or difficult to follow may actually bring us to new realizations, accomplish justice, and even facilitate transformation. But we get ahead of ourselves.

As we seek to mediate effectively, we hold trickster as a resource and a talisman. As a resource, she models fluidity, flexibility, vitality, and creativity. She reminds us to bring a sense of humor into the room, to be used with subtlety and respect. As a talisman, she reminds us that good practice is steering clear of the perils of pride and ego for mediators and parties alike. Observing trickster, we recognize the paradoxes that pepper our processes: the surrender that may lead to results; the apparently indirect route that can lead us to discover answers in unexpected places.

Most of our mediation literature has not welcomed trickster, neither as a familiar character nor as a source of inspiration for untying the knots of conflict. Benjamin's contributions stand virtually alone in suggesting trickster as a role model for mediators. But trickster is there in conflict notwithstanding his lack of invitation. He is there confounding, stirring things up, raising questions and doubts about the status quo. He brings invention and vulnerability, the release of laughter, the magic of shape-shifting. He looks at the recipes we devise for intervening in conflict and reminds us of the ingredients that wait to be discovered on the path to the kitchen.

Trickster as Resource in Conflict

Trickster stories playfully invite us to reflect on the qualities and roles that most animate and impassion our work:

- Boundary crosser

- Shape-shifter

- Creative disrupter

- Peacemaker

- Storyteller

As we acknowledged earlier, all conflict is about boundaries, where they are or are not, and how they can be righted or coconstructed. Trickster stories teach us about boundaries and how to negotiate them with ease and grace. They also warn that those of us who deal with boundaries should remain humble, since we inevitably run into the occasional electric fence.

Conflicts often touch us at the level of identity. Trickster helps us transform identities, from victim to survivor, from wounded one to resilient leader. Trickster normalizes the discomfort that comes with conflict: its knots, confusion, and frustration. We do get into conflict. Divorce happens. Neighbors get into conflict about fences, dogs, shared driveways, and overhanging trees. Communities get into conflict about resources, ways of doing things, and development. Groups get into conflict about identity, security, resources, and history. What can trickster show would-be mediators about these situations? Listen to this trickster story from an old Norse tale.

The trickster Loki had made all the other gods angry, so he had to hide by day so they would not find him. Loki built himself a house with doors on every side so he would not be surprised by their approach. During the long days, he amused himself by turning into a salmon, darting and playing in clear mountain streams. As Loki was sitting by his fire one morning, he imagined how he might be captured and twisted a linen string into the first fishnet. No fishnet had existed on the earth before, and Loki was proud of his ingenious invention. But at that moment, the gods approached. Quickly, he threw the net into the fire, turned himself into a salmon, and swam away. But the gods found the ashes of the net and made a new one, finally capturing Loki.

What does this tale tell us about the qualities we need to culti-vate as mediators?

Boundary Crosser

The story shows trickster as a boundary crosser. He moves freely from the human world to life as a fish. He moves from ingenious inventor to victim of his own trap. He reminds us that all conflict involves boundaries, and that the boundaries we erect between our-selves and others may impede our ability to entertain alternative stories.

Boundaries may be between edges or ideas, between our sense of in and out, OK and not OK. Or they may be social boundaries, between good and bad, sacred and profane, clean and dirty. We get into conflict about which kind or degree of development is accept-able and sustainable, about what kind of compensation is appropri-ate for a particular wrong, about how our identities, needs, and interests are reflected, or not, in proposed solutions.

Trickster the boundary crosser reminds us that there are no clear or formulaic answers. Heroism is in the journey, in engaging each other's stories, rather than in the loss for another that a win might entail. The ingenious inventor is the same fool who gives himself away. The transgressor in one scene is victim in the next. Parties in conflict often both identify as victims, pointing fingers at the other.

Trickster reminds us that the boundaries between victim and aggressor, virtuous and underhanded, are seldom as clear as we might wish.

Trickster is the creative fool, the wise child, showing us paradox and questioning the givens we bring to the table. Trickster is the mythic embodiment of ambiguity, doubleness, and contradiction. Because trickster travels between heaven and earth, he reminds us to draw from a universe of ideas and spheres to fashion our approaches. He disturbs the order and boundaries we re-create, reminding us that cocreating resolutions is an ongoing process that requires our love as well as our minds.

Trickster also speaks to us of our mediation processes and their roles in addressing inequity and exclusion. Structures, including mediation, always involve both exclusion and inclusion. We constantly select some topics and comments as ways to move forward, eliminating or muting others. As we do this, we participate with parties in exploring and creating meaning. Selection and discernment is always a part of our mediation processes, moment by moment.

We can see this more clearly if we think of a concrete task. Consider, for example, how we might design a flag. The world has endless colors, and there are many geometric patterns that might be used. To make a flag, we select only a small number of available colors. From the infinite ways we might arrange them, we settle on one. Only by narrowing like this and building ownership among a group of people does the flag get identity. Then it means something. We can salute it, be its heroes, keep it out of the dirt. Even if we abuse it, we are responding to it as an item of meaning. So, in our mediation processes, we facilitate the process of creating new meanings, and new symbols for meanings.

This analogy reveals some questions that address our effectiveness as mediators. As we seek to organize and structure dialogue, do we impose controls and limits that may inadvertently foreclose transformation? Do we call on parties for input into the colors and their arrangement on the flag or do we seek to impose order ourselves? In many processes, mediators provide leadership in color and shape selection. Trickster reminds us that we are never neutral, so we are wise to attend to the way our points of view create or constrict space from which solutions may emerge.

Our processes and process choices reflect not only our individual personalities but our development at a point in human history, enveloped in worldviews, assumptions, and common sense, all of which are constantly changing. When we listen to trickster, we cultivate comfort with the ambiguity inherent in the process of finding order in chaos. We recognize that a work of art may begin with a muddied canvas, one that looks to the outsider's eye like a mess. From the initial marks ventured on the white canvass, we work hand in hand with parties to help images emerge that speak to their issues in comprehensive and balanced ways. We draw our processes not from a series of ordered rice paddies but the overflowing grain that nourishes all life.

Shape-Shifter

The story of Loki shows trickster as shape-shifter. He plays many roles and shifts into them as the situation demands. He shifts playfully, and also out of necessity. He is fluid and inventive in the roles he assumes.

Trickster reminds mediators that we play many roles in the course of our work. We are listener, educator, salve, and catalyst. We are reminder, referee, respectful observer, champion of the process. Effective practice means being able to shift gracefully among these roles, and to know which is called for and when. This is something difficult to teach; it is a characteristic of experts that they usually do it unconsciously. For those of us on the road to becoming experts, we can constantly work to develop our creativity and discernment so that we will know which role to assume and when, and have the flexibility to transform.

As an inexperienced mediator, I had a rigid and fairly narrow idea of appropriate behavior. But as I gained experience, talked with others, and read such books as Deborah Kolb's *When Talk Works* (1994),

I came to realize that there are many ways to be effective as a mediator. As Parker J. Palmer reminds us about outstanding teachers, it is not so much the methodology they use that makes them effective but their ability to connect with others and to dance with shifting interpersonal dynamics (Palmer, 1997). Mediators too are most effective when they connect genuinely with parties, modeling the shapeshifting that parties must do to heal and continue relationships.

Creative Disrupter

In the story, Loki creates the first fishnet known to humankind. We don't know what he did to anger the gods before the invention, but it must have been something significant for them to spend so much time in his pursuit. The trickster Loki then tries to use his ingenuity to avoid the conflict of capture, but he is finally unable to do so.

This reminds us that we may lack the tools to extricate ourselves from the conflicts we create. Especially when we follow old patterns (Loki turned himself into a fish, as he had previously), it is hard to escape the consequences of our actions. Conflict, it seems, catches up with us. It is amazing but true that many times we try more of a solution that has not worked, rather than changing strategies altogether. As mediators, it is our job to help parties see unproductive patterns and make new choices. It is also important for us as mediators to reflect on our practice strategies, noticing those that lead to spaciousness and those that narrow our ability to maneuver.

The Loki story also reminds us that conflict may stimulate social change, and that this is not necessarily bad. Through the conflict between Loki and the gods, a new tool (the fishnet) was invented and Loki was ultimately accountable for his actions. Justice and peace were both present, each part of the other. Since we know from many other trickster stories that Loki is ultimately freed to engage in new adventures, the possibility of transformation is in the air.

Peacemaker

We do not know exactly what happened to Loki after he was captured in the reconstituted net. But similar stories are repeated about trickster over and over again. Loki may be captured and bound for one of his misdeeds, but this brings a curse onto the earth. Eventually, he is freed and does something to create balance or bring great good. Trickster figures in world stories are credited with bringing fire to humans and journeying to distant lands to gather and bring scriptural truths back home. In this, they remind us to look for redemptive aspects of stories; to hold the possibility that everyone has the capacity both to hurt and be generous with others.

Trickster stories remind us to value conflict for how it highlights what is sacred and precious. Loki valued freedom, creativity, and his independence. The gods valued order and justice. Peace came about over time, as Loki experienced the consequences of his behavior and then returned to contribute to the world with his ingenuity and spirited ways. For both Loki and the gods, conflict sharpened their focus on what they valued and what they were willing to do to preserve these things.

Think back to conflicts you have experienced. Painful as they may have been, they probably revealed aspects of yourself and what you deeply cared about as they unfolded. We contend with others over things that matter, usually not over trivial issues. Because we seek to protect that which we treasure, conflict is a mirror of our convictions, our courage, and our willingness to take a strong stand even when it might be easier to sidestep or deny a difference. In a recent mediation, an ah-hah moment saw one of the parties pull her chair back from the table and observe that her story was so important and precious to her that it stood firmly in the way of her hearing her counterpart's story. Even as she found room to accommodate another story, she became more aware of what she treasured about her own.

Trickster is a teacher for mediators because he is a being of intelligence and courage with human flaws. He is out on the edge of what is acceptable, stretching boundaries and bringing disparate ideas together in new forms. Aren't mediators also in the process of bringing new ways, traveling to distant lands to bring information back home, ultimately working to invent a more peaceful world?

Surely this work takes courage. I remember one of my mentors, Jim Laue, who worked as part of the Community Relations Service in the United States with the late Reverend Martin Luther King Jr. Jim, who was white, had the courage and the audacity to think he could accompany King in the South and make a difference. He did not hide behind his identity, his guilt, or any other ways he might have felt or been perceived to be bound. Apparently Reverend King initially asked him, "Do you really think a white guy like you can help with this struggle?" Jim answered a confident, but still humble, "Yes."

As third parties, we seek not to inflict new hurts, while bringing the tools and the courage necessary to help parties transition to a more comfortable, equitable place. Trickster shows us how to move fluidly, mindful of our human frailty and tendencies to try well-worn solutions when new ones are needed. We are admonished not to get caught up in pride about our peacemaking, or we may get snared in the fishnet we invented. We seek to help with awareness of the possibilities and the limitations inherent in stories.

Storyteller

Trickster stories take ordinary life and materials and transform them into something novel or surprising. They show us that much of our work as mediators involves rearranging what we already have. Tricksters do not create new life; they work with existing pieces, forming new patterns. Trickster stories are anti-idealist; they are made in and for the world of imperfections. They are tailor-made for mediators, because we cannot always expand the pie but find ourselves working with parties to rearrange it and view it from new perspectives.

Though tricksters are at home in an imperfect world, they are not tragic. Great shape-shifters that they are, tricksters show us that we can take the givens of our lives and form them into a number of designs. We can make new stories with the ingredients we have, and find new ways to live with those givens that surround us (death, sleep, impulse, waterfalls, sunlight). Surely this is an important message for mediators, faced as we are with the discouragement and damage that conflict carries in its wake.

Trickster's message is ultimately one of hope and renewal. The story is not over with Loki's capture or the myriad setbacks and conundrums encountered in other trickster tales. Reading these stories, we are reminded that we are not passive in our storytelling. Rather, we are actively creating and re-creating our experiences as we tell stories again and again. Mediators help parties tell old stories in new ways. Trickster, riding along in our back pocket, gives us ideas about how to do this when the going gets tough.

The Story's End: Coming Full Circle

What can the storied trickster tell us in the end? We look to Hermes, the classical trickster figure. He is described in many ways in the various stories about him. In some, he is a peacemaker; in others, he is the patron of youths and the protector of flocks. When we make a lucky find, we thank Hermes, and he is also the original chef, bringing ingredients together in delicious combinations to delight palates and warm friendships. Stories of Hermes emphasize connections between humans and between humans and deities. Conflict happens when connections are ruptured.

Hermes shows us that the job of the mediator is to find the opening for something to occur that weaves the rent fabric back together. Using a weaving metaphor, our task is to find the *kairos*, or the space that appears between the warp and the weft threads into which the shuttle can be placed. How do we do that?

We draw upon Eros, the personified principle of connectedness and nurturing. The work of making connections between people, multiple sets of ideas, is the sphere of the erotic. Eros is the way people were originally drawn to each other, and it has a much broader classical meaning than the sexualized way it is thought of today. Through Eros, relationship is rightly placed at the center of our work.

Hermes teaches us to foster associations and relationships, bringing people together to accomplish things they dream. From his example, we facilitate but do not force connections. Hermes takes messages into the underworld and back again. He links deities and humans by inventing sacrifice, and this sacrifice brings together members of political and religious communities. Hermes shows us that connectedness comes not just from personal relationships but from peaceful social intercourse, business, religion, travel, education, athletics, politics, and even magic.

Following his lead, we invite a range of activities into our thinking about peacemaking. We go where parties are, greeting them in the ways they greet, taking our cues from them. We break bread with them, following them into the field to see the mineral deposits that are the subject of their conflict; we listen to their stories. We do not wait for the moment to be ripe for rational thought. We think outside the box, inspired by examples of peacemaking and mediation in the midst of conflict, not only in formal rooms far removed from the conflict. Organizations such as Search for Common Ground and the Public Conversations Project encourage us through their actions to widen the way we think of mediation and peacemaking. One of Search for Common Ground's initiatives was to go to Angola and persuade the most popular rock artists on either side of the civil war to record a peace song together that the whole country joined in singing.

We ask what is needed rather than selling a generic prescription. We learn from trickster that invention and vitality arise from uncovering and discarding limiting assumptions about who we are and how we can create stories to connect us across differences.

Reflective Practice Questions

1. Do you agree with the author's description of mediators as "boundary crossers"? If so, to what extent are you comfortable or uncomfortable with that role?

2. Does the concept of mediator as trickster broaden the range of personal qualities that you would feel comfortable deploying in a mediation? If so, in what ways?

3. To what extent is the role of mediator as trickster consistent or inconsistent with the concept of bringing peace into the room?

References

Benjamin, R. D. "The Constructive Uses of Deception: Skills, Strategies, and Techniques of the Folkloric Trickster Figure and Their Application by Mediators." *Mediation Quarterly*, Fall 1995a, *13*(1), 3–18.

Benjamin, R. D. "The Mediator as Trickster: The Folkloric Figure as Professional Role Model." *Mediation Quarterly*, Winter 1995, *13*(2), 131–149.

Kolb, D. M., and Associates (eds.). *When Talk Works*. San Francisco: Jossey-Bass, 1994.

Palmer, P. J. "The Heart of a Teacher." *Change*, 1997, *29*(6), 14–21.

6

Emotionally Intelligent Mediation

Four Key Competencies

Marvin E. Johnson, Stewart Levine,

and Lawrence R. Richard

The concept of "emotional intelligence" began arousing the public's interest in 1995, when Daniel Goleman published *Emotional Intelligence*, a book that has since become a runaway bestseller. The concept of emotional intelligence, which has spawned a cottage industry of research applying the lessons described in Goleman's book to workplace, family, and everyday life, seems to have particular relevance to the work of mediators. Before exploring the connection to dispute resolution, however, it is worth considering what emotional intelligence is and describing the core competencies that make people emotionally intelligent.

The emotional intelligence field got its start in 1983 when Harvard education professor Howard Gardner first began writing about "multiple intelligences" (Gardner, 1983). Gardner contended that among the various forms of noncognitive intelligence—or "personal intelligences"—were two groups: interpersonal intelligence (the ability to understand and relate to other people) and intrapersonal intelligence (the ability to understand and manage one's internal feelings). An Israeli psychologist, Reuven Bar-On, published research on emotional intelligence in 1988 and developed a measurement instrument for what he called EQ. Psychology professors Peter Salovey and Jack Mayer also published early research on emotional intelligence, which helped explain how seemingly "smart" people often do stupid things (Salovey and Mayer, 1990).

This body of work, along with the outpouring of more recent studies prompted by Goleman's books, has expanded to include a body of work known as "competency modeling," which examines the central role that "people skills" play in leadership, management, and overall competency in life. More recently, researchers have begun to look beyond the intellectual and social realms to forms of "spiritual intelligence." (See, for example, psychologist Richard Wolman's recent work *Thinking with Your Soul: Spiritual Intelligence and Why It Matters*; Wolman, 2001.)

Goleman defines emotional intelligence (EQ) as "the capacity for recognizing our own feelings and those of others, for motivating ourselves, and for managing emotions well in ourselves and in our relationships" (Goleman, 1998, p. 317). His research has shown that the various competencies that make up such intelligence play a much larger role than previously thought in one's overall success. For example, the factors often assumed to govern success—academic intelligence or IQ, work experience, and mastery of a technical area—appear not to be accurate predictors, although they can predict who will gain initial entry into a field. After one enters a field, EQ appears to be a more important predictor of success. Indeed, Goleman claims that, on the basis of statistical studies of performance in the workplace, emotional competencies are "twice as important in contributing to excellence as . . . pure intellect and expertise" (p. 320).

Some Principles of Emotional Intelligence

All the competencies identified by Goleman and others are teachable and learnable, so an individual who is sufficiently motivated has the potential to improve his or her emotional intelligence performance and therefore his or her success in life. Goleman and his colleagues have identified twenty emotional intelligence competencies to date (Goleman and Cherniss, 2001). Mastering one of the twenty identified competencies is predicated on developing a set of learned skills that serve as a cumulative series of building blocks for that particular competency. The premise of this research is that people who routinely behave in a way that demonstrates mastery of a certain competency tend to benefit or receive a payoff down the road by becoming more successful in aspects of life that are affected by that competency.

Not only does there appear to be a large payoff for mastering an individual competency but when one consistently masters a cluster of related competencies, the individual receives an even larger secondary payoff. For example, three of the twenty emotional intelligence competencies are related to self-awareness: emotional self-awareness, accurate self-assessment, and self-confidence. Although mastery of any one of these three produces a benefit in one's self-awareness, mastery of all three produces an exponential benefit that is greater than the benefit of mastering one or two.

Here are the twenty competencies that Goleman and his colleagues have identified, shown in the four clusters that are internally related:

Self-Awareness

1. Emotional self-awareness

2. Accurate self-assessment

3. Self-confidence

Self-Management

4. Self-control

5. Trustworthiness

6. Conscientiousness

7. Adaptability

8. Achievement orientation

9. Initiative

Social Awareness

10. Empathy

11. Organizational awareness

12. Service orientation

Social Skills

13. Developing others

14. Leadership

15. Influence

16. Communication

17. Change catalyst

18. Conflict management

19. Building bonds

20. Teamwork and collaboration (Goleman, 1995)

What Are the Implications of Emotional Intelligence for Mediation?

After some experience in mediation, we begin to discover that, by creating a safe space for the expression of emotions, we can help the parties open the emotional blocks that are preventing resolution of their conflicts. We begin to see that a root cause of almost every conflict is an emotional block preventing the parties from seeing the conflict with objectivity. Unless violence is anticipated, a mediator typically encourages the parties to express their emotions, giving them the missing experience of feeling heard. Even though an emotional discussion may become intense, new information often emerges that can move the parties toward resolution. If the discussion becomes too intense, a mediator can use a caucus to address the emotional concerns more directly. When the mediator encourages the parties to talk directly about their own experience—why they are feeling the way they are feeling and what is going on for them—they often move through the emotional block to a place of clarity.

Allowing emotion to emerge in a mediation, however, requires a mediator with a high degree of emotional intelligence. Some mediators resist dealing with emotions, on the theory that expressing emotions is not necessary to resolving conflicts. This view is often expressed by mediators who are also attorneys, because the field of law has historically not been receptive to emotional expression. Other mediators simply fear their own emotions and, as a result, fear the emotions of others. In either case, the lack of EQ in the mediator prevents him or her from using emotional release as a technique for achieving resolution of a conflict. For this reason, we believe that improving one's emotional intelligence is an essential developmental path for mediators. As EQ improves, a mediator becomes more comfortable with his or her ability to manage an emotional process successfully.

For example, during a difficult labor-management mediation, a union president became highly emotional during the mediation session whenever she became stuck on rights rather than underlying interests; the mediator would remind her that mediation agreements were nonprecedental, meaning the fundamental rights of union members were not affected by the process. The mediator saw that the union president was becoming emotional about an issue that did not have to be a barrier to resolution. Her emotions were taking control and reducing her effectiveness as a negotiator. The emotionally competent mediator acknowledged the union president's self-awareness of the unproductive emotion in a way that enabled her to move forward rather than slide into impasse around the irrelevant issues.

The Four Emotional Intelligence Clusters

It is our contention that Goleman's twenty emotional intelligence competencies, which Goleman groups in four clusters described here, are a sweeping list of personal qualities to which any mediator should aspire. These competencies relate directly to many of the fundamentals of mediation.

Self-Awareness

The self-awareness cluster is an essential initial step in developing one's EQ. Until one becomes sufficiently aware of one's own emotions to feel and diagnose them accurately, one remains emotionally incompetent. It is always easier to gain awareness of the emotions we perceive in others. We perceive anger in another long before we recognize our own. Until we develop emotional self-awareness, we will project our own unrecognized emotions onto others. Such projections are a fundamental source of most conflict. One of the most important insights to emerge from the emotional intelligence research is that gaining awareness alone is one of the most powerful engines of human behavior and especially leadership. Without self-awareness, it is difficult, if not impossible, to master the other competencies. Self-awareness is the foundation. As mediators, it is all too easy to become so focused on the emotions of others in the process that we forget to notice our own emotional reaction to the parties. Accordingly, such self-awareness is as important for us as for the parties.

One of the competencies within the self-awareness cluster is self-confidence. We all know the importance of projecting self-confidence to parties who are in conflict. They are looking to the mediator for clarity and support. It takes self-awareness to project self-confidence. The initial assessment we commonly make upon meeting a new person is not based on rational thought but on a visceral, emotional response and is sometimes known as the "seven and a half seconds" rule. With this awareness, before entering the mediation room, an emotionally competent mediator pauses to reflect on how he is about to present himself to new clients. It is vital for a mediator to "show up" with self-confidence; otherwise, the parties may have diminished confidence in the mediator for the rest of the session.

But how do we show up with self-confidence when we are not feeling self-confident and still maintain our authenticity? By turning to another competency in the self-awareness cluster, accurate self-assessment, we can take a few moments to review our abilities and previous experiences in mediation or in other professional endeavors. No matter how new we are to mediation, we can find areas of life where we have shown the reliability necessary to be, and authentically project, self-confidence. Through practicing the competency of self-awareness, we know from experience that all emotions, positive and negative, come and go like ripples in a pond. By affirming this experience, we learn to allow unproductive emotions to pass through us and regain our emotional balance, giving us the authentic self-confidence necessary to be an effective mediator, rather than failing to serve our clients by succumbing to our own unproductive emotional state.

Self-Management

The second cluster of competencies, self-management, is composed of six individual competencies. Half of them relate to affirmative self-management, such as motivating ourselves to do something that we do not want to do (for example, filling out our tax returns). The others have to do with negative self-management, such as restraining ourselves from doing something that we have the impulse to do but know we should not (for example, exploding inappropriately in a meeting or hitting Send on an inappropriate e-mail without taking time for necessary reflection). These latter competencies can be thought of as impulse control, which is certainly an extremely important competency for anyone in a leadership position.

Goleman describes the absence of self-management as an "amygdala hijacking" (Goleman, 1995). The amygdala is the ancient reptilian stem of the brain that produces fight-and-flight hormones. These amygdala hijackings can be sudden and involve powerful emotions, and yet afterward the average person feels guilty or ashamed. We are all familiar with the "gunnysacking" experience in which one person in a relationship saves up all the little annoyances and irritations. Then one day his relationship partner fails to put the cap on the toothpaste, and wham! The partner who has been gunnysacking the annoyances and irritations loses his self-management and explodes with emotion all out of proportion to the specific offense.

When we explained this self-management competency to the audience for our presentation on this topic at the twelfth annual conference of the Center for Alternative Dispute Resolution, one audience member related a story of a coworker who innocently said something to another coworker that hit an extremely sensitive spot. The latter "clocked" her unaware coworker, physically knocking her out cold.

A classic cartoon depicts a king mentoring his young son who is sitting on the throne. The king says, "Son, you cannot say *on* with their head after you've said *off* with their head." Developing the emotional competency of self-management gives us greater emotional control, while still maintaining our authenticity, so that we can refrain from taking a client's head off metaphorically. An emotionally competent mediator is able to choose his or her response instead of reacting. An emotionally incompetent mediator is likely to lose control and react inappropriately.

A fundamental tenet of mediation is that the mediator must remain impartial. But how does one maintain impartiality in the face of emotional outbursts? On occasion, as we all know, one of the parties to a mediation will say something inflammatory or utter a trip-wire phrase that might cause us, outside our role as mediator, to respond emotionally or to view that person differently and even treat him or her differently. The mediator who is aware of his or her own emotional reactions and who is adept at emotional self-management is better able to take these situations in stride and maintain neutrality.

On the other hand, a mediator with a low EQ in the self-management competency may respond inappropriately. Such behavior is almost certainly perceived as biased and may result in the mediator losing the trust of the parties. If the situation is not corrected, it can lead to an unsuccessful mediation.

The trigger could be something as simple as a misstatement. If one of the parties makes a statement that the mediator believes is inaccurate, the mediator may have the impulse to jump in and correct the statement, making the party feel shamed or scolded. Regardless of whether the party's statement is correct, there are more effective ways to handle the situation and maintain both the appearance of, and actual, impartiality. The emotionally competent mediator might say, "I'm not really certain about that point. Maybe we can take a look at the documents together and discuss this point further." Whether an expert or a document is brought into the session, the impact on the process is much more effective than an impulsive correction or challenge from the mediator.

Social Awareness

The third cluster of competencies is called social (or other) awareness. This cluster includes three competencies related to one's effectiveness in understanding other individuals and social systems. The first, empathy, refers to one's ability to step into the shoes of another and see things from the other's perspective. This competency is so fundamental that it serves not only as a competency in its own right but also as the foundation for a number of other competencies. Goleman breaks down gaining empathy into mastering at least five of six skills:

1. Listening
2. Active listening
3. Reading nonverbal cues
4. Being open to diversity
5. Seeing others' perspectives ("tipping point")
6. Understanding others (Goleman, 1995)

According to Goleman, if an individual masters the first three skills and no more, her ability to project empathy improves, but she might not experience a payoff in terms of improved relationships at work or home sufficient to lead to greater long-term success in life. When one has consistently mastered up to skill level five, one experiences a long-term payoff in life. For this reason, the fifth level in this example is called the "tipping point." Goleman's research identifies a tipping point for each of the twenty competencies. Mastery of the ladder of skills up to or beyond that point yields a significant payoff in improving one's EQ.

The Mediator's Use of Empathy

A skilled mediator has the ability to recognize whether either of the parties has been, or is, seeking someone to be empathic. The parties may not have received empathy, and the mediator may be the first person to provide it. Without agreeing with a party's story or appearing to take sides, an emotionally competent mediator can acknowledge the fundamental need to be heard.

We may have heard these admonitions many times, but increasing our competence at social awareness reveals to us those particular conflicts with the potential to hook us emotionally and undermine our ability to express appropriate empathy. The deeper challenge for mediators is to go beyond the expression of empathy to actually feel it, especially in those cases where the party who needs the mediator's empathy is acting in such a way as to alienate the mediator and others as well. When that occurs, the mediator might do well to remember the words of Henry Wadsworth Longfellow: "If we could read the secret history of our enemies, we would find in each life a sorrow and suffering enough to disarm all of our hostility."

Role Reversal

In some cases, resolution of a dispute calls for the parties themselves to achieve a higher degree of empathy for each other. One technique to develop the parties' empathy is role reversal. The mediator asks party A, "If you were in party B's shoes, how might you feel and/or what might you do when faced with the story you have just told? How do you imagine that party B might react?" With more emotionally aware parties, it is even useful to ask them to exchange chairs and speak to one another as if they were the other.

If party A has developed enough social awareness of how party B felt when the events that gave rise to the conflict occurred, he or she will be able to respond effectively to the questions and speak what party B felt or still feels. Sometimes the ability to express this level of social awareness will cause the parties to shift fundamentally and be able to pursue possible resolutions to their problem.

Social Skills

The last cluster of competencies, social skills, includes win/win influencing, conflict resolution, leadership, and communication. The essence of the social skills competencies is that they build on the other clusters—that is, one must achieve a level of social awareness and self-management to be effective in the social arena. For example, one of the most important social skills competencies is influencing skills. It is easy, of course, to influence another person with duress, force, or threat. But all of these approaches damage and ultimately destroy relationships. The real art is being able to influence others in such a way that the influence makes the relationship stronger.

The Skill of Communication

A frequent statement in mediation training is "do the parties no harm, or do not leave them worse off than when you met them." Given this important principle, a mediator must develop the important social skill of communication to gain full awareness of the importance of choosing words carefully during the mediation sessions, maintaining awareness of not only what we say but how we say it. Research shows that people can actually feel certain words that are spoken to them (Hersh, 1986). Parties come to mediation with some level of pain arising from their inability to resolve their conflict. Words used during the mediation, without sufficient emotional intelligence, may add insult to injury and increase their pain.

The Skill of Influence

Developing the social skill of influence reveals another critical success factor: whether we are directive or nondirective in our behavior and speech. Some mediators consider this difference to be fundamental to their definition of "correct" mediation. Here, we are not considering the philosophical issues associated with facilitative versus evaluative mediation, but instead we are focusing on another of Goleman's EQ competencies. If we are directive in a certain situation in mediation, we may ask, "Why did you take that action?" On the other hand, if we are nondirective, we might say, "Tell me more about how it happened." Depending on our choice, our inquiry sets a certain tone for the parties and generates a particular reaction. This choice of approach has to do with the importance of being aware of social process and developing the social skill of influence, which allows an emotionally competent mediator to get information on the table that is necessary for the parties to discuss if they are to resolve their dispute. As we develop our competency in this skill, we recognize that different situations and individuals require us to use different approaches. Thus if we are locked into just one approach, we retard our own emotional intelligence and limit the kind of dispute we can help resolve. Developing the emotional skill of influence calls forth a deeper awareness of our intentions as mediators. If we have also honed our emotional competency in service orientation, our intentions are pure, and the technique that we choose has less importance to the outcome, because our intentions more effectively guide our words. If instead we are focused on achieving a certain result to build our résumé, we may fail to serve our clients appropriately, and our lack of authenticity is often apparent.

The Skill of Change Catalyst

When people come to mediation, the disputed issue is often the tip of the iceberg under which rests a deeper history of the conflict. Sometimes people elaborate emotionally on concerns that may not seem directly related to their complaint. Just because what they say does not appear relevant to us does not necessarily mean that it is not important to the change necessary for resolution. A mediator with undeveloped skill as a change catalyst may think this information is extraneous and limit or stop the parties from discussing their concerns, or conversely, not be able to place appropriate boundaries around issues that can be resolved in the time and place of the mediation sessions. Without a skilled awareness of what it means to catalyze change, the mediator may block the parties from reaching resolution because the underlying emotional concerns that are driving their dispute are not articulated or addressed.

We have all seen situations where people never got to tell their entire story because every time they started to tell it they were interrupted or cut off. Some mediators cut people off without being aware, because they want to ask questions to gather the data that they believe, from their perspective, are needed to resolve the dispute. A mediator skilled in catalyzing change remembers whose dispute it is. Some mediators act as if the dispute is theirs and seek to resolve it in a manner suitable to them. If we are doing all we can to help the parties move toward resolution and they do not agree, they are not ready. A skilled change catalyst knows that change can never be forced.

Conclusion

Goleman and his colleagues have outlined important emotional competencies that are especially applicable to mediation and mediators. It is vital, in our view, that mediators work to develop a high

EQ. Absent the ability to deal with emotions, the true power of mediation is lost. Absent the ability to create space for parties to express difficult emotions, it is unlikely that any resolution reached will last. A participant in our workshop on emotional intelligence beautifully expressed the importance of EQ: "As mediators, we must work to feel comfortable with, not afraid of, emotions. We can't always keep everything smoothed over. Emotions are present like an elephant in the room. As mediators, it is vital for us to acknowledge the elephant and invite it to be present. Emotions are a very powerful mediating tool because the conflict is really about emotions." For all of these reasons, we believe that developing emotional intelligence is essential for a successful mediator.

Reflective Practice Questions

1. To what extent do you experience the management of emotion—your own and that of the parties—as central to your work as a mediator?

2. In what ways have you seen emotional intelligence (or the lack of it)—either your own or that of the parties in a mediation—influence the resolution of a dispute?

3. As you look at the list of twenty competencies that make up emotional intelligence, where—on the scale from unconscious incompetence to unconscious competence—would you place yourself with regard to each one?

References

Gardner, H. *Frames of Mind: The Theory of Multiple Intelligences.* New York: Basic Books, 1983.

Goleman, D. *Emotional Intelligence.* New York: Bantam Books, 1995.

Goleman, D. *Working with Emotional Intelligence.* New York: Bantam Books, 1998.

Goleman, D., and Cherniss, C. *The Emotionally Intelligent Workplace: How to Select for, Measure, and Improve Emotional Intelligence in Individuals, Groups, and Organizations.* San Francisco: Jossey-Bass, 2001.

Hersh, P. "Heart to Heart: The Physical Correlation of Verbal Communication." *Human Potential,* Mar./Apr. 1986, pp. 16–22.

Salovey, P., and Mayer, J. "Emotional Intelligence." *Imagination, Cognition and Personality,* 1990, 9, 185–211.

Wolman, R. *Thinking with Your Soul: Spiritual Intelligence and Why It Matters.* New York: Random House, 2001.

Paradoxes of Mediation

David A. Hoffman

When you come to a fork in the road, take it.
—Yogi Berra

According to Zen Buddhism, one way enlightenment can be achieved is by holding two contradictory thoughts in the mind simultaneously. This, I have found, is more easily said than done. Perhaps I am handicapped in this endeavor by virtue of professional training: as a lawyer my mental functioning has shifted decidedly to the left brain. I know one lawyer-turned-mediator (or, as the joke goes, a recovering lawyer) who describes law school as a process in which the left brain circles around the right brain and eats it.

If that is the case, learning to practice mediation has presented me with the task of recovering the right-brain function, the place where creativity and nonlinear thinking flourish. Indeed, restoring the balance between the two hemispheres may be necessary to succeed at mediation because the work is inherently difficult, is multidimensional, and requires not only logic but also inventiveness.

This chapter is excerpted from a two-part article with the same title, published in the American Bar Association's *Dispute Resolution Magazine* (Fall/Winter 2002), and is reprinted here with permission. The author wishes to thank Frank E. A. Sander, Beth Andrews, Diane DiLeo, Melissa Filgerleski, and Lily Hoffman-Andrews for their comments on a prior version of this article, and Bhavani Murugesan for research assistance.

Managing Complexity

As mediators, we must hold in the mind simultaneously the perspective of each of the parties—perspectives that often have little in common and are usually contradictory or mutually exclusive. As we manage the interactions of these parties, we find ourselves enmeshed in a breathtakingly intricate matrix of psychological issues; negotiation dynamics; communication problems; subtleties of inflection and body language; barriers of gender, culture, race, and class; and disagreements about legal issues and the facts that gave rise to the dispute. The very complexity of the work is one of the things that make it so appealing: no matter how much experience we have, no matter how skilled we may become, mastery always eludes us. For people who love challenges, mediation is a natural calling.

The division of labor between left brain and right brain is a good metaphor for considering the paradoxes of mediation because it exemplifies how, as mediators, we often need to be engaged in multiple, and often mutually exclusive, activities simultaneously. Because of these many layers of complexity, one must consider adding to the list of personal qualities that enable mediators to function effectively a high tolerance for ambiguity, an enjoyment of multitasking, and a willingness to accept the possibility that reality is riddled with paradox.

I am also struck by the similarity in these paradoxes to those identified by psychotherapist and scholar Sophie Freud in her article "The Paradoxes of Parenthood: On the Impossibility of Being a Perfect Parent" (Freud, 1988). Freud's article says the missteps that we make as parents are inevitable because of the conflicting responsibilities involved in raising children. For example, we must protect them, while at the same time letting them make their own mistakes. We must praise and encourage them, but without overdoing it, so that they learn how to manage criticism.

Freud also identifies the dilemma of "fostering simultaneous attachment and separation" as perhaps the most difficult parental task: "It involves promoting individuation and autonomy, essential life goals, while also offering the child an experience of attachment profound and meaningful enough to evoke a lifelong capacity to love, feel, and care. . . . [This is a] paradox of parenthood: disenchantment with and rebelliousness against parents is a necessary part of the relationship; a [parent-child] relationship is flawed if it remains conflict free and apparently totally harmonious" (Freud, 1988, p. 183).

The moral of Dr. Freud's article is that perfection in parenting is unattainable because there is no perfect balance of these conflicting duties. Certainly, this is true from the standpoint of our children, who, as silent critics or voluble detractors, often tell us we're doing our work as parents wrong if we're doing it right. It is unattainable in our own eyes as well. Our children are mortal and therefore fallible—in a word, imperfect. Likewise, our efforts as parents are inherently imperfect.

Similarities to Mediation

Is our work as mediators different? It seems to me that mediators try to balance some of the same tensions and deal with some of the same paradoxes that parents encounter. For example, if the parties in a mediation leave the process annoyed with us but reconnected with each other, have we succeeded or failed? Do we not have to manage the tension in mediation between attachment and separation, relationship and autonomy?

I have had occasion over the years to observe some gifted mediators at work and to talk with lawyers about their experience with these same mediators. I have been astonished to hear mixed reviews on mediators whom I regard as some of the most skilled practitioners in the field. *Perhaps the mediator had a bad day*, I thought. But more often, I suspect, the mediator's style did not fit the particular people or circumstances of the case; the techniques they used were a mismatch for one or more of the parties or their lawyers. Or perhaps the inherent tensions in the perspectives or negotiation styles of the parties made success impossible. In short, the mediators may have found themselves in a situation where no amount of skill would have sufficed.

Striving for Perfection

I do not underestimate the difficulty of getting it all right; indeed, the complexity of the work is one of the premises of this chapter. What I am suggesting is that by exploring the fundamental and to some extent irreconcilable tensions in what we do, we mediators will gain a fuller understanding of how very difficult—indeed, sometimes impossible—our work is, thus enabling us to do a better job while relinquishing the ambition of doing a perfect one. We all know the saying about the perfect being the enemy of the good. So it is with mediation.

What are these irreconcilable tensions, these paradoxes if you will?

Mediator "Presence" Versus Party Control

One paradox can be found in a phenomenon noted by a number of mediators: the positive impact that a mediator's "presence" can have as a factor in promoting resolution (Bowling and Hoffman, 2000; Gill-Austern, 2000; Gold, 1993). The reasons for the effectiveness of a mediator's presence not only are difficult to define but also vary from one mediator to the next. Some mediators seek, by their demeanor, to "bring peace into the room" (Bowling and Hoffman, 2000). Other mediators may, by virtue of their charisma, credibility, or charm, create an environment in which the parties find themselves motivated to achieve settlement.

Yet, as mediator Gary Gill-Austern has pointed out, the very effectiveness of the mediator's presence is problematic: "The mediator's role is complex, even paradoxical. A mediator must be remarkably and uniquely present—a full participant. At the same time, and more fundamentally, the mediator must be present in a manner that embodies an understanding that she or he has no significance at all to the dispute and its resolution. . . . The mediator must function within a paradox: how to be central and matter not at all" (Gill-Austern, 2000, p. 353).

There is the further paradox of mediator presence that mediators try to be present in the moment (putting to one side any concern about the future) while at the same time trying to attend to the strategic direction and effectiveness of their interventions; that is, they seek to influence the future while simultaneously ignoring it.

Empathy Versus Candor

Ken Cloke has described empathy and honesty as two of the principal qualities of effective mediators (Cloke, 2001). Although it is possible for a mediator to be both empathic and honest at the same time, the effort calls for exquisite balance. For example, in a recent mediation in which such balance was not achieved, I suggested to divorced parents who were engaged in a tug-of-war over their kids that each of them might be feeling a personal stake—beyond the best interests of the children—in winning. Unready to hear this, both denied caring which of them "won," and I came away with the feeling that I had perhaps tipped the balance too hard in the direction of honesty. *— + necessarily!*

Empathy requires engagement; honesty requires objectivity and detachment. Engagement fosters safety, while candor may create difficulty. The paradox is to be both engaged and detached at the same time.

A number of mediators describe mediation as "making a safe place for a difficult conversation" (see, for instance, Stone, Patton, and Heen, 1999). Thus the mediator's job is to strike a balance between the difficult and the safe in a way that motivates change and the taking of fresh perspectives, while at the same time creating a level of comfort that fosters resolution.

Emotion: Encouraging Expression by the Parties While Suppressing Our Own

A seasoned plaintiff's employment lawyer once told me that her cases usually do not settle in mediation until her client cries. To be sure, venting emotion is an essential part of most mediations. No matter how dry a business dispute may be, it probably arose because of decisions by people who in all likelihood have strong feelings about the matter. Likewise, as noted earlier, mediators cannot avoid having an emotional reaction to the parties, but they must avoid letting such reactions create an appearance of partiality. The paradoxical element is that part of our job as mediators is to encourage the parties to vent their emotions while we must suppress our own.

Impartiality Versus Bias Toward Problem Solvers

Mediators aspire to be impartial. Indeed, impartiality is an ethical requirement. Most mediators are able to act in ways that appear to the parties to be impartial. Yet even the most experienced mediators will admit to feelings of bias that begin to develop shortly after the mediation has begun—often within minutes. Perhaps the most common bias is in favor of the party or parties who, like the mediator, embrace a principled, interest-based style of negotiation. Mediators generally do not like belligerent, positional bargainers who are uninterested in expanding the pie and who focus instead on seizing the largest obtainable piece of it. Mediator and author Ken Cloke describes the mediator's role as being "omnipartial" (Cloke, 2001, p. 13).

The paradoxical element is the mediator's need to identify with, and support, people whose positional bargaining seeks to undermine, and in some cases take advantage of, the mediator's problem-solving, interest-based orientation. Mediators are bargainers in the mediation process, seeking cooperation, disclosure, and concessions, just as the parties do. Moreover, mediators pursue ends of their own—principally, a successful outcome. The meaning of success may vary from case to case and may not always require a settlement of the underlying dispute. But it is naïve to assume that mediators are indifferent as to outcome, and thus it is remarkable that mediators succeed in remaining omnipartial to those who stand in the way of success.

A related paradox arises when the parties begin to trust the mediator (perhaps because of her omnipartiality) and share with her secret information about themselves—perhaps an admission of culpability—that causes the mediator to feel less omnipartial. To earn the parties' trust is an important mediator skill, requiring a good deal of empathy. The fruit of that trust, however, can sometimes leave a bitter taste in the mediator's mouth and cause her to question whether the empathy was misplaced.

Trust Versus Transparency

One of the mediator's principal tasks is to win the trust of the parties. From the first moments of her involvement with the parties or their counsel, the mediator seeks to convince them that she will be fair and evenhanded. In theory, transparency—candor by the mediator about the process and the mediator's role in it—enhances such trust (Moffitt, 1997). Yet there are aspects of the mediator's work that, according to some, involve deception and manipulation. In Chapter Four of this book, describing the mediator as trickster, Robert Benjamin discusses one aspect of the mediator's role: playing the part of the wise fool, a role not unlike that of Peter Falk's television character, Lt. Columbo. Playing such a part successfully, of course, cannot be done transparently. Does the mediator seek to win the parties' trust only to take advantage of it, in the way that Lt. Columbo lulls his suspects into complacency? If the mediator is truly transparent, might such a stance not only undermine her effectiveness but also cause the parties to question their ability to trust such a mediator? Transparency is hardly the norm in our dealings with others, who tend to keep their agendas and methods to themselves. Thus the effort to win trust may have the opposite effect.

Honesty Versus Protection from Fraud

Mediators occasionally learn more than they want to know. When one side or the other shares with the mediator confidential information that might affect the other party's willingness to settle, the mediator must decide whether disclosure of that information to the other side is necessary to avoid perpetrating a fraud. For example, in a recent case, three brothers and their father were in a real estate dispute with their elderly neighbor, who did not know that title to the land in question had been completely transferred from the father to the sons. From the standpoint of the settlement terms, it did not seem to matter who owned the land. But to the elderly neighbor, it did: after signing a settlement agreement, he sought to revoke the deal when he learned of the change of ownership. The mediator had been given the information, on a confidential basis early in the mediation, by the father and his sons, who rejected the mediator's advice that they disclose the change in ownership. The mediator, of course, could not find out from their neighbor whether the change of ownership would matter to him because the inquiry itself would amount to an impermissible disclosure.

The paradoxical aspect of this situation is threefold. First, the mediator has conflicting ethical duties (honesty to the parties, confidentiality, and refraining from perpetrating a fraud), all of which must be honored. Second, the mediator's participation in the process may have enhanced the parties' level of confidence that they were receiving honest treatment, when in fact the mediation may have lulled one of them (the elderly neighbor) into a false sense of security, while at the same time satisfying the need of the others (the father and sons) to confess the true state of affairs. Finally, although the parties may have believed that the mediator's involvement would enhance the likelihood of achieving an enforceable agreement, the mediator's nondisclosure gave the neighbor grounds for challenging the enforceability of the settlement terms. (The case, by the way, settled, but only after a second round of mediation—and new settlement terms, more favorable to the elderly neighbor—when the title issue came to light.)

Mediator "Pressure" Versus Party Autonomy

Robert Baruch Bush and Joseph Folger (1994) have pointed out how mediators unavoidably affect or steer the process of mediation, even when they believe that their exclusive role is to carry out the parties' intentions. Their solution to this dilemma is to participate in the process in such a way as to promote empowerment and recognition.

For other mediators, the solution is to promote settlement. Their dilemma is different: how to manage the tension between parties, each of whom wants the mediator to apply settlement pressure to their *opponents* (through reason, appeals to emotion, and other means) but not to them.

In his article "Mediator Pressure and Party Autonomy: Are They Consistent with Each Other?" mediator and professor David Matz notes that "for a mediator to encourage the free expression of a party's will, the mediator may (and in some circumstances must) . . . pressure a party to enable that party to achieve autonomy" (1994, p. 362). For some mediators, there is a paradox within this paradox, because often the most effective pressure is simply agreeing with the parties. As Benjamin (1995a, 1995b) has noted in his pair of articles on mediators as tricksters, mediators sometimes use what are known among psychotherapists as "paradoxical interventions" to move the process along; that is, suggesting one thing while meaning another. For example, when we talk with a party who is hellbent on proving her case in court, we might discuss all the advantages of a trial because discussing the disadvantages would simply deepen her resistance to settlement: "Only by first exploring and supporting the parties' thinking and encouraging them to hold on to their entrenched positions can the mediator move them to allow themselves to consider other options. Thus is the paradox: intensifying the commitment to a stated course of action allows for the lessening of that commitment. Conversely, [disagreeing with the parties' views] will only serve to bolster the resistance" (Benjamin, 1995a, p. 10).

As a mediator, I have found that in the final, hard-bargaining stage of a mediation in which the dispute often boils down to money and a zero-sum negotiation (after full consideration of the possibilities for mutual gains, integrative bargaining, and expanding the pie), I am often skating a fine line between the parties' desire to get the deal done and their annoyance with me for extracting yet another concession from them. This situation presents an equally paradoxical dilemma for the parties, because they must skate the line, in their communications with me, between resisting concessions firmly enough to achieve their bargaining objectives without overdoing it and sabotaging the opportunity for a settlement.[1]

Mediator Knowledge Versus Party Expertise

One of the most frustrating paradoxes for mediation clients is that they look for mediators who are knowledgeable, only to find that mediators are often reluctant to share with them what they know. Divorce mediators, for example, acquire a good deal of knowledge over the years about the various arrangements that lawyers and the courts consider customary with regard to asset division, custody, alimony, and child support. The parties often prefer mediators who have such knowledge, but we mediators send the parties off to lawyers to get answers to their questions because, when serving as mediators, we are not permitted to give legal advice or engage in the practice of law. (Even if we are lawyers, ethical principles prohibit us from mixing the two roles, and those mediators who are not lawyers are also prohibited by statute from practicing law.) Thus parties who came to us to minimize the role of lawyers in the resolution of their dispute are being sent to the law offices they sought to avoid. The hoped-for result of these referrals is better-informed parties. But often the result is to inject a higher degree of contentiousness into the process, thus undermining one of the reasons the parties chose mediation.

Confidentiality: Keeping Secrets Versus "Noisy" Communication

Mediators usually begin a mediation session by assuring the parties that their communications will be confidential—not only from outsiders but also from each other, if the mediator meets with the parties separately and they disclose information they do not wish the other party or parties to know. The conventional wisdom is that confidentiality fosters candor, which in turns fosters settlement.[2] Ethical rules for mediators also require confidentiality.[3] Nevertheless, some commentators have noted that the mediator's success in settling cases may depend, at least in part, on her ability to make indirect disclosures to each of the parties concerning their opponent's position (Brown and Ayres, 1994). Mediators make such disclosures (assertedly without violating ethical rules) by cloaking the disclosures in what Jennifer Brown and Ian Ayres describe as "noise," a smoke screen of hemming, hawing, and what-if-ing—that allows the parties to discern more effectively each other's perspectives and bargaining positions, while at the same time protecting them from being asked to make bargaining concessions that are not likely to be reciprocated.

The paradox here is that the parties are counting on the mediator to keep their confidences while at the same time disclosing them—albeit noisily—to the other side. "Mediators," write Brown and Ayres, "can productively control the flow of information between the parties by filtering or inserting noise into their private disclosure" (Brown and Ayres, 1994, p. 330). Mediators learn to manage this tension with time and experience, and the parties learn, during the course of the mediation, whether they can trust the mediator to manage it successfully. The parties gauge, to some degree, what the mediator is doing in meetings with the opposing party by what she does with them. Although the mediator can bargain with the parties for leeway in making disclosures, there is usually a need, even without such bargaining, for noisy, filtered, indirect communications by the mediator that enable the parties to navigate their way to a settlement (Honeyman, 1999).

Providing Normative Data Versus Promoting Party Self-Determination

Mediators are frequently asked, "What do *you* think is fair? What do *you* think is reasonable? What do most people do? What do the courts do? What do *you* think we should do?" The parties seek benchmarks, norms against which they can measure their own sense of fairness or reasonableness. Yet the mediator ordinarily resists these efforts to drag her into the fray, because party autonomy (including letting the parties apply their own standards of fairness) is a vital principle of mediation. The paradoxical element here is that, notwithstanding the mediator's efforts to avoid injecting her own normative views, her influence is unavoidable.

Social scientists have demonstrated that observation produces change in the behavior of the observed. Known as the Hawthorne effect, this phenomenon is at work whenever a mediator sits at the table with the parties (Bowling and Hoffman, 2000). Most often, the effect is to improve the parties' ability to negotiate effectively, as they seek to impress the mediator with their reasonableness. Occasionally, however, mediators observe what can be described as reverse Hawthorne effects—that is, parties who seem to negotiate *less* productively if a third party is present. For example, in some cases, explosive personal issues (such as the emotional distress caused by an abrupt termination of employment or the discovery of infidelity in a marriage) cannot be discussed productively without a third party present, and the seemingly unproductive discussions that take place in the mediator's presence are nevertheless valuable.

Either way, the parties are affected by the norms that the mediator brings to the table, explicitly or implicitly, because they are keenly aware of the mediator's reactions to the stories, positions, and interests that they articulate at the bargaining table.[4]

Some mediators consider this type of normative impact on the parties not only inevitable but also desirable. Sara Cobb describes this aspect of the mediator's presence as "witnessing," which is not a passive activity: "On the contrary, this 'witnessing' involves very active participation in the evolution of narrative content. [Notwithstanding the injunction to be neutral] mediation is thus a very moral practice, and mediators are deeply implicated in the nature of the moral worlds that emerge in [mediation] sessions" (Cobb, 2001, p. 1031). Thus no matter how strenuously we may assert that the only norm we bring to the table is a commitment to assisting the parties in reaching their own self-determined solutions, our reactions to them as people, and to their stories, unavoidably shape those solutions.

Conclusion

What are the implications of these tensions and paradoxes for practice?

First, despite our all-too-human craving for order, rationality, and logic, we mediators—particularly those who have suffered right-brain atrophy in law school—need to get comfortable with the mysterious, irreconcilable, ambiguous, and paradoxical elements of our work. Peter Adler once commented that "one should never underestimate the power of a good ambiguity." The same is true of paradox.

Second, there is no obviously correct way to practice mediation. Perhaps we already knew that, but I believe that examining the inherent tensions in our work underscores this point, which should give us some degree of humility as we consider such issues as credentialing and regulation.

Third, even if we develop the personal qualities that make us good mediators (such as candor and empathy, and an ability to tolerate paradox and ambiguity), their attainment does not solve the dilemmas of mediation practice because of the inherent tensions between and among those qualities.

Finally, a detailed examination of the paradoxes of mediation should give us a renewed appreciation of not only the difficulty of this important work but also the value of reflective practice. Reflection is likely to persuade us that the very complexity of mediation—and the paradoxical nature of its goals and methods—causes success to be an elusive horizon that (like enlightenment) we seek, perhaps with many years of practice approach, but never fully reach.

Reflective Practice Questions

1. Do you share the author's view that mastery as a dispute resolver is essentially unattainable? Is this perspective necessarily inconsistent with Peter Adler's view of mastery as achievable in moments of "grace"?

2. The author analogizes the paradoxes of dispute resolution to those associated with parenting. Are there other roles or activities in your life that generate the same type of fundamentally irreconcilable tensions? If so, what are the personal qualities that connect these roles and activities for you?

3. Do you find it possible, in your work as a dispute resolver, to hold in mind simultaneously such inconsistent goals as "seeking to influence the future while simultaneously ignoring it"? If so, what personal qualities enable you to maintain such "binocularity" in your focus?

References

Benjamin, R. D. "The Constructive Uses of Deception: Skills, Strategies, and Techniques of the Folkloric Trickster Figure and Their Application by Mediators." *Mediation Quarterly*, Fall 1995a, *13*(1), 3–18.

Benjamin, R. D. "The Mediator as Trickster: The Folkloric Figure as Professional Role Model." *Mediation Quarterly*, Winter 1995b, *13*(2), 131–149.

Bowling, D., and Hoffman, D. "Bringing Peace into the Room: The Personal Qualities of the Mediator and Their Impact on the Mediation." *Negotiation Journal*, 2000, *5*(10), 5–28.

Brown, J., and Ayres, I. "Economic Rationales for Mediation." *Virginia Law Review*, 1994, *80*, 323.

Bush, R. B., and Folger, J. *The Promise of Mediation: Responding to Conflict Through Empowerment and Recognition.* San Francisco: Jossey-Bass, 1994.

Cloke, K. *Mediating Dangerously: The Frontiers of Conflict Resolution.* San Francisco: Jossey-Bass, 2001.

Cobb, S. "Creating Sacred Space in ADR." *Fordham Law Review,* 2001, 28, 1017–1031.

Freud, S. "The Paradoxes of Parenthood: On the Impossibility of Being a Perfect Parent." In *My Three Mothers and Other Passions.* New York: New York University Press, 1988.

Gill-Austern, G. "Faithful." *Journal of Dispute Resolution,* 2000, no. 2, 343.

Gladwell, M. "The Naked Face." *New Yorker,* Aug. 5, 2002, p. 38.

Gold, L. "Influencing Unconscious Influences." *Mediation Quarterly,* 1993, 11, 55–56.

Green, E. "A Heretical View of the Mediation Privilege." *Ohio State Journal of Dispute Resolution,* 1986, 2(1), 1–36.

Honeyman, C. "Confidential, More or Less." *Dispute Resolution Magazine,* Jan. 1999, 5, 12–13.

Matz, D. "Mediator Pressure and Party Autonomy: Are They Consistent with Each Other?" *Negotiation Journal,* 1994, 10, 359–365.

Moffitt, M. "Casting Light on the Black Box of Mediation: Should Mediators Make Their Conduct More Transparent?" *Ohio State Journal of Dispute Resolution,* 1997, 13(1), 1–149.

Sander, F. "The Obsession with Settlement Rates." *Negotiation Journal,* 1995, 11, 329.

Stone, D., Patton, B., and Heen, S. *Difficult Conversations: How to Discuss What Matters Most.* New York: Viking Press, 1999.

8

Mediation and the Culture of Healing

Lois Gold

The 21st Century will be spiritual or not at all.
—*André Malraux*

The notion of healing and invoking higher principles to deal with a range of contemporary problems is weaving its way into the mainstream. We can see it in experimental programs such as teaching transcendental meditation in prisons; the Fetzer Foundation's support of the Center for Contemplative Mind in Society, which has given courses in meditation as part of the curriculum at Yale Law School; and new professional associations such as the International Association of Holistic Lawyers. Many medical schools now include courses on spirituality and health in their curriculum. Certainly in the behavioral sciences, one cannot pick up a journal or conference brochure without seeing titles like Awakening Our Wisdom, Spirituality and Family Therapy, or Tribal and Shamanistic Social Work. It is clear we are all part of a larger social yearning for more meaning, spiritual connection, and healing for our times.

I think this movement raises two questions for the mediation profession. First, have we, as mediators, been constrained by our role definition as a neutral from sharing more of our humanity? Have we been prohibited from drawing upon our higher consciousness or spiritual center to be present to the dispute in a way that might foster healing and inspire parties to seek the highest good? One could say we have preciously guarded neutrality as the standard at the expense of examining the role of compassion. We have honed our skills as conflict technicians, not conflict healers. I think we have an opportunity to ask if there is a way we can bring who we are at a higher level into our practice.

Second, are we asking enough of our disputants? Can we raise their goal aspirations, asking them to reach deeper into themselves than their self-interest to look at resolutions that bring genuine peace and healing or that address the greatest good? Are we doing enough as conflict interveners merely to bring about settlement without encouraging healing between parties who have continuing obligations or impact on the wider community? We are never just one side against the other; we are always two parts of something larger. Should we have a responsibility to the whole—the greater good?

> What befalls the earth, befalls the sons of the earth;
> what he does to the web, he does to himself.
> —Chief Seattle

If we consider the example of divorce mediation, twenty-five years ago the notion of cooperating with an ex-spouse and sharing child rearing was unheard of. Now the cultural expectation is the cooperative sharing of parental tasks. There has been a paradigm shift about what it means to be a family after divorce, and the mediation profession was largely responsible for this. It established a new expectation. In the words of Goethe, "If you treat a man as he already is, you make him worse than he is. But if you treat a man as if he already were what he potentially could be, you make him what he should be."

When we talk about augmenting the healing potential of mediation, we are talking about a twofold approach. How can we remain connected to the highest and best within ourselves? How can we inspire the highest and best within our clients? There is more to all of us than the elements of the dispute, and calling all of who we are into play is the untapped potential of mediation. Although Bush and Folger (1994) in the transformative models emphasize the relational field, that is, the parties' sense of empowerment and acknowledgment of each other, I am suggesting that we also need to look within. We cannot ask participants to know or touch a part of themselves that we do not know and cannot reach within ourselves.

As a mediator who is also a therapist, I have always been interested in the healing dimensions of mediation practice. In the last decade, I have studied the healing traditions in cultures from Brazil to Bali. This chapter explores methods to augment mediation's potential to foster healing resolutions by focusing on the quality of the mediator-client relationship, drawing from the mediator's higher self or spiritual center, and the use of indirect and embedded suggestion to assist clients in bringing their best forward. It is an invitation to experiment with how we can reach beyond strategy into the deeper levels of human experience in which healing can occur.

The Relational, the Whole, and the All: The Importance of Context

What happens psychologically to people in the crisis of protracted conflict is that all context is lost. Crisis narrows perspective; the domain of the self reigns. A myopia sets in, at the center of which is the individual's sense of self—what is owed, the damages done, the redress or retribution sought. There are three levels of disconnection and subsequent disempowerment.

The first is from the *relational field*, which is what mediation traditionally addresses: understanding the needs and concerns of the other and developing a willingness to address those needs and concerns. This is the Fisher-Ury (1981) interest-based model and the Bush-Folger (1994) transformative model. The second level of disconnection that occurs is from the *whole*; the dispute is part of a larger social and human context, be it the immediate family, neighborhood, community, or the global community. The third level of disconnection is from the *all*; that is, we are part of a larger order that generates questions of ultimate meaning, why we are here, what our purpose is.

If the mediating process can draw from the sense of the all—meaning the religious or spiritual values that guide a person at the highest level—it can help parties address the whole, which is what William Ury in his book *Getting to Peace* (1999) seems to be referring to as the "third side" and what Chief Seattle and many Native American traditions refer to as the "web"—the sense that we are all fundamentally interconnected. I am not suggesting that mediation adopt any type of religious orientation, but rather that it find a context to encompass the values of compassion, right action, forgiveness, and inclusiveness that are the basis of all spiritual practices. Conflict draws parties far away from these principles and valuable spiritual resources. We need to think about how we can help clients access them if we are interested in fostering peacemaking or agreements that address the greater good or a broader range of constituencies.

The Fundamental Principles of Healing and Their Relationship to Mediation Process

Any discussion of the healing potential of mediation has first to ask, What do we mean by healing? What heals? Where does the power to heal reside? How do we invoke it? Healing is a complex phenomenon that has physical, spiritual, and emotional components. It is not very well understood. We understand the process of disease and dysfunction more than we understand the process of recovery. It is beyond the scope of this chapter to rigorously define healing or to create some standard to apply to the mediation process, but I would like to draw upon elements of the healing arts that relate to what we do as mediators.

Let me begin by emphasizing that all healing is self-healing. The healer does not do the healing, and I am not suggesting the mediator become a healer. Dr. Christine Northrup observed, "Healers don't heal, but they do facilitate the process by holding the energy of possibility. They help a person wake up to what he or she already knows" (Northrup, 1995, p. 58). The role of the healer is to create conditions that activate the person's innate healing capacities. People are healed by so many systems because the real healer is within. Dr. Robert Moss writes, "Healing always involves a transformation of some sort. It is not the same as curing. It is more than returning to a former condition. In true healing, the circle grows larger, more inclusive, more capable of loving" (1989, p. 36).

In the book, *Healers on Healing* (1989), Carlson and Shield have identified common elements of healing in the writing of well-known healers, from Dr. Carl Simonton, the pioneer in the use of visualization in the treatment of cancer, to Ram Dass. What follows is a summary of these central principles. Mediators also hold these values. If we can focus on them with a greater intentionality, I believe we can augment mediation's peacemaking and healing potential. In mediation they are values; in healing work they are the method.

- The role of unconditional love and caring, the nonjudgmental acceptance of a person's humanity. Healing's opposite is judgment. We lose our effectiveness when we emotionally react to the client. Our task is to remain open and receptive even in the most challenging situations.

- The quality of the relationship. Rapport, emotional support; healing does not occur in isolation. When there is a real connection between two people, something beyond them opens up. All healing occurs in the relational field.

- The importance of the return to wholeness. The root of the word *heal* is "whole"—bringing back into balance what has fallen out of balance. Do not underestimate the universal desire for wellness.

- Helping clients find and listen to their higher intelligence and inner wisdom. People want to bring their best forward and are often compromised by the adrenalin and stress of conflict. Our goal is to help them access the wiser, more knowing part. We need to go beyond asking them to be reasonable and logical. We need to help them touch their wisdom.

- Stimulating a healing attitude and hope. Believing change is possible and working toward a better future. Hope energizes behavior. Without hope, motivation is lost. Disputants often feel defeated or feel like a failure. In this sense, we lend them our energy.

- The realization that healing is our natural state. The organism strives toward health and restoration. The brain and body have templates to right themselves. Our task is to foster conditions that nurture this movement. The surgeon sets the fracture. The bones mend themselves.

The Healing Dimensions of the Mediation Process

Although our work does not have healing as a focus, the mediation process shares the fundamental principles just listed. Although we describe what we do differently, mediation, like other helping professions, operates within this core framework. We see ourselves as caring individuals who believe that clients have the inner capacity to find their own solutions. We activate the hope that life can be better, that solutions are possible. We value self-determination and empowerment. We are oriented toward the future, supporting clients in moving forward and constructively coping with change.

Disputes that are honorably resolved open the way for the wounds they created to mend. A process that is respectful of each person and encourages the expression of mutual respect heals the ravages of hateful and angry diatribes. A process that supports people in retaining control of the decisions that affect their lives is empowering. A process that encourages awareness of mutual needs, mutual losses, and shared concerns reduces feelings of victimization and blame. In divorce, a civilized parting in which the parties retain their integrity honors the marriage and the life that was shared. All this is healing.

In this context, I think we could agree that at its best the mediation process itself, independent of particular interventions or techniques, has considerable healing potential. Perhaps the unrealized potency of mediation lies in the experience of a collaborative, constructive process, which as a whole has an integrity and healing power that is greater than the benefits derived in any given session (Gold, 1988).

With this in mind, I see four assumptions as fundamental to accessing and augmenting mediation's healing potential: (1) there exists a part of the psyche that has preference for peace; (2) every person has a capacity for growth, change, and good; (3) people prefer to bring forward their highest and best; (4) each participant has a higher wisdom and better self than is manifested in the dispute. Core beliefs of this kind, about the latent potential for good in the mediation clients we see, whether they are trying mediation as a last resort or are highly committed, become part of the presence the mediator projects.

The Use of Self and the Concept of Presence

An area that has been largely neglected in the mediation literature until recently (see Chapter One of this book) is how we use ourselves and what we bring of our own personal being. Narrow role parameters have defined practice, ignoring exploration of the relationship between client and mediator or the personal presence the mediator brings to the negotiation process. This may have been necessary in the nascence of the profession to carve a professional identity, develop skills as negotiators, and guard neutrality, but we have not had permission to consider our own unique personas in our work. It is almost as though being a neutral carries with it significant constraints on being a person. Mediation is task-oriented; consequently, we are only beginning to explore the skills and interventions that do not bear directly on negotiating and bargaining.

It is these intangibles in the person of the mediator that I want to discuss first. The ability to be fully present, work from the heart, and connect with the highest in our clients is a powerful force in any helping profession. I refer to these abilities as elements of the presence of the mediator. To have a presence that can foster conditions for healing, we need to learn to open our hearts and release judgment when it begins to cloud our view and tighten our bodies, move away from our egos when our need for success or settlement is overactive, and learn to be in the present moment when we can no longer hear what is in the clients' hearts. If we are centered or grounded in who we are, when we can get out of the way of ego and come from a place of authenticity, congruence, and compassion, we have a different impact.

I first came to think about the concept of presence through my association with the late Virginia Satir. An element of her charisma as a teacher, therapist, and pioneer in the field of family therapy was what she described as being "fully present." Steeped in the humanistic tradition, her belief in each person's capacity for growth, change, and transformation was in her bones. She described it as "feeling these things in every cell of my body." A master reframer, she was able to find positive intention behind even the most maladaptive behavior and never wavered from seeing the potential for change in even the most difficult of circumstances. She regarded authentic human connection as fundamental to change processes and perhaps was most remarkable in her ability to make contact with each person on a human level, eyeball to eyeball, navel to navel.

As mediators, we share a commitment to similar humanistic principles. Satir had an extraordinary presence because she was connected to her belief system at the core of her being. Although the most remarkable example of presence is charisma, most of us experience effortless flow when there is a congruence of mind and action. When we lose all self-consciousness we are fully present. Healing occurs in these expanded states of consciousness. If we can access these places within ourselves, we can help others access theirs, because we experience them in their wholeness.

The Elements of Presence

There are four elements of presence that can increase our effectiveness as mediators: (1) coming from center, (2) compassion, (3) connection to central and governing values and higher purpose, and (4) congruence (i.e., permission to be authentic). We can think of them as the four C's.

Coming from Center

Being centered is a state of physical and mental alignment in which one experiences an almost transcendental connection to one's being or to the larger universe. It is an egoless state of being in which all thinking and judgment is suspended. There is a feeling of harmony, as if boundaries disappear. To achieve it, you empty your mind and simply focus your awareness on what is, observing present experience without judging or evaluating it. A shift of consciousness occurs allowing you to see things not ordinarily seen because experience is not filtered or mediated through the ego.

Psychologist Larry LeShan, speaking of the centered state of healers, elaborates: "One can only be in this mode when one has, if only for a moment, given up all wishes and desires for oneself . . . and just allows oneself to be, and therefore to be with and be one with all of existence . . . any awareness of doing interrupts this mode" (Dossey, 1993, pp. 197–198).

Being centered, however brief, is an altered state of consciousness. Most of the time in mediation we operate in the linear analytic mode. However, we shift consciousness all the time, and each state of consciousness produces new opportunities for problem solving because the mechanisms that operate within it organize experience differently (Lankton, 1985). Working from the center can bring you to a point of clarity or new perspectives on the problem. At any time during or before a mediation session, you can momentarily shift consciousness by taking a few deep breaths, emptying the mind of all thought, and simply focusing awareness on the present moment.

When the mediator is centered in a conscious appreciation of his or her own humanity, not the ego's requirement of performance, this translates to an appreciation of the client's humanity, enabling the mediator to see the client apart from the context of the dispute, beyond the angry and harsh words, and to relate to their higher concerns: family, survival, security, and desire for peace and well-being. When the mediator comes from his own center and speaks his own truth, it inspires trust and allows others to reflect their own truth.

The ability to find your center and return to it is an extremely important tool. In high-conflict disputes or with difficult or contentious parties, it is easy to lose sight of their real concerns. We can become frustrated and react internally despite our best efforts to be neutral, impartial, and empathic. We are constantly being thrown off center. When you recenter yourself through the breath, it opens you and puts you back in a receptive state. You are fed rather than depleted. This practice is for those moments when you don't know what else to do.

Compassion: Connection to the Humanity of the Clients

The day will come when,
after harnessing the winds, the tides, and gravitation,
we shall harness for God the energies of love,
and for the second time in the history of the world
man will have discovered fire
—*Teilhard de Chardin (1975)*

Compassion is the ability to see with the heart and connect with the essential humanity of the client. It is about developing an attitude of openness and receptivity, especially to the negative other. It is the ability to open your heart to even the most difficult of clients, to step back and see their fundamental human striving, not the problematic survival behavior; the ability to see their lost hopes, spent dreams, and pain. It is "seeing with the altered eye" (in the Buddhist sense)—i.e., who they were before they were born and to make a felt connection with them on the level of their humanness.

A person is able to go beyond the narrow confines of her story when she has been seen and acknowledged. When you are a source of positive sponsorship, when you are able to see the humanity, specialness, or good intentions, others may be able to act on those intentions more directly and constructively. Whatever the nature of the dispute, an underlying element is often a threat to a basic human need, whether family, freedom, respect, identity, land, food, shelter, security, or love (Ury, 1999). It is human nature to react when we perceive these things as endangered.

Learn to become aware when you are closing off or becoming judgmental. Take a deep breath and let go. Stephen Levine, a psychologist and Buddhist meditation teacher who works with death and dying, has said, "Healing involves learning to keep your heart open in hell . . . it is about sending love (compassion) to the hard places" (Levine, 1991, p. 247). As mediators, we have to periodically remind ourselves to relate to the level of clients' pain and fear, not their defensive posture.

Many experts suggest that connection is the key to helping and that the quality of the relationship is what makes the difference in enabling others to bear their pain and garner strength. The successes of Dr. Carl Simonton, the pioneer in the use of visualization in the treatment of cancer, may have had as much to do with him and the relationships he established as the techniques he used (Capra, 1988).

This kind of connection comes from the ability to acknowledge and simply be with what is—the loss, sorrow, pain—and not need to do anything about it. There is a healing power in the act of just being there. Roslyn Bruyere writes, "Healing arises out of compassion. Compassion is a genuine concern for another's pain. Suffering is a soulless state. Part of the role of ritual is to coax the soul into participating in a time of need. The compassionate healer whose soul is present awakens the other's soul" (Bruyere, 1989, p. 107). When you enter another's world, acknowledge an experience that they may not have been able to communicate to others, and make it more understandable and real to them, something transformational occurs. A profound feeling of trust and intimacy is created at having been understood at the deepest level. Hugh Prather describes this connection this way: "Love is the uniting principle in all healing approaches. Any system or practitioner loses its effectiveness when it becomes judgmental. The true healer merely gives the gift of healing, but does not watch over the patient to say in what form it is to be received. This frees the healer to heal unhampered by anxiety over the possible results" (Prather, 1989, pp. 14–15).

It is interesting to compare your mediation cases in which the issues were competently resolved and those in which there was a real feeling of connection between you and your clients. You can notice it in the good-bye. It is in the hug instead of the handshake. I invite you to review cases in which you felt the deepest connection to the clients or in which there was a fundamental shift or transformation in the parties' relationship. What characterized those situations? Was there a part of yourself that you allowed into the process? Here are some of the themes that have emerged from workshop participants when I have posed this question:

- The disputants finally came to a point where they realized the situation was so broken, there was nothing left to do but to try to heal it.

- At the heart of the dispute, the desire to heal was stronger than the desire for money.

- The parties developed a real sense of trust and connection with the mediator, and this took time.

- Mediators responded from their gut, trusted their intuition, and allowed themselves to express real emotion.

- There was an experience of shared grief, for the mediator as well.

- There was an emotional breakthrough between the parties; they were able to see the good in the other or see their common humanity, vulnerability, or suffering.

- There were heartfelt apologies and the beginning of forgiveness.

- Compassion was aroused, and disputants wanted to help each other.

Connection to One's Governing Values, Beliefs, and Purpose

The more emotionally connected we are to our highest intention in choosing to become a mediator, the more the power of that intention is expressed in our work. When we are aligned in body, mind, and spirit with the meaning and purpose of our work, we are empowered. Because the decision to become a mediator for many represented a radical shift or a desire to bring about change, there is a sense of purpose and mission in this profession. The more the highest intention in making that choice is clarified, made conscious, and amplified, the more it becomes a guiding force. Centering on our purpose, on our highest values, and on why we answered the calling affects the presence we project. To the extent we convey the highest possibilities of this work, we enable our clients to recognize and clarify their highest possibilities. The further away we are from our roots, from our core values, because of busy schedules, anxiety about success, and so forth, the less fully present as human beings we become. Periodically, we ought to remind ourselves why we are doing what we are doing.

A focusing exercise such as a short meditation or visualization before a session can be useful to reconnect with your central and governing values and highest purpose, and access the deeper reasons you were drawn to mediation. Sit comfortably, close your eyes, take several slow and deep breaths, and review your belief in mediation, why you chose to become a mediator, the skills and resources you have acquired as a negotiator, and what you sense are the deepest concerns and hopes of the clients you are about to see.

The Concept of the Wounded Healer

For some, the calling comes from deeply personal reasons that are not always entirely conscious but that nonetheless can be a powerful part of one's gifts as a mediator. If you want to go deeper in aligning with your core values, in the focusing exercise just described, ask yourself if there was something that called you on a personal level to this work. Ask if you were drawn because of an experience in your childhood or family. Were you the mediator in a family with conflict or did you watch helplessly as parents or family members fought destructively? If you were touched or "wounded" in your family by issues of abuse, destructive family conflict, or were compromised growing up because of your family's inability to handle conflict, you may have a special part of you that has knowing and compassion about what this experience is like for others.

There are two ways of thinking about this concept. One is the traditional psychological theory about countertransference, which refers to how we overreach or overreact because of our own personal unresolved issues, problems, or vulnerabilities. The other view is drawn from the mythological. In mythology, the concept of the wounded healer speaks to how it is out of our wounds that true compassion and gifts emerge. The healing for the person is in the serving, and the serving is more profound because of the compassion born of the wound. It renders the person available to meet the client in the place of suffering. In this respect, we want to be touched by our client's struggle; it activates our own wounds and makes us more human and compassionate. Examples of this principle are service associations, such as Alcoholics Anonymous, Mothers Against Drunk Driving, or any number of self-help groups where those who have been through a life challenge help others with a similar struggle. I am not suggesting this is the core of the mediation profession, but any profession has within its ranks many individuals who have a special passion, motivation, and compassion born of a deep desire to serve that is based on their own wounding and struggle. I do not think we have to compromise our impartiality to share our humanity and to sit with people in the grief, loss, or tragedy of a situation.

Rachel Naomi Remen has written eloquently about this concept: "What fosters healing is the way we stand in relationship to each other. My woundedness allows me to connect to you in your woundedness and there is a trust. I know what suffering is. I know of your feeling of isolation, loss, and fright. My woundedness allows me to be with you in a non-judgmental way and my very presence facilitates something. In a true healing relationship, both heal and are healed" (1989, p. 92).

Being Congruent

A fourth element of presence is congruence. Being congruent is the condition of being emotionally honest, being who you are and not allowing your anxiety, pride, or ego to be a mask. It is being authentic, not having to be perfect and have all the answers. Carl Rogers has said: "There is something I do before a session. I let myself know that I am enough. Not perfect. Perfect wouldn't be enough. But that I am human, and that is enough" (Remen, 1989, p. 92). The power of congruence comes from the permission to be who you are, unencumbered by "shoulds" and self-consciousness. It is about not being so locked into the role that you are less a person. It is allowing your human vulnerability to show. If you speak from your truth, it can have great impact.

Presence Is About Holding Two Fields

Maintaining a generative presence is the ability to hold two fields simultaneously. It is about focusing on the dispute and listening for the essential person; dealing with the level of crisis and holding the level of possibility; working on the transactional level and being informed by the transcendent. It is difficult to remain centered, open, and compassionate amid demanding negotiations. Clients induce us to the dark self. We often see them at their worst; their best is hidden. You have to repeatedly find in your heart the person's humanness and goodness and hold the field. Reenergize it with the breath when you lose it, and develop a practice of sitting quietly before clients arrive to become fully present and open.

Spiritually Based Strategies to Augment the Healing and Peacemaking Potentials of Mediation

Mediators can use a variety of spiritually oriented strategies to augment the healing potential of the process.

"Purification"

All traditional healing work involves ritual purification, setting an intention, and calling for guidance. Preparing oneself to be fully present, as I have suggested, can be considered modernity's version of ritual purification. It is a release of judgment and centering on purpose, similar in intent to "smudging" or cleansing with burning sage, which is used by many Native American groups in preparation for ceremony, important gatherings, or meetings. Like mindfulness in Buddhist traditions, it is "Be here now." That we pay more attention to why we are doing what we are doing through any manner of preparation, ritualized or other, can only strengthen us and help us act faithfully on our highest purpose. If we can prepare or allow ourselves to be present in body, mind, and spirit, we project an ambiance that is calming, supportive, and hopeful.

Develop your own way of centering and preparing yourself before a session. You can do a short meditation or visualization. For example, sit with your eyes closed and focus on your heart center and the energy of love and compassion. With the breath, open your heart to your clients and try to see their vulnerabilities, fears, and hopes; release any frustration or negative thoughts about the disputants or the mediation session.

The Role of Intention and Directed Intentionality

On a psychological level, intention unconsciously organizes behavior. We tend to act consistently with our intentions, whether or not we are aware of them. Intentions are frequently below conscious awareness and are often deduced after the fact when our behavior is questioned, as in "Was your intention to hurt interest X?" I would like to address how we can use intentionality proactively to cull our unconscious creative resources and to amplify the potency of our clients' highest aspiration and goals by making them more explicit and motivating forces.

For example, if you, as a mediator, set an intention to be in the service of healing and peacemaking, you are "seeding" your unconscious creative mind to look for opportunities to act on that intention. It is not a linear process, a thought followed by an action. You are influencing the unconscious mind to be of service in ways that cannot be determined or measured linearly. Ericksonian models of hypnotherapy, based on the groundbreaking work of psychiatrist Dr. Milton Erickson, see the unconscious mind as a creative resource, a repository of stored learning, skills, and latent potential. By setting an intention, in a sense you are activating a search engine in your unconscious that brings ideas and behaviors forward consistent with that intention.

On another level, setting an intention can be a prayerful act. In this sense, it is in collaboration with higher mind, or a communion with higher powers. When you say, "May I be of service at the highest level" or "May this session be a vehicle for peace and healing," you are directing that appeal or energy to the universe or whatever you believe to be its divine sourcing.

There is a difference between having an intention, which is often outside awareness, and setting an intention. When we consciously set an intention, that is, when we verbally state or say to ourselves what it is that we desire, we are calling upon or asking the forces of body, mind, and spirit to act. In my experience, if I am aligned with my highest mind and ask that the session be a vehicle for healing, something beyond problem solving often occurs. In very contentious, seemingly unresolvable situations, when I set the intention "May the parties find a path to peace or healing," something in the session shifts. It moves in a more positive, productive direction. I do not understand this, but it does occur. Perhaps it is coincidence or readiness. Perhaps the energy I am projecting changes when I go inside and center on the higher.

We can help clients home in on their highest aspirations, and similarly create a framework to turn these aspirations into intentions, by asking them if they would be willing to state their intentions from a place of honest and deep desire. We can ask, for example, "Are you willing, or do you think it would be helpful, to make these goals or aspirations be your intention as we begin this mediation process? Or can we say that it is everyone's intention here to try to resolve this matter at the highest? Or can each person state what their highest intention is?"

Prayer, Meditation, and Guidance

Sometimes there might be a benefit to approaching an intractable problem with an attitude of prayerfulness. I am not suggesting petitionary prayer in which a specific outcome is requested, but rather calling ourselves or our clients into communion with what is greater than ourselves.

At a minimum, prayer brings the person praying into a harmonious relationship. It calls us into a deeper sense of personhood (Spong, 1998). It sheds the delusion that we are at the center of the universe and places the dispute and our claims in some perspective to the larger order. It can bring a person out of emotionality or ego-driven blame and attachment into a perspective of greater understanding and empathy. I do think it is appropriate, in certain situations, to ask participants who are stuck to go home and pray or ask for guidance about an impasse.

Physicist Peter Russell speaks of calling for guidance as posing the question of the deep self, "Is there another way to see this?" (2003, p. 96–97). Guidance then is about a change of perspective and a change in the context. It gets us out of a materialistic mindset. In the words of Albert Einstein, "You can't solve a problem on the same level it was created."

There is a noteworthy Mennonite tradition. When people are in serious conflict, someone prays to the higher intelligence of the disputing parties, asking that their higher intelligences enter into a dialogue with each other. It is hoped that through these prayerful intentions, the parties find their way toward more reasonableness, empathy, and understanding.

Prayer or calling for guidance can be a powerful tool because mediation is all about how we see things, how we frame things, and understanding a multiplicity of perspectives. Again, this is not about imposing one's religious or spiritual beliefs or practices on others or bringing religion into mediation but about the value of calling yourself or the parties into communion with whatever is a spiritual sourcing. Praying for clients with whom you are having personal difficulty gives rise to feelings of compassion and brings you into a more harmonious relationship with them. This, in and of itself, regardless of any religious beliefs about the value of prayer, is beneficial.

Use of Silence and Reflection

In stillness, the mind becomes clear. Silence can access higher mind rather than reactive mind. A moment of silence can be used in the beginning of a session as a focusing device, either open-ended or with a specific question to reflect on. For example, participants can be asked to reflect on their deepest concerns or what they hope to achieve in the session. A moment of silence with the eyes closed creates a shift in energy and allows them to reach a higher place of clarity before they begin. Parties can also be asked to reflect on an obstacle; for example, "Is there something you need to understand about the other side that you are missing?"

Use a moment of silence during a session when parties are not in a constructive or resourceful state. At a minimum, it calms the mind and can interrupt unproductive interactions. For example: "Can we all take a moment of silence and ask ourselves if this is the way we really want things to be? Can we have a moment of silence and go to that higher place inside and ask ourselves if there is another way to view this situation?" In the words of Fr. Thomas Keating, "Silence is the language God speaks, everything else is a bad translation" (Keating, 1994, p. 44).

Role of Ritual

Ritual calls us into alignment with purpose and meaning. It takes us out of the rush of the ordinary into a place of contemplation. It moves people away from the prepared, rehearsed, or well-worn story and creates a space for something new to emerge. It enables people to speak more from their core or from their hearts because the ritual context imbues what is about to occur with importance.

Simple opening rituals can create a more positive ambiance, prepare parties to be more constructive, and create a container for dealing with hard or contentious issues in a constructive manner. It calls the group together, emphasizing the common purpose. The message is that we have something hard to do, but we are going to do it in a good way. Ritual indirectly asks parties to draw from their higher and wiser selves. I have found, for example, an opening silent meditation on "How can we be present (or resolve this conflict) at the highest level?" has helped angry, hurt clients to shift away from these emotions.

Many mediators have experimented with the ritualization of dialogue. One example is the Native American or Quaker tradition of using a "talking stick," which is passed from speaker to speaker. The stick is a revered symbol of respect, and each holder of the stick in turn is given the full attention and respect of the group.

Ceremonial practices such as smudging with sage, Buddhist meditation, lighting candles, or chanting can be used in a culturally sensitive way to sanctify or honor the process. In considering ritual, elicit ideas from participants and, if appropriate, invite participants from other cultures to offer ritual or ceremony from their traditions.

Ritualized or ceremonial acts need to be organic, not imposed, or they will be perceived as false and empty. The mediator has to trust his or her intuition in suggesting a ritual. If the mediator or group wishes to construct a ritual, there are four basic components: stating the purpose or intention, choosing a symbolic object or representation, developing a method of enactment, and closing the ritual and honoring what has taken place (van der Hart, 1983).

Because rituals are not intellectual but rather multisensory experiences involving symbolic objects or enactment, they touch the deep and can bring up powerful emotions that the mediation process may not be equipped or have the time to handle. Rituals cannot go by the clock. They take time. The time frame needs to be open-ended before engaging in anything ritualized beyond simple acknowledgments.

Cognitive Strategies for Cultivating Higher Principles and Stimulating Peacemaking and Healing

In addition to being aware of the quality of the relationships we establish with our clients, the presence we bring to our work, and the role of spiritual contexts, there are a number of cognitive strategies that can foster peacemaking and healing. The next section focuses on what I refer to as "strategic communication," meaning purposeful language, statements, and questions designed to bypass conscious resistance or rigid positions and access or engage a client's creative capacities and highest self in working toward a solution.

The unconscious mind is particularly receptive to suggestion at times of emotional crisis or life transition. A person searches for information to resolve the crisis on both a conscious and an unconscious level. The well-timed indirect references or suggestions you make about healing, peacemaking, or forgiveness can have a potent effect on the subconscious.

Frame mediation in terms of the potential to be healing. During times of emotional crisis or life transition, the unconscious mind is looking for information to help resolve issues and ease psychological pain. The person is suggestible, and suggestions are likely to have a deep level of receptivity. The opening statement or informational "monologue" can be strategically used to convey information that is conducive to negotiating success, cooperation, and healing, because the unconscious is paying very close attention. You can embed suggestions about healing and higher purpose as discussed earlier, preempt potential roadblocks by describing a set of behavioral norms associated with successful outcomes, or describe others' successes. You may notice times when the client's rapt attention to your words is almost trancelike. The intensity of their absorption in what you are saying allows your words to penetrate subconsciously. In this sense, the introductory monologue can be used as an induction into a more healing and cooperative process.

There are a number of ways in which one can frame mediation in terms of healing in the opening statement. Draw from what you suspect are the issues or obstacles in the particular situation. For example, you can describe how mediation can pave the way for healing by helping parties to lay aside old grievances, increase mutual understanding, build trust, become less angry, begin to forgive each other, and so on. If there is a high level of conflict, telling an anecdote about other clients who achieved a remarkable end result, despite how unlikely it seemed at the beginning, plants a seed without challenging how the parties currently view things. With more receptive clients, you can suggest that if they make healing one of their personal goals, they might find that negotiations go more smoothly. Whenever you refer to the potential for healing in the mediation process, you plant a seed in the back of the mind and open the possibility for behaviors that support the healing process.

It is important to remember that even though people come to mediation primarily to get matters resolved, a part of them often seeks something more: to be acknowledged, affirmed, their core values recognized. Whenever I describe mediation in terms of these unspoken universals or in terms of paving the way for wounds to heal, I can see I have touched a responsive chord. The mediation session is a rare opportunity to respectfully acknowledge profound human concerns at a point where parties are together and capable of listening. We speak to the part of the psyche that Gerald Jampolsky (1983) describes as "having a preference for peace," the part that recognizes the sorrow, loss, or broken spirit and that longs (in even the angriest of clients) to be whole. Do not underestimate the power of tapping into the universal desire for wellness that exists even in the most bitter of disputes. With divorcing clients, you can ask them to consider making self-healing a guiding principle in interacting with each other; they can ask the question of themselves, "Will this action promote my healing, or make matters worse?" (Gold, 1992, pp. 73–74).

Reinforce the choice of mediation as a healing choice. Committing to a cooperative resolution process and moving in the direction of what seems right promotes healing. Help clients appreciate the full significance of the choice they have made in using mediation. Marsha Sinetar, in her book, *Elegant Choices, Healing Choices,* writes, "How we do things counts" (1988, p. 25). The act of choosing a peaceful path is a healthy choice. Choices change us in the quality and direction of the choice. Reinforce the importance of the peaceful choice as a commendable effort toward the higher moral ground.

Clarify the highest intention. The more you can help clients become aware of their highest intentions in making positive choices, the more they are guided by those intentions. Embedded in the choice to mediate, especially in divorce or another situation in which there was once a meaningful relationship, are unspoken hopes that can be a potent force in helping clients get the most out of the mediation process. By helping them clarify their highest intentions or goals in choosing mediation, those intentions become more concrete, visible, and attainable. In the opening discussion of what they hope to achieve from mediation, probe to help them articulate what may be higher aspirations. The question to pose is not just "What is important to you?" but also "Why is that important to you?"

Relate to the larger contexts. Disputes narrow vision. When needs, interests, or survival is threatened, an exaggerated self-interest dominates. What should be held in reverence is treated like a bartered commodity, be it children, a family residence in a divorce, or the meaning of the land in an environmental dispute. When parties in conflict become polarized, they lose all awareness of what things mean in a larger human context. Sometimes demands and expectations are simply not achievable, but this is not seen. In divorce, for example, parents often have not fully faced that neither will be able to see the children whenever they wish, as they would in the intact family. They may know this intellectually, but it has not penetrated, and the conflict over every precious hour or overnight is often rooted in not having accepted this sad reality.

Where appropriate, help clients relate their experience to fundamental truths and universals: no life is without loss; pain is a great teacher; all things change; bringing children into the world is a gift. Reframe a dispute in terms of a higher or transcendent principle: "This dispute is about the inevitability of change"; or "This dispute has to do with the limits of our knowledge"; or "This dispute reminds us that life is fragile." Sit with the silence that comes with facing fundamental human truths. Perspective comes with seeing our small experience in relationship to the human experience. If the mediator can speak congruently with heart, and from personal authority, these statements are not clichés but potent reminders of our place in the larger order.

Helping Parties Speak Their Truth

People in conflict have lost the ability to speak to each other from their core. Much of the discourse in mediation comes from some level of defensive posturing. There is usually a substratum of advancing one's position, making a point, justifying oneself, or trying to convince the other side in even the most articulate and calm speaker.

If clients can speak from their center, without an agenda, and simply describe what is true for them without blaming or casting aspersions on each other, if they are able to express the heart of their experience, their words have tremendous impact. This does not occur frequently in mediation, but when we hear it we know its truth and are moved. If just one person can speak this way, it can lead to a breakthrough or a new level of emotional honesty.

Speaking one's truth carries no agenda other than to be what it is. It is the unrehearsed story. It doesn't try to persuade, convince, or justify, and it is precisely because of this that its inherent honesty can be felt. It is very difficult to speak from this place of utter congruence of mind and heart, both for participants and mediator. One way to access it is to pay attention to how you formulate questions as you ask for information. Ask people if they could respond or describe a situation as objectively as they possibly can or if they could try to express the heart of the matter. You can also simply ask them to speak their truth: "Can you speak your truth about this? Can you just say what is in your heart about this and not worry about defending yourself or trying to convince the other side of anything?"

Honor Grief

Once a dispute has reached a level where third-party intervention is required, something of value in a person's life has been compromised, threatened, or lost. It may be livelihood in a personal injury case, previous well-being in a medical malpractice case, the solace and serenity of one's home in a siting and land-use case, the family and children in a divorce case. Often neither the loss nor the grieving is acknowledged. Yet unrecognized or denied grieving in the form of unrelenting anger, blame, or the inability to let go may be one of the elements emotionally driving a dispute.

Loss needs to be recognized and its significance acknowledged and honored. There is a healing power when a mediator acknowledges the loss without judging, explaining, or trying to fix it. It is seeing and being with what is, and allowing clients to say what it means to them. This kind of compassionate listening and presence touches parties and helps them face their pain. If parties can recognize and acknowledge each other's loss and show any level of compassion, it opens the door to forgiveness.

The mediator can also speak about loss and grieving in general terms if it is not appropriate to deal with it directly on an emotional level. Especially in a contentious divorce case or other situation where there has been deep personal loss, speak to the importance of honoring the loss and needing time to grieve, perhaps comment on the stages of grieving, or make a preemptive statement about the

fact that the anger and blame of intense conflict or endless negotiation can keep people from the grieving necessary for healing.

Use of Indirect or Embedded Suggestions

Indirect or embedded suggestions address change at an unconscious
level. The tendency of the conscious mind is to see a singular solution or perspective and to conserve that perspective. Indirect or
embedded suggestions help bypass the limitations of the conscious
mind and access a person's creative resources (Lankton and Lankton, 1983). They are effective when there is a high level of conflict,
resistance to cooperation, or strong positional arguing. These
interventions enable shifts in perception or attitude to take place
without challenging the person's defenses.

You can embed suggestions about healing by posing questions
containing a presupposition about healing that must be accepted to
answer the question; for example: "What is the most healing way
you can think of to address the contentiousness of this matter?"
"How do you see yourselves healing the family (partnership, company)?" "How do you see this settlement honoring what was good
in your partnership?" "What do you need to see happen in the
process to feel safe and be at your highest?" This kind of question
carries an implicit directive: *You can do it—that is, be at your highest,
honor, or heal.*

Questions with embedded suggestions that contain a presupposition about the clients' ability to act in a positive or healing way
require them to search internally for positive solutions. You create
an opportunity for the participants to draw on their strengths to
answer the question. To resist answering these questions is to
acknowledge that one is not being positive. For example, "What
good would you like to be remembered for in this community
(business, family)?" or "What good would you like to come from this
resolution?" Another example is "I would like everyone to take a
moment to get settled and centered so you can be here at your
best despite the tension surrounding our work." The embedded

suggestion compels disputants to try to be at their best or else be viewed in a negative light.

Use of Language Associated with Healing or the Spiritual

Another way to use embedded suggestions is to frame questions in language associated with healing and spirituality. You can weave in words such as *mend* instead of *solve*, *harmony* instead of *outcome*, *honor* instead of *recognize*, *seek* instead of *want*, *wound* instead of *anger*, or *what is the heart of this matter* instead of *what is the real issue here?* These words speak to a deeper part of the psyche. They alter the accessibility of information consistent with these principles and require parties to reorganize a response in terms of mutual benefit rather than individual posturing; for example: "How can this misunderstanding be mended?" "How can you bring more harmony into the transition between households, in the relationship between divisions?" "How can the issues in this community be healed?" Questions or potential impasses can be framed in terms of "What would be the most healing solution?" A concession can be reframed as a healing gesture or as a gift for the "higher good of the group."

Make an Alliance with Parties' Higher Intelligence

To the extent a dispute has a reactive emotional component, the capacity for rational, mature reasoning and impulse control is compromised. Clients' actions, demands, and behaviors are often based on strong emotions. However, each of us has a wise, more knowing part of ourselves. I refer to this as one's higher intelligence. You can access that part of a person by addressing it directly or through a hypothetical. A particularly angry client who was a college professor regularly launched into a diatribe of "I can't believe you are doing this to me" whenever his wife brought an issue to the bargaining table. When I finally asked if his higher intelligence could address the issue, he understood immediately. He offered a reasonable proposal and became a more cooperative negotiator from that point forward.

When trying to engage the wiser mind or higher intelligence of contentious, angry, or mistrustful disputants, it is important to acknowledge and work with dualities: the part that seeks the high road; the part that is responding out of hurt, anger, or a sense of injustice; the part that wants to hurt the other side; and the part that wants to heal itself. "I appreciate how hard it is to put aside your feelings about the past. Can the objective side come up with a high-minded proposal for the next step?"

Another way you can help clients find and listen to their higher intelligence is by asking questions that require them to hypothetically put aside their angry, mistrustful, or other negative feelings and think of a solution *as if* these feelings did not exist. For example, "If he had not had the affair, what solutions do you think could be found for the disagreement about overnight visits?" You can also ask questions directly of the higher intelligence: "What would your higher intelligence say about this dilemma?"

Try to make an alliance with this wiser self. Let angry disputants know that you believe they have a wiser, more knowing side. Ask them to try to operate more from this part, and as Fisher and Brown suggest in *Getting Together: Building a Relationship That Gets to Yes* (1988), be "unconditionally constructive," that is, to act in the direction of good regardless of whether the other reciprocates.

When asking clients to share their concerns or state what the issues are in the opening session, I frequently word my initial line of inquiry something like this: "Can you please share your highest, objective understanding of the issues?" This is a difficult question, but I think clients appreciate the opportunity to speak from their wiser self.

Increase Hope and the Belief in the Potential for Success

Hope operates to energize and organize a person's resources. The client's confidence and beliefs about the help to be received affect healing. Skillful healers may bolster what Jerome Frank refers to as the healing power of expectant faith (Walsh, 1990). This new sense of hope may account for the frequent reports of improvement, between initial phone call and first appointment, that have been noted in a variety of helping professions.

Even on the telephone, be encouraging about the potential for success. Conveying your faith increases theirs. Create a picture of positive future expectancies. Tell stories of others' success. Help them see how far they have come. Describe the behaviors and attitudes most associated with success in mediation.

Postmediation Suggestion and the Closing Statement

Clients' attention is often as riveted on your closing statement as on the opening statement. The unconscious mind is similarly receptive and searching for helpful information. The mediator can use the closure phase of the last session to seed future growth and healing. In hypnosis, this is referred to as posthypnotic suggestion. In essence, you suggest that the parties can continue to learn and benefit from the mediation experience in a variety of ways. You can describe how the knowledge gained in mediation may help them handle conflict better in the future; how they may find, as time goes on, that this experience has allowed old wounds to heal; or that the mediation experience may enable them to relate to each other differently in the future. By describing the possibilities for future success or change, you create a future expectancy that may increase the likelihood of unconscious behavior supporting that expectancy.

Conclusion

It has been my intention in this chapter to raise our awareness of the healing potential of mediation and to bring more into our consciousness what we already understand and do. Some readers will regard certain of the ideas presented here as inappropriate to a goal-oriented, structured, strategy-driven process, or as imposing on clients more than they are asking of mediation. I am of the belief it is good to raise the bar, to raise the level of parties' aspirations, and to tap into the "more" that is within each of us. I find these words of Dr. Albert Schweitzer particularly inspiring: "Patients carry their own doctor inside. They come to us not knowing that truth. We are at our best when we give the physician who resides in each patient a chance to work."

Reflective Practice Questions

1. To what extent are you comfortable or uncomfortable, in your work as a dispute resolver, with the role of healer?

2. In this work, what are the personal qualities you bring into the room that foster healing? Do you agree with the author's list of the four C's? How, if at all, would you modify or expand the list?

3. The author suggests that it may be valuable at times for us to share with the parties in a dispute the personal wounds we have suffered, because they might connect us more fully with the parties or help illuminate their path. What are the wounds you carry with you that seem particularly relevant to the cases you mediate, and how can you use those experiences in your mediation work?

References

Bruyere, R. "The Compassion Factor." In R. Carlson and B. Shield (eds.), *Healers on Healing*. Los Angeles: Tarcher, 1989.

Bush, R. B., and Folger, J. *The Promise of Mediation: Responding to Conflict Through Empowerment and Recognition*. San Francisco: Jossey-Bass, 1994.

Capra, F. *Uncommon Wisdom: Conversations with Remarkable People*. New York: Simon & Schuster, 1988.

Carlson, R., and Shield, B. (eds.). *Healers on Healing*. Los Angeles: Tarcher, 1989.

de Chardin, T. *Toward the Future*. London: Collins, 1975.

Dossey, L., M.D. *Healing Words: The Power of Prayer and the Practice of Medicine*. San Francisco: Harper San Francisco, 1993.

Fisher, R., and Brown, S. *Getting Together: Building a Relationship That Gets to Yes*. Boston: Houghton Mifflin, 1988.

Fisher, R., and Ury, W. L. *Getting to Yes*. Boston: Houghton Mifflin, 1981.

Gold, L. "Lawyer Therapist Team Mediation." In J. Folberg and A. Milne (eds.), *Divorce Mediation*. New York: Guilford Press, 1988.

Gold, L. *Between Love and Hate: A Guide to Civilized Divorce*. New York: Plume/Penguin Books, 1992.

Jampolsky, G. *Teach Only Love*. New York: Bantam Books, 1983.

Keating, T. *Intimacy with God*. New York: Crosswords, 1994.

Lankton, S. "A States of Consciousness Model of Ericksonian Hypnosis." In S. Lankton (ed.), *Ericksonian Monographs, No. 1: Elements and Dimensions of an Ericksonian Approach*. New York: Brunner/Mazel, 1985.

Lankton, S., and Lankton, C. *The Answer Within: A Clinical Framework of Ericksonian Hypnotherapy*. New York: Brunner/Mazel, 1983.

Levine, S. *Guided Mediations, Explorations and Healings*. New York: Doubleday, 1991.

Moss, R. M.D. "The Mystery of Wholeness." In R. Carlson and B. Shield (eds.), *Healers on Healing*. Los Angeles: Tarcher, 1989.

Northrup, C., M.D. "Heal Me." *Utne Reader*, Sept.–Oct. 1995, *71*, 58–59.

Prather, H. "Love Is Healing." In R. Carlson and B. Shield (eds.), *Healers on Healing*. Los Angeles: Tarcher, 1989.

Remen, R. N. "The Search for Healing." In R. Carlson and B. Shield (eds.), *Healers on Healing*. Los Angeles: Tarcher, 1989.

Russell, P. *From Science to God: A Physicist's Journey into the Mystery of Consciousness*. Novato, Calif.: New World Library, 2003.

Sinetar, M. *Elegant Choices, Healing Choices*. New York: Paulist Press, 1988.

Spong, J. S. *Why Christianity Must Change or Die*. San Francisco: Harper San Francisco, 1998.

Ury, W. *Getting to Peace*. New York: Viking Press, 1999.

van der Hart, O. *Rituals in Psychotherapy: Transition and Continuity*. New York: Irvington, 1983.

Walsh, R. *The Spirit of Shamanism*. Los Angeles: Tarcher, 1990.

9

Creating Sacred Space

Toward a Second-Generation Dispute Resolution Practice

Sara Cobb

There have been times, during the course of a mediation or facilitation, when I have had the impression that something happens in the room, something more important than the agreement that is emerging, that the conflict is itself just a vehicle for the creation of something sacred, something whole, something holy. This experience of mine often coincides with confessions on the part of the disputants and a quality of sharing that exceeds the technical boundaries of problem-solving processes; apologies are offered, personal stories exchanged, even pictures of children, grandchildren, and vacation homes appear. It is as though the process of conflict resolution cannot contain the often spontaneous and reciprocal expressions of relief and renewed hope that emerge not only as a result of the agreement but also in the course of its construction. Interaction patterns shift[1] and people express wonder and curiosity about the source of these changes in their sense of the "other," as well as their experience of themselves, and about their sense of a new morality (or their return to a very old morality) that permits the existence of the other without compromising deeply held values. Alternative dispute resolution (ADR) is, in these instances,

---

more than the sum of its parts, and the resulting mystery remains inexplicable within the vocabulary of ADR (Davis, 1989).[2]

Although the field of conflict resolution acknowledges that agreements can alter the nature of interaction between disputants, it constructs this shift as a function of the agreement, as a result or an outcome of the process. Practitioners use this shift in interaction as evidence of (1) the presence of respect or recognition on the part of one party for the other,[3] (2) the viability of long-term improvements of relationships between parties,[4] and (3) even as evidence that parties are able to transfer the experience (skills) of the conflict resolution process to other conflicts.[5] Thus the benefits of altered interactions are instrumentally construed; relationships are improved, the agreement is more durable, and parties are more able to apply the experience of one positive conflict resolution process to another conflict, by themselves, in the future. Although these benefits may well appear, as a result of the structure and process within mediation, they do not describe either the experience of the relational space or the emergence of morality itself.

Beyond these instrumental accounts, there lurks the presence of a relational process that defies our explanation as practitioners. Even further, attempts to define or describe these processes in noninstrumental terms, as communion (rather than the convening of stakeholders), as a process of witnessing (rather than listening), as a process of giving testimony (rather than stating interests), and as the creation of a covenant (rather than an agreement), constitute a serious transgression, blurring ADR's secular language with a language from religion(s), defying the boundary between church (synagogue, mosque, temple) and state. The tenacity of ADR's secular discourse grows out of the strength of our collective fear of blurring this boundary.

This secular discourse is itself what Foucault has called a "regime of discourse," completely consonant and resonant with the state; "neutrality," rather than morality, is celebrated; "turn taking," rather than reframing, is the vehicle for ensuring "equal participation";

and "consensus," rather than understanding, is the objective (Foucault, 1991). ADR has adopted, in a rather wholesale fashion, the discourse of the (democratic) state, a discourse of decision making, not by majority rule but via consensus building. This discourse struggles to erase its own moral commitments—equality, participation, voice, and personal responsibility—precisely so that it can position itself within value-based disputes, as an alternative, neutral frame. This is possible because these moral values are so pervasive within our democratic culture that we do not notice them as moral commitments; we do not notice them as a frame for containing moral discussions that is itself a moral framework.[6]

Furthermore, this secular discourse transforms any discussion of morality into a pragmatic discussion of needs and interests. The coincidence of the pragmatist view of conflict as based on competing needs and interests maps completely onto the discourse of the state; our secular state is founded on the notion that there is a diversity of views, and that there is no Archimedean moral frame from which to judge, other than the values of the state itself, expressed in the U.S. Constitution (equality, voice, participation), as these are seen as values that ensure the possibility of diverse values. However, even though these may well be "meta-values" in that they function to permit other values to flourish, they are still values and retain their privilege as frames for negotiating moral discussions. As the values of the secular discourse mask themselves, morality itself is expunged from our ADR discourse; the moral frames of ADR itself are enveloped by the discourse of the state, and the moral frames of parties are disguised as "needs" and "interests," rather than described explicitly as moral commitments. So relative to both the content of the process, as well as accounts about the process (in training manuals, theory, and research), the process and experience of moral discussion is effaced in our ADR practice.

Clearly there is a regime of discourse in ADR that systematically eludes discussion of the functional accounts of relational space and moral discussion. Experience is flattened into "satisfaction" with outcomes; the moral frameworks that emerge as the infrastructure of this relational space are either effaced by a discourse of neutrality or collapsed into a discourse of participation. What we know about ADR is a function of the vocabulary that is harnessed to describe and prescribe its practices. Since prescriptions for practice carry, like a DNA code, moral frameworks for evaluating practice, the discourse that houses our prescriptions for practice determines what moral frameworks we use to evaluate practice, as well as to train others. An examination of this regime of discourse reveals how the moral frameworks of ADR, buried in our prescriptions for practice, paradoxically disable attention to the pragmatics of moral discussion. Given that we cannot understand what we cannot name, I shall attempt to provide a new vocabulary for describing the pragmatics of moral discussion, as well as a prescription for ADR practice that reinstates moral discussion as central to conflict resolution processes.

Moral Discussion as (Sacred) Narrative Practice

Morality is not a set of abstract decontextualized rules collected into a set of prescriptions for behavior; it is a story about a set of events, characters, and themes that exemplifies what to do and what not to do, carried within embedded metaphors that make sense of the world (for example, "She acts like a princess") and materialized in a narrative form. In ADR processes, moral discussion involves the negotiation of the past that builds toward instructions for the present and the future. Parties in conflict are captured by the stories they tell about the problem, its antecedent, and the roles played, and there is always a moral to their story, a theme that usually reconfirms, as do all the other parts of the story, their description of the problem. Inevitably, the moral of the story is that the other has to change in some way, as well as offer restitution.[7] As a narrative operates as a system, its entire component parts function in an interrelated fashion to maintain the integrity of the meaning of the whole narrative. Likewise, any change to a portion of the narrative (roles, plotline, themes) shifts the meaning of the whole narrative. Moral discussion, from this perspective, is often simply the reiteration by each party of their story, as they elaborate plotlines, values, or character roles that reconfirm and anchor the moral of the story. To generate shifts in the moral of the story, there must be some evolution of the story content of both parties. Seen from this perspective, productive moral discussion is not simply talking about values; it is the process of evolving the content of narratives so that there is a shift in the moral corollaries associated with a story.

Consider this case: I was asked to mediate a dispute within a partnership of a small accounting firm. The three partners included two young women, Beth and Anne, brought up through the ranks by Steve, who initiated the firm. Steve was convinced that one of his partners (Beth) was behaving destructively and fomenting coalitions against him within the firm. He asked for a mediation to develop an agreement about how they would work through their differences, as she had repeatedly had "tantrums" on occasions when he tried to air his views.

Beth agreed to the mediation, eager to have a forum in which she could air a host of complaints against Steve. She routinely felt he ignored her input; Beth also felt that the other partner, Anne, functioned too much like Steve's (favored) daughter, never standing up to him, which put all the responsibility for contestation (airing differences) on her. Anne indicated, in an initial interview,[8] that she was concerned about Beth's "hot temper" and felt sorry for Steve, even though she often agreed with Beth that Steve functioned, all too frequently, in an authoritarian fashion.

At the opening of the public session, I asked Steve to choose an instance that he felt exemplified the problematic interaction with Beth. Steve told of a time when Beth stormed into his office, shouting about a set of bookcases that were in the process of being built in the corridor, outside the staff kitchen area. He described his shock and dismay over her behavior and his distress that the staff knew they were in conflict, which he felt diminished his authority in the firm and feared could lead to triangulations between staff and partners.

Like most stories that appear at the opening of ADR processes, Steve's story is a victim story, carefully constructed so as to position Beth as morally inappropriate; no doubt he practiced this story with others, perhaps his wife and other family members and close friends. Victim stories are public; they do not become relevant unless and until they are witnessed by others. Girard has described this process of witnessing victimization, noting that victims call for witnesses (Girard, 1977).[9] He describes victim stories as sacred processes through which community, morality, and law itself are born as people gather together, form through collective inquiry, to make sense of what happened to the victim (Girard, 1977). He argues that victimization is essential to the birth of law and community, which can only materialize as people work collectively, in some public realm, to assign causality and develop moral corollaries as a way to redress "the body of the victim" (Girard, 1977).[10]

Examining mediation (or ADR) as a process of "tracing the victim"[11] offers a window into the sacred process through which community and morality emerge. However, because conflict stories are morality tales, the repetition of a morality tale by either party does not constitute the creation of community; community requires the creation of some consensus about the body of the victim. Paradoxically, the body of the victim disappears as a new story (about who did what to whom and why) emerges, as this case study demonstrates.[12]

Steve describes himself as helpless either to predict or to affect Beth's "emotional storms," which "toss him about," and he feels "capsized." Steve links events together in a way that construes Beth as irrational and in such a fashion that the consequences of her action could well bring about the demise of the firm that he worked so hard to build. The morality that emerges is one that heralds Steve's sacrifice and hard work over the years, his rationality, and the overall goal of coherent leadership of the firm, toward not only its profitability but also the maintenance of the sense of family that helps foster trust and good relations across staff and between staff and partners. This opening permitted Steve to elaborate his position as victim, as well as the moral frames that function as the platform for his legitimacy and Beth's delegitimacy (she had not made similar sacrifices—in fact many "goodies" had come easily for her—she was not rational, and she cared little for the long-term viability of the firm, much less the family environment).

Like almost all disputants in mediation, Steve externalizes responsibility, locating the cause of the problem in Beth's action. As a plotline, Steve's victim story is linear (Beth causes the action sequence) rather than circular (they interact together in a way that brings about the action sequence). Second, in Steve's story there is no account of variation in Beth's (negative) character; the story is intended to exemplify the problem, and within this story there is no account of how Beth does things that exemplify traits other than those attributed here in the victim story (for example, thoughtfulness or being hardworking). Beth is portrayed in this victim story as a flat character with little variation in her behavior or complexity in her character. Third, the values are portrayed as a polarized (and polarizing) framework; Steve is advancing a moral framework (totally consistent with the framework of mediation itself) that valorizes "respect" for others, exemplified by listening, rather than flying off the handle; and "trust," rather than malicious gossiping behind his back. Across all three dimensions of the narrative (plot, character roles, and values or themes), Steve's victim story offers a "morality" in which there is little or no account of how his actions may have prompted Beth's response. That is, there is no interdependence; Steve delegitimizes not only how Beth behaves but also who she is as a person.

Through the telling and elaboration of Steve's victim story, Beth sighed, changed position in her chair, shook her head, muttered, and made exclamations ("That is ridiculous!"). I persisted in my efforts to witness Steve's pain and elaborate his moral perspective, asking Beth to monitor her upset feelings and if she got to a six (on a one-to-ten scale) she should just leave the room, and I would call her in when Steve was finished. However, I also told her that I was sure that she would learn things she did not know if she stayed, and that she might need the subtlety of this information to tell her story. She stayed put.

Before she told her story, from her perspective, I asked her to help me elaborate Steve's perspective:

AUTHOR: I am sure it has been hard to sit and listen. . . .

BETH: Yes, it has, especially since—

AUTHOR: Wait a minute, before you start with your view, I want to let Steve know that the problem is not one of not understanding—that you fully "understand" his viewpoint . . . so I will ask you a couple of questions that help him see that you are competent in his worldview. . . . Can you imagine with me, who, on the staff, you think he has been most concerned would be vulnerable to this conflict between you and Steve?

BETH: Who I think he thinks. . . .

AUTHOR: Yes.

BETH: Ummmmm, it would have to be Susan. She is a new and very promising accountant on staff. He really wanted to bring her on and thinks she is partner material eventually, and he will be worried that this conflict, which is very visible, would scare her away.

AUTHOR: Do you share his view that Susan is worthy of support—that she may indeed be partner material?[13]

BETH: Well, of course I am worried that she may not be able to stand up to him, but part of the support that I want to give her is to help her find her voice with him, so she knows that this is a place where her views count.[14]

AUTHOR: OK. A second question, before you tell your story. . . . If I were to ask Steve what he has done to try to reduce the tension, what would he tell me?

BETH: I think he would say that he tries to avoid me, that he tries to avoid conflict, and that he has gone so far as to cut down the frequency of the meetings, just to reduce the opportunities for conflict between us. While I disagree with his method, I do see that he has tried.

AUTHOR: OK. Thanks for being willing to show him you are able to take his perspective. Steve, I do not know if she hit the nail on the head, but I do not want to take time at this point checking in with you—she needs to be able to give her perspective at this point, so I will ask her to do that now. As I told her, if you get to a six on a scale of one to ten, just leave the room, and I will have an idea as to how you are faring. Otherwise, please try and listen, so when I ask you to take her perspective, as she did yours, you will be able to do so with some texture and precision. OK, Beth, let's hear your side of this. . . .

Beth proceeded to tell a victim story about how, over time, Steve had become progressively more authoritarian, less collaborative, and even secretive. She came to the firm, in the first place, because she thought it was a place where she could grow and take on increasing responsibility for the firm, in an environment that was "human" as opposed to cutthroat ("like firms in L.A."). However, as her victim story notes, she has not been able to grow, as Steve has become less and less willing to share decision-making processes with her. As an example, she discussed with the staff the possibility of expanding the staff kitchen area, so that a table could be added. But before she had time to bring it to a partner meeting (which Steve regularly canceled or postponed), Steve had installed bookcases that made the kitchen addition impossible. By her account, Steve had misrepresented himself to her and the firm, pretending to be open to others' participation. In fact, he was unwilling to share power and information. Furthermore, he kept others "down" by pretending that the firm was his family, which made it difficult to address substantive differences that others may have had with Steve. According to Beth, he positioned himself as a "patriarch."

Through this discussion, Steve sat quietly, at times shaking his head and making notes. When Beth was finished, I asked Steve if he was willing to show Beth that he understood her perspective, that he could walk in her shoes. He agreed to do this, so I asked him:

AUTHOR: Has there ever been a time in your life when you felt somehow betrayed or shut out?[15]

STEVE: Well, I am not sure. . . . I usually have good relations with others. . . .

AUTHOR: But relationships are never always perfect, so there has been some point at which—

STEVE: Well, I guess the closest I had to this experience was with my older brother—he usually made unilateral decisions about things we should do, in our group of friends. I was the younger "tagalong," and although I almost always went along with him, I was sometimes either worried I would not be able to keep up, or resentful that it was not exactly what I wanted to do. So maybe that is similar. . . .

AUTHOR: And were you ever able to alter that pattern with him? It is hard to do. . . .

STEVE: No, I was never able to change this, as he has always been my older brother.

In this exchange, I asked Steve to begin to elaborate the moral framework that Beth had advanced (being inside or shut out of decision making), and interestingly enough he used an example from his family as a way to illustrate his experience. On the basis of this example, combined with the complaint he had about Beth, I surmised that Steve uses familial relations as a standard for assessing his professional relations with others. This may function in a deterministic way, by restricting the roles that others can play with him, as well as what roles he can play with others. In a private conversation I had with Steve, he described his "fatherly" feelings for Beth and Anne, and he expressed hurt over Beth's unreasonable behavior. He was using a father-daughter role set as a frame for morally assessing Beth's behavior.

Beth experienced this, as Steve had often admonished her as if she were a child, with a "you should know better" tagged onto complaints he made about her work. This infuriated Beth and made it much more likely that she would be, in her own words, a "rebellious daughter" at the same moment she was trying to break out of the father-daughter frame altogether. We discussed this in front of Steve, and then I asked Beth what she would need to do to really break free of the rebellious-daughter frame.[16] She indicated she could write memos that detailed her concerns, adding them to the agenda for partner meetings. She also indicated she would not discuss Steve with Anne or any other staff member, in an effort not to "rebel" by speaking badly about the "father." We discussed these strategies in front of Steve, as ways to help him remember that Beth was not his daughter.

In turn, I asked Steve whether he thought his role as father was working and he indicated that, despite his comfort with that role, it was not working. In fact, over time he wanted to "not have to be the father" because he was hoping to put more and more responsibility on other, younger partners. I asked him what he could do to break his pattern of acting like a father, and he suggested four things[17]: (1) that all partner business be discussed at partner meetings, not in informal settings between meetings; (2) that he would take the notes at the meetings because this would require him to listen and record the input of others; (3) that each partner be assigned a functional role, so that at every meeting each partner would be in charge of reporting about work within their domain and asking for input from other partners, yet with ultimate responsibility for the area; and finally (4) he offered to pay for a facilitator for the partner meetings for the next three months, hoping that if he got himself out of the role of convening and running the meetings, there would be less conflict and more substance to the discussion. These were substantive suggestions that grew out of our conversation about both the content and the process of partner meetings.

Contrary to the dominant mediation ideology mandating that mediators attend to process without affecting the content of what disputants say (about the nature of the problem or its solutions), I was quite involved in the emergence of this content, shaping questions and making comments that developed the options. However, this did not mean that Steve was not involved; I interacted with him in such a way that these options and this plan emerged. I played a role but did not originate these "solutions." To say these solutions were socially constructed means that they emerged from the interaction between Steve and myself, and that they rested heavily upon the history of the conversation, both in the mediation and prior to the mediation. It was my intention to favor versions of "reality" that (1) clearly established the suffering of each party; (2) created descriptions of the suffering that connected it back to their own actions, without minimizing the suffering or blaming the victim; (3) positively connoted the intentions of each actor with other actors; (4) created variation in character traits; and (5) added complexity to the value sets in use, that is, incorporating more and different values.

This is a highly engaged mode of mediation practice, recognizing that mediators participate in the social construction of meaning, regardless of what questions they ask and what they do not ask; regardless of whether they remain silent or make summaries; regardless of whether they actively reframe or whether they simply repeat descriptions that disputants offer. This kind of engagement on the part of the mediator requires calibration with disputants and careful ongoing observation of self-in-interaction. This kind of observation is consistent with the features von Foerster attributed to second-order systems in which the process of observing the conflict system brings forth the conflict system (von Foerster, 1984). In other words, the nature of the reality that is constructed is dependent on the nature of the descriptions that observers make of the system. This implies that mediation is a second-order process in which the mediator's interaction with others (elaborating observations) has an impact on the evolution of the conflict, both by the content of the conversation as well as by the nature of the interaction in which the content emerges. This is a radical departure from what could be called first-generation mediation practice, where the mandate not to influence the content of the dispute is thought to be essential to preserving the privilege the parties have of defining their own problems and building their own solutions. However, once we adopt an interactionist or social constructionist perspective, the mandate to separate content from process dissolves, as mediators recognize the inevitability of their impact on the content of the dispute. This attention to the evolution of the content calls for a second-generation mediation practice in which mediators interact with disputants so as to evolve the conflict stories, reformulate relationships, reframe the past, and rebuild the future. This second-generation mediation practice requires careful attention to both the nature of the morality that is advanced in the session and the process by which it is advanced.

In this session, the morality that was advanced grew out of the metaphors surrounding father and rebellious daughter roles; in our conversations, these roles were progressively defined as both inappropriate and unworkable. Once the new normative stage was set (the new moral frame created), Steve and Beth could work on the agreement. After receiving compliments for their contributions, Steve and Beth signed an agreement that stipulated all the suggestions each had made. They spent some time trying to discuss the functional distribution of responsibility within the partnership, until we realized that this was an agenda item for the next (facilitated) partner meeting.[18] The session closed with an agreement. Follow-up interviews with Steve and Beth (at one, three, and six months) showed that there were still issues in the partnership,[19] neither Steve nor Beth felt Steve was trying to function as a father to Beth, and neither felt Beth was resorting to acting as a rebellious daughter. On the contrary, they felt the pattern between them had shifted radically and the quality of their relation had improved. Rather than attribute this to the "magic" of mediation, I prefer to try and recount how we "traced the victim," and in the process elaborate the nature of moral discussion that distinguishes first-generation from second-generation mediation practice.

Retracing Morality in Mediation

Moral discussion in mediation often works against the very goals of the first-generation mediation process. Parties tell their story, launching moral frames that are the basis for their own legitimacy, while delegitimizing the other. Paradoxically, mutual blame is the outcome. From this perspective, value frames are tools that parties use to negatively position the other in discourse (Davies and Harre, 1999). As the accounting firm case study shows, there is moral discussion in mediation; however, it only serves to reconstitute problematic relationships. Moral frames emerge and are deployed as weapons to position the self as appropriate and the other as inappropriate. Following Girard, this kind of moral discussion does little to generate either law (social rules) or community, as there is nothing "sacred" in the act of mutual blame (Girard, 1977). On the contrary, in the process of mutual blaming in which values are weapons, both sides refute the victimization of the other in a struggle to occupy the place of the victim. It falls to the mediator to create what Girard calls a sacred place by functioning as "witness" to victimization of both sides (Girard, 1977).

A sacred place is one that, according to Girard, does more than simply recount the victimization in the presence of others; it elevates violation of an individual to the level of the collective, as others witness and elaborate the violation in public spaces (Girard, 1977). What happens to one person becomes something that reasonably happens to anyone,[20] and thus the collective is itself at risk for similar violations. Second, in the course of this public process, there is also transformation of the victims; they become a symbol for the collective, a sign of both danger and immorality, signifying a practical breach of security as well as a moral breach of someone's social obligation. The public story about how the violation occurred functions to increase the security of the collective if strategies to avoid future violations can be created; the public story about who contributed to the violation and why it happened generates morality tales about how people should behave toward each other. It is in this process, according to Girard, that the collective comes to witness itself as a connected whole; relationships are affirmed, social norms created and acknowledged, and social harmony restored (Girard, 1977). Therefore, a place is sacred if it can create the conditions for the victim to be recognized; for the victimization to be accounted for, both practically and morally; and for social relationships to be anchored on that emergent morality. All of this involves the creation of a space where the community can witness itself as a community in which social obligations and norms materialize.

But this act of witnessing is not a passive activity[21]; on the contrary, this witnessing involves active participation in the evolution of narrative content. For example, both Steve and Beth told stories that had problematic features[22]: although each of these stories functioned to display the speaker as the victim, neither witnessed the victimization of the other. My role in the session was to enable each person to see the other as the victim, and in the process build a new moral framework. So it is not only that I functioned as a witness; I asked questions, created summaries, and made comments that enabled each party to witness the other and to witness their own role in creating the conditions of that victimization. In this case, Steve victimized Beth by treating her as a daughter (Beth's story) and she responded by acting in a rebellious fashion, confirming Steve's worldview, participating in her own victimization, and victimizing Steve in the process. This kind of "double witnessing" involves tracing the victim, as well as tracing the role that each plays in the victimization of the other. Double witnessing functions to create a set of doubled values; a new value system emerges that is used by each party to understand the new problem frame, and there is a new set of meta-values, which celebrate personal responsibility and reciprocity. In this mediation, a common value set emerged that defined familial relationships as inappropriate frames for navigating professional settings. Treating a colleague as a daughter is unprofessional, and acting like a daughter is unprofessional. At the meta-level, however, the act of creating contributions toward the resolution of the conflict functions as a performative; it enacts personal responsibility and reciprocity, materializing these values as second-order values, as a morality for talking about morality. At this moment, community is formed as new social rules emerge.[23]

Like the great Wizard of Oz revealed behind the curtain, the purported magic of mediation is revealed—shifts in relationships, which themselves bear witness to shifts in how we see self and other, are not mysteriously produced by the mediation process itself but by the careful process of double witnessing in which both pain and accountability emerge as features of the problem, and its solution emerges via the evolution of the narratives that parties tell. By implication, double witnessing requires that mediators themselves own their participation, as witnesses who do not only reflect the pain of parties but also actively construct it, along with its link to responsibility (the ability to respond). They must witness themselves as witnesses to others. This definition of the role of the mediator defies the injunction to be neutral, but it does contribute to anchoring a second-order morality that celebrates taking personal responsibility for mediators' participation in, and accountability for, the nature of the community that is created in mediation, as well as the social norms and rules that frame the community as a community. Mediation is thus an entirely moral practice, and mediators are deeply implicated in the nature of the moral worlds that emerge in sessions.

In the first-generation mediation practice, we learned that there was a formula that could be useful for resolving conflicts. We learned to bring parties to the table, to structure the process so each side had a turn to speak, and to help parties invent options on the basis of the elaboration of their interests. In the first-generation practice, we practitioners clung to our belief that the process alone could yield outcomes that not only resolved disputes but also increased the humanity of those involved. We trusted neutrality as well as the ground rules of turn taking. We worked to witness the pain of the parties and struggled not to tamper with the content of their stories, as that was thought to constitute a violation of our practice as neutrals. However, as I have tried to show in this chapter, mediation is a moral practice at two levels: (1) it is about moral frameworks and (2) it advances a morality of personal responsibility and accountability as a way of dealing with others. If we adopt this view, we then must let go of some of the assumptions so central to first-generation mediation practice and embrace what could be called a second-generation practice, in which we come to witness the role that we as mediators play, with parties, in the social construction of moral frames for evaluating action past, present, and future.

In this second-generation practice, we are not only freed from the arbitrary constraints imposed by the secular discourse of mediation. We also are obligated to initiate ourselves into vocabularies through which we can track our role as moral practitioners. Defining ADR as a sacred practice does not signal its link to a particular religious tradition, but instead it calls attention to the transformative capacity of the practice; through the transformation of victim stories, community is brought forth, enabling it to bear witness to itself as a community, as a set of intertwined relationships. Defining ADR as sacred practice enables us, as practitioners, to witness the moral frames we contribute to create, both in discrete sessions as well as across our practice, over time.

Reflective Practice Questions

1. Have you experienced what the author describes as the creation of something sacred, something whole, something holy in the course of a mediation? If so, what qualities did you bring that contributed to that process?

2. The author describes a "sacred" space as one that does more than simply recount victimization in the presence of others; it elevates violation of an individual to the level of the collective, as others witness and elaborate the violation in public spaces. Do you agree with that description as it applies to mediation? If so, how do you reconcile impartiality with the process described here?

3. Do the qualities and behaviors of the mediator unavoidably create, as the author suggests, a "moral frame" for the mediation? If so, what are the moral frames that you help create in the mediation process?

References

Bush, R. B., and Folger, J. *The Promise of Mediation*. San Francisco: Jossey-Bass, 1994.

Cobb, S., and Rifkin, J. "Practice and Paradox: Deconstructing Neutrality in Mediation." *Law & Social Inquiry*, 1991, 16, 35–62.

Davies, B., and Harre, R. "Positioning and Parenthood." In R. Harre and L. van Lagenhove (eds.), *Positioning Theory: Moral Contexts of Intentional Action*. Oxford: Blackwell, 1999.

Davis, A. M. "The Logic Behind the Magic of Mediation." *Negotiation Journal*, 1989, 5, 17–24.

Foucault, M. "Politics and the Study of Discourse." In G. Burchell, C. Gordon, and P. Miller (eds.), *The Foucault Effect*. Chicago: University of Chicago Press, 1991.

Girard, R. *Violence and the Sacred* (P. Gregory, trans.). Baltimore, Md.: Johns Hopkins University Press, 1977.

Innes, J. E. "Evaluating Consensus Building." In L. Susskind, S. McKearnan, and J. Thomas-Larner (eds.), *The Consensus Building Handbook*. Thousand Oaks, Calif.: Corwin Press, 1999.

Loewenstein, J., and Thompson, L. "The Challenge of Learning." *Negotiation Journal*, 2000, 16, 399–408.

MacIntyre, A. *Whose Justice? Which Rationality?* Notre Dame: University of Notre Dame Press, 1989.

McKenna, A. J. "Tracing the Victim." In *Violence and Difference*. Champaign: University of Illinois Press, 1992.

Pearson, J., and Thoennes, N. "Divorce Mediation: Reflections on a Decade of Research." In K. Kressel and D. Pruitt (eds.), *Mediation Research: The Process and Effectiveness of Third-Party Intervention*. San Francisco: Jossey-Bass, 1989.

Retzinger, S., and Scheff, T. "Emotion, Alienation, and Narratives: Resolving Intractable Conflict." *Mediation Quarterly*, 2000, *18*, 71–85.

Rifkin, J., and others. "Toward a New Discourse for Mediation: A Critique of Neutrality." *Mediation Quarterly*, 1991, 9, 151–164.

Scarry, E. *The Body in Pain*. Oxford: Oxford University Press, 1985.

Sluzki, C. E. "The 'Better-Formed' Story: Ethics and Aesthetic Practice." Unpublished manuscript on file with author.

von Foerster, H. "On Constructing a Reality." In P. Watzlawick (ed.), *The Invented Reality*. New York: Norton, 1984.

10

The Personal Qualities of the Mediator

Taking Time for Reflection and Renewal

Jonathan W. Reitman, Esq.

Like many of us with busy mediation and training practices, I
have learned how important it is to the quality of my service to
clients to step out of the river periodically and take time to think
and reflect on what I do and why I do it. Sharing my reflections with
others deepens their value to me. Invariably, when I plunge back in
after this time out, I am refreshed and renewed.

Moreover, this process of reflection and renewal produces a paradoxical result: it allows me to be more conscious and deliberate in
my choices of the personal qualities I exhibit during a mediation,
and it makes those qualities so much a part of my "style" that I do
not have to overthink those choices. The qualities are more present
and available. This is the point of a reflective practice and its value
in my work: it allows me to be more fully present to whatever direction emerges during mediation and thereby respond with more
authenticity.

When taken together as a collective time-out, it is my intention
that reading the chapters in this volume renews and refreshes
the field, just as writing my contribution has renewed and refreshed
me. Reflection on my experience led me to identify the nine
personal qualities I discuss here. They are listed in no particular
priority order, but taken together they form parts of my theory of
practice.

Genuine Curiosity

When I practiced law, I knew what I wanted to know in the intake interview with the client. I listened for certain catchphrases, and as the client spoke I was mentally checking off the presence or absence of the elements of proof I needed to establish, if I were to prevail in representing that client. My mind was very busy, but I trained myself to screen out or ignore those aspects of the client's story that did not fit the structure with which I was working.

By contrast, when I mediate I am genuinely curious about everything contained in the party's story. Everyone has a story to tell in mediation, and they want the chance to tell that story. I let the parties know how curious I am, how interested in them as people. How? By asking open-ended questions, by identifying with one behavior or another, by inquiring more deeply about why certain things seemed so important to them. I want to know not only what they did but why they did certain things.

This curiosity is *not* a technique, and parties can tell if I am asking questions in some formulaic way. Curiosity is not genuine, as a technique. Perhaps genuine curiosity is something innate, which cannot be learned, but we know it when we experience it.

Finding the Place of Love in Your Heart

We all know that some parties are a pain in the neck. Or worse, they may be deceitful; manipulative; or prone to aggressive, insulting, or condescending outbursts. It is natural for the mediator to have personal reactions to these parties and their behaviors. My initial reaction may be as mild as irritation ("Why don't they just get with the program?") or as strong as intense dislike ("What a jerk! Don't they know they are alienating everyone in the room and destroying any chance for settlement?").

Several years ago, I was co-mediating a multiparty, multi-issue public policy dispute. We seemed to be making good progress, but every time we moved forward, the general counsel for one particular state agency would insist that the proposed solution would not work. He was hypertechnical. He was sarcastic. He was intransigent on matters others readily agreed to. I grew more and more irritated with him, seeing him as a stumbling block to progress.

My co-mediator saw him in a different light. To her, this lawyer was understandably defending the traditional prerogatives of his agency. He was defending his turf. He was doing the best job he could. Once I was able to reframe the way I looked at him—to find the place of love in my heart—I began to appreciate him. I let him know. When he saw that I was no longer resisting his suggestions, and in fact that I understood why he was making them, he softened his approach.

The lesson I learned was a simple but profound one that I had somehow forgotten: when the mediator can find a way to deeply value what each party brings to the table (sometimes despite the mediator's initial reactions of irritation) and can express that appreciation to the party, the party feels truly heard and valued. Often, it is the need for this affirmation that is the source of the party's intransigence. Whether you think of it as the mediator's gift to the process or as a technique for settlement, this quality has a direct and immediate impact on the mediation. It works.

Doing the Footwork, Then Letting Go of the Outcome

When parties hire any of us as their mediator, they want help in resolving the case. Understandably, we (and I definitely include myself) sometimes define "success" as meeting the parties' expectation of settlement.

What I have learned is that there are *many* reasons a case does not settle, only a few of which have to do with my skills as a mediator. If I have carefully created a problem-solving environment and genuinely worked a creative process, I have to let go of my understandable desire to get to settlement. In twelve-step recovery programs, one often hears, "Let go and let God."

Whenever I take time to reflect, I remember how much this truth applies to mediators.

Being the Eye of the Storm

Once I was co-mediating an extremely heated discussion among Serbs, Croats, and Muslims in Bosnia. It was the first time since open warfare that these groups had been in the same room with "the other." Their rage was just below the surface. Predictably, someone said something that infuriated another ethnic group, and within seconds the room was full of shouting adversaries, who were pointing fingers and moving as if they would either stalk out or physically attack the enemy. I felt my breath shorten and my brain short-circuit. I did not know how to stop the incendiary escalation.

Then I looked over at my co-mediator. She was breathing slowly and rhythmically, with a half smile on her face, sitting with her feet on the floor, her arms at her sides, in a vulnerable and open posture. She was clearly the calmest person in the room in that moment, and her presence calmed me and, eventually, the participants. Part of our job as mediators requires us to "hold the form" even when the accusations and anger are directed toward us. Last summer, my Arab and Jewish Israeli students (in a course on negotiation, mediation, and conflict management) were voicing their displeasure with me in their typical, wonderfully blunt (and loud) way. They accused me of being "unfair," of changing the rules in the middle of the course. They were angry. Seeing this situation as a "teaching moment," I was able to hold the form, to be the calmest person in the room, to use all my active listening and reflecting skills. My students felt heard. We came into dialogue with each other, and we eventually found common ground.

The Ability to Compartmentalize

Last year I bought a new television. Although I did not really want it, the television came with a "picture-in-picture" feature, which allows the viewer to watch two channels simultaneously and to switch back and forth between the larger, background channel and the smaller channel displayed within a box.

On reflection, I see that I often use the picture-in-picture feature in mediation. While listening as carefully as I can to what is being said, I am also thinking about how hot the room is, how long we have been working without a break, what the likely reaction of the other side will be to what is being said, and what is *not* being said. The need for this quality arises from the complexity of the mediation process: there is an understandable tendency for any one of us to focus only on the substance of what is being discussed. Experienced mediators have come to understand, however, that there are underlying, core issues, the discussion of which is essential to any lasting resolution of the conflict. Those issues emerge only if the parties feel safe enough to share their true interests. In turn, that safety depends, in part, on the mediator's ability to hold (be aware of) several aspects of the mediation at once.

The ability to simultaneously think about several aspects of the mediation (teenagers call it multitasking) is a learned skill. I have become better with practice. Perhaps I will get even better by using this unwanted feature on my new television.

Honor the History of the Conflict

I often ask, somewhere near the start of a mediation, "How did we get here, to this point?" I am really asking the parties to tell me about the history of their conflict. Although I find this inquiry useful in domestic mediations, it is essential in cross-cultural mediations, especially in cultures that prize their history more than we tend to value it in the United States.

For example, several years ago in Bosnia, I was talking to several young Serb students who had participated in one of our workshops. They expressed the importance of their history in trying to understand the current conflict in the Balkans. They began to tell me in some detail about a battle that had occurred in Kosovo Polje, the

Field of Blackbirds as it is known in English. They described troop movements, leadership, and the result (the Serbian forces were defeated). They told me about the impact of that defeat on Serbian identity. Because of the detail with which they recounted this event, I thought certainly they were describing one of the battles that had occurred in the 1991–1996 Balkan Wars. When I asked, I learned that this battle occurred in June 1389. In that moment, I learned that in their culture, history had a powerful and living influence on the parties' current actions.

In my trainings, I sometimes give a questionnaire designed to elicit certain cultural values. My questionnaire contains this statement: "While the past is important, it is much more important to focus on what we can do in the future." This attitude is typical in the United States, where I often find more than 75 percent of my students agreeing with this statement. Among my Middle Eastern students, fewer than 10 percent of the students agreed. I fully admit that my questionnaire is not a scientific sample, but it suggests that, in many cultures, to be effective the mediator must recognize and respect the history of the conflict. In those cultures, a solution that does not attend to history is not likely to have lasting value.

Persistence and Optimism

When parties have been engaged in protracted conflict, they often lose perspective and even the ability to believe that a solution is possible. Their hope has been extinguished. In the hundreds of conversations I have had with Arabs and Jews in the last year, virtually none of them believe that peace is possible between Israel and the Palestinians. Even Dennis Ross, the longtime mediator in the region, was quoted recently as saying, "There is no process, and there is no hope."

This example is only a dramatic picture of what we see from parties in many mediations. Parties will tell us before the mediation or in the first caucus, "I gotta tell you. This case will never settle."

Because we mediators have the advantage of detachment from the conflict, we often find ourselves as the only one in the room who truly believes that a solution is possible. This optimism allows us to be persistent in the face of the parties' discouragement. Such optimism is not the same as the mediator pushing for a solution when it is clear the parties do not want one. Rather, it is a personal quality that directly affects the parties' actions. I often listen for a sentiment something like this: "Well, I don't really think it will matter, but if you [the mediator] think it will help us close the deal, I'm willing to consider it." When I hear that, I know that persistence and optimism work.

Lateral Thinking

Because my son is halfway through college, I am interested in the state of the current job market. So I read with interest a story in the *Wall Street Journal* not long ago in which several CEOs were asked what background or qualities they were looking for in their new hires. I suppose I thought they would all be looking for young people with MBAs. To my surprise they said (in different ways) that they were looking for people capable of "lateral thinking": people who could take apparently dissimilar facts or events and discern within them a deeper pattern or meaning, which could give direction to decision makers or policymakers.

So it is with mediators. It is often helpful to connect the dots between pieces of data or information that at first blush seem to be totally unrelated. For instance, I was recently speaking with a corporate executive involved in a protracted dispute with his workforce. We spent the first forty-five minutes of our time together with him telling me about his father's death the year before and its impact on him. With little prompting from me, this led him to reminisce about his childhood of poverty growing up in a European country and his subsequent rise to corporate power in the United States.

Perhaps anyone listening to this conversation would have been able to connect the dots, to trace his childhood fears to his current dispute. Somewhere in our conversation, I realized that his childhood fears about not having enough caused him to be unnecessarily stingy with his workforce. His was a profitable business. In classic distributive thinking, he assumed that if the employees took a bigger piece of the pie, there would be fewer resources available for management. Because of his formative experiences, he had a scarcity mentality. Moreover, his history, personal ambition, and talents persuaded him that the key to success was to pursue his own agenda with single-minded determination. He would not be distracted by the needs of others. No wonder his workforce told him, directly and indirectly, that he was a terrible listener and communicator!

As a mediator brought in to perform a conflict assessment, I found that lateral thinking made all the difference in my ability to help the CEO see how his personal history related to the current conflict. That awareness led to a genuine change in his style.

Courage

Whether you are mediating one of your first cases or you have been mediating for years, you (and all of us) experience a moment somewhere during the mediation—the moment when your inner voice tells you to take a risk and do or say something unusual, or controversial, or out of character. To tell a joke or a story. To tell someone off. Or to just keep silent. My experience with these moments is that if I listen to this inner voice, more often than not my action, inaction, or silence produces a positive turning point in the mediation. But sometimes I do not follow the inner voice, usually because I lack the courage or I care too much about what the parties may think.

It takes courage to do the work we do, to act despite the ever-present risk of failure, ridicule, or disdain. But when it works, ahhh . . . our courage is more than rewarded.

Conclusion

As Hoffman and Bowling have suggested in Chapter One of this book, the personal qualities that the mediator brings to the process can, and do, have a direct impact on what happens in the mediation room. The nine qualities I have discussed are not unique to me, nor are they necessarily original. They are not always appropriate in every situation, and sometimes they serve me better than at other times. Or perhaps on those occasions, I am more skilled in my practice of them. Regardless, through my consistent reflection and renewal practice, I have learned to ground these qualities in my experience. This experience teaches me to be humble about my impact on the process, and to be conscious and mindful about the choices I make in the mediation room. The ultimate question always remains the context for my choices in the mediation room: "Which of these personal qualities will best serve the parties' needs and interests in this moment?"

Reflective Practice Questions

1. What are the qualities you value in yourself as a conflict resolver? What are the qualities you seek to develop further? Do you consider some of these more essential to your conflict resolution work than others? What qualities would you add to the author's list?

2. One of the qualities the author describes as important for mediators is courage. In what ways have you found it necessary to be courageous as a mediator?

3. The author describes the extraordinary calm of his co-mediator in a bitter ethnic dispute as "holding the form." What are the qualities that enable you to hold the form, and bring peace into the room, when you are, as he puts it, at the eye of the storm.

11

Style and the Family Mediator

Donald T. Saposnek

Mediation is both a science and an art. The *science* of mediation is grounded in the body of systematized knowledge regarding interpersonal conflict that describes the structure, methodology, and logic of the practice, and the predictability of people in conflict. Having this knowledge allows the mediator to formulate principles derived from observation, study, and experimentation. These principles help to elucidate the steps for teaching, learning, and evaluating particular skills used to resolve interpersonal disputes.

The *art* of mediation consists of the intangible, spontaneous, flowing, unpredictable, intuitive aspects of the expertise. Art does not follow the rules of logic but operates more on intuition and feeling. Through the art lens, a problem is viewed holistically, creatively, systemically, and from numerous angles, and the parts are seen in their relationship to one another. One does not gain this view by breaking the problem into teachable steps; instead, the view is developed organically. Art demands of the student an intuitive grasp, the gaining of impressions based on emotions, and then a conceptual integration.

As is true for learning any area of expertise, the mediation student first must learn the science of the practice, to establish a systematic basis for the work. This includes an overview of the well-recognized approaches, details of the structure and process, specific steps for task completion, techniques for assessing the outcome, and ways to use feedback to improve the specific techniques employed. However, as the mechanics of practice are mastered, the more experienced practitioner begins to use this knowledge base differently, expanding beyond technique into more creative, intuitive, and artful ways of practicing. It is at this level that the mediator first begins to discover the artist within (Lang and Taylor, 2000) and begins to notice a unique "style" of practice emerging.

Style and Its Development

Style—that unique blend of science and art—was best described by Eugene Emmanuel Viollet-le-Duc, one of the mentors of the late architect, Frank Lloyd Wright: "Nature, in all her works, has style, because, however varied her productions may be, they are always submitted to laws and invariable principles. The lilies of the field, the leaves of the trees, the insects, have style, because they grow, develop, and exist according to essentially logical laws. We can spare nothing from a flower, because, in its organization, every part has its function and is formed to carry out that function in the most beautiful manner. *Style resides in the true and well-understood expression of a principle* [emphasis mine], and not in an immutable form; therefore, as nothing exists in nature without a principle, everything in nature must have style" (cited in Hoffman, 1995, p. 3).

Indeed, it is the development of a style that ultimately makes an accomplished mediator. Once the mediator has solidly established a theoretical framework, has mastered the basic principles, purpose, and methods for resolving conflict, he or she expresses these well-learned principles and techniques in the craft of mediation through a particular style.

In the psychotherapy literature, it has been empirically documented that effective and experienced therapists all have more in common than they have differences, in spite of their respective models of therapy (Beutler, Machado, and Neufeldt, 1994; Luborsky, Diguer, Luborsky, and Schmidt, 1999). Korchin and Sands (1983), for example, in a survey of highly effective therapists, concluded that effective therapists of any type may practice more similarly than they preach. Though not yet empirically confirmed, it appears that this is also likely to be the case for mediators. The commonalities are the shared bases of knowledge of experienced mediators. Yet each practitioner is unique in his or her style. As such, it may make more sense to describe forms of mediation not so much as differences in models but as differences in styles—those unique "expressions of common principles."

Shifts in Thinking Toward Common Principles

In the early stages of the development of one's style of mediation, there are necessary shifts in thinking. These fundamental shifts occur across a number of dimensions. The basic shift is from linear, logical, analytical, rational, task-oriented thinking to nonlinear, intuitive, holistic, emotional, metaphorical thinking. In particular, this includes shifts across several specific dimensions.

From an Individual Perspective to a Systems Perspective

With this first shift, the practitioner moves from seeing two opposing disputants who have opposing views that compel the mediator to sort out who is truthful and lying, who is right and wrong, and who should prevail and yield; to viewing the participants as engaged in a systemic dispute that has no single truthful or right outcome. This necessitates that the mediator maintain a bigger frame, with the details of the dispute having less importance than the development of an integrated, systemically workable outcome to the mutual benefit of the parties.

From a Problem-Solving Perspective to One of Compassion and Healing

This requires the mediator to connect with the parties on a deep, empathic level that may include acknowledging and helping to process pain, anger, sadness, grief, anxiety, guilt, and regret. It also involves proactively looking for the good in people, which benefits not only the disputants but also the mediator himself or herself. Looking for good in people can increase one's overall optimism and hope, which has been well documented to be health-enhancing.

This shift creates a powerful psychological atmosphere for beginning to heal the wounds of divorce. This is especially necessary in getting through impasses of divorce in which negotiations get stuck on an emotional level until they are processed in some fashion (Johnston and Campbell, 1988; Saposnek and Rose, 1990). The ability of the mediator to operate on this level, from a basis of genuine compassion beyond technique alone, can effectively facilitate lasting resolution of parenting disputes.

From Just Another ADR Approach to Better Than the Adversarial Process

For cases in which there are no contraindications for mediation, such as a chronic history of abuse within the family, a shift is needed from the view of mediation as just another ADR approach to a proactive view of it as better than the adversarial process.

This view maintains the personal conviction that mediation (especially in child custody disputes) is better for minimizing conflict within the coparenting relationships, is better for the child by optimizing cooperation between the parents, and operates from a principle that maximizing positive adjustment of the children is a higher goal than winning in court. Maintaining this view also has implications for the larger social sphere, by modeling for all the participants and their children an attitude of harmonious resolution of conflict, so urgently needed in our global community (Saposnek, 1993).

Personal Qualities for an Effective Mediator Style

What are the qualities and attitudes of a mediator that contribute to an effective style of practice? In general, because the very nature of the work is dealing with interpersonal disputes, the mediator first of all must be comfortable with conflict. This is not to say that he or she must enjoy conflict, since it is commonly known that mediators are often conflict-avoidant in their own lives. However, they must enjoy the challenges inherent in managing and helping to resolve the conflicts of others. Whether mediating is motivated by a subconscious attempt to overcome one's own aversion to conflict by managing the conflict of others, or by an attraction to interpersonal intensity, or simply by the joy of achieving resolution and helping people, the fact remains that effective mediators must comfortably embrace conflict.

In addition to being able to manage interpersonal conflict, an effective mediator style requires that the mediator have the personal capacity to tolerate and contain ambiguity and unpredictability. Because most divorce mediations have much emotionality, both in the origins of the disputes and in the negotiations leading to resolution, the process, as it unfolds, is neither clear nor linear in its progress. At any time, it can suddenly flare with hostilities, escalate to the point of impasse, or resolve peacefully. As such, the mediator must personally serve as a container for the couple's unpredictable emotions and actions. As with the ability to comfortably manage conflict, this ability to tolerate and contain ambiguity for the couple is very important for a mediator. Those who tend to become too anxious with ambiguity do not fare well as a family mediator.

Frequently, the position or utterances of one or both of the parties can trigger emotional responses on the part of the mediator (termed *countertransference reactions* by psychoanalytic theory). Issues arise in family disputes that touch every person on some level. The mediator is confronted with a broad range of emotional triggers, from the pain of children and parents going through divorce to neglectful, destructive parental beliefs and practices. To maintain effectiveness, the mediator must have the capacity to keep such reactions in check and remain nonjudgmental regarding such content. This requires the mediator to be aware of, and reasonably resolved about, his or her own familial issues and personal values, which can readily be aroused during the course of family mediation.

Because of the often intense, emotionally driven, compelling stories that each party typically tells the mediator, it is quite easy to get swallowed up in the perspective of only one side of the dispute. Those whose style allows them to resist such pull have the capacity to consistently maintain a systems view of the dispute (that there are no right or wrong perspectives, no good or bad people, only functional balances of multiple and conflicting realities). They also have the capacity to remain calm and poised amid flying allegations, and the ability to empathize with and fully appreciate the point of view of each person involved in the dispute. This is similar to Lovenheim's idea (2002) that successful mediators need to "maintain professional detachment." Again, it is important for a mediator to "look for the good in people," which allows the parties to feel validated, regardless of their particular points of view on a given matter.

Mediators must also be able to rigorously maintain balance between the parties. Although some suggest that this means maintaining neutrality, others clarify that, because the mediator must lean on one party at some times and then on the other at another time during the mediation process, it is balance, rather than neutrality, that is the more accurate organizing principle. So, over some unit of time the mediator must equalize, or balance, the emphasis of the interventions between the parties.

The importance of empathy and good listening skills as a mediator cannot be overemphasized. This capacity for being able to understand and connect with the feelings of others is a skill that, according to research, lies on a continuum. At one extreme (as in the pathologies of Asperger's disorder and sociopathy) are people who either do not have, or are extremely deficient in, the capacity for empathy. At the other extreme are effective mental health practitioners, who are high in what Daniel Goleman (1995) refers to as emotional intelligence. This innate, intuitive capacity to understand and feel what other people are feeling and to read the emotions of others, by both verbal and nonverbal cues, is crucial for an effective mediator. It cannot easily be taught but is invaluable in facilitating helpful communications in mediation.

An important coquality to empathy and good listening skills is patience. It is very important that the mediator be comfortable with letting clients proceed at the pace of the one needing most time to process. Mediators who are impatient with clients tend to hurry things along, often missing important opportunities for empathy and listening, and creating tension in one or both clients—tension that can build into resentment toward the mediator. As Mosten (2001) points out, mediation clients (or more often just one of them) may negotiate in a tortuously slow way, or else make demands for quick results when they don't know what to do, both of which put pressure on the mediator. If a mediator cannot remain patient and proceed in a responsive but optimal pace, mediation is bound to fail. An effective mediator must have the ability to wait, and even to sit with silence, if the clients need to process the content slowly.

Although it may seem obvious, being trustworthy is also an important quality for a mediator to have. Trustworthiness includes being organized, responsible, responsive, following through on promises and commitments, being truthful and accurate in reporting information, and admitting ignorance when that is the truth. Being trustworthy allows clients to reveal essential information, knowing that such revelations will not be used against them nor used to make them feel badly about themselves. It gives implicit permission for clients to count on the mediator to help resolve their disputes in as honest, effective, and efficient a manner as possible. It establishes confidence in the mediator's effectiveness and fosters full and safe participation in the mediation process.

Effective mediators must also have the skill of reframing (Saposnek, 1983; Watzlawick, Weakland, and Fisch, 1974) well practiced and on automatic pilot. Being able to relabel and reconceptualize a point uttered by one party so that it is palatable to the other party is basic to mediation work. Such a skill is not only inherent within the empathy necessary to simultaneously address the needs of both parties, but it even goes beyond. When the parties are stuck in their perspectives, it is essential for the mediator to be able to spontaneously generate a new point of view that both parties may be able to embrace. Such new and alternative realities frequently lead to the resolution of an impasse.

Lastly, it is essential for a mediator to have well-developed skills for thinking and intervening strategically. A mediator must read people quickly and be able to influence them directly and indirectly by his or her own words, intonations, and body language. This model of influence derives from similarities between mediation and the martial art of aikido (Saposnek, 1986). The mediation session is viewed as a systemic field of energy, and conflict and impasses are seen as energy that has become stuck. The mediator must keep the energy moving in constructive directions, by blending (empathizing) with the clients and redirecting (reframing) their energy toward resolution of the conflict. Maintaining a stance of eclectic flexibility ("being light on your feet") optimizes effective use of a range of strategies of intervention (Saposnek, 1998). It affords the mediator a conceptual agility that allows rapid and responsive shifting of frameworks and meanings toward constructive interactions. Practitioners who are too rigid of personality, inflexible, or unable to rapidly and responsively shift gears as needed do not succeed in either of these crafts.

Conclusion

An effective family mediator's style is best characterized as active, assertive, directive, organized, goal-oriented, businesslike, and systemic in its scope. The mediator must be technically proficient in crisis intervention techniques, negotiation skills, organizational development, and counseling. He or she must be knowledgeable about child development, marital and family dynamics, and divorce dynamics; he or she must also be sensitive to and able to manage the emotional and psychological aspects of the mediation process. Moreover, he or she must be able to maintain an optimal degree of control over the process, lest it get out of hand and become nonproductive.

Finally, the personal qualities for effectively blending the science with the art of family mediation into an effective style include:

1. Maintaining a systems perspective to disputes, which allows one to get beyond right and wrong, and good and bad, when faced with compelling but equal and opposite perspectives of each party.

2. Maintaining a perspective beyond simple problem solving, toward compassion and healing.

3. Being a proactive believer in the process of mediation.

4. Being comfortable with handling and managing conflict.

5. Being able to tolerate and contain ambiguity and unpredictability.

6. Being capable of remaining calm and poised in the face of flying allegations.

7. Being able to find the good in all people.

8. Maintaining balance and neutrality between the parties.

9. Having strong abilities for empathy, good listening skills, and high emotional intelligence.

10. Being patient and trustworthy.

11. Mastering the skills of reframing.

12. Being comfortable thinking and intervening strategically.

13. Maintaining eclectic flexibility so as to optimize rapid and responsive shifting of conceptual gears.

Although some of these mediator qualities are simply inborn and not teachable, others can be learned with good training and much practice. It stands to reason that not everybody can become an effective mediator. Many who begin the practice self-select out after realizing that it is not their natural calling to help people resolve or manage their conflicts. However, if one does persist in learning and practicing family mediation, it behooves the person to learn the science of mediation well and to practice and refine the artful aspects of mediation under wise guidance and experienced tutelage. Not only is this good for increasing the personal effectiveness of the mediator but it also enhances the quality of the profession as a whole.

Reflective Practice Questions

1. How would you describe your own "style" as a conflict resolver?

2. To what extent has that style been borrowed or adopted from others? How much is it grounded deeply in your authentic self?

3. Do you agree with the author's description of mediator style as the "expression of principle"? If so, what are the principles that are the foundation of your style? Are aspects of your style that you have borrowed or adopted from others accurate expressions of your principles?

References

Beutler, L. E., Machado, P.P.P., and Neufeldt, S. A. "Therapist Variables." In A. E. Bergin and S. L. Garfield (eds.), *Handbook of Psychotherapy and Behavior Change*. New York: Wiley, 1994.

Goleman, D. *Emotional Intelligence*. New York: Bantam Doubleday Dell, 1995.

Hoffman, D. *Understanding Frank Lloyd Wright's Architecture*. New York: Dover, 1995.

Johnston, J. R., and Campbell, L.E.G. *Impasses of Divorce: The Dynamics and Resolution of Family Conflict*. New York: Free Press, 1988.

Korchin, S. J., and Sands, S. H. "Principles Common to All Psychotherapies." In C. E. Walker (ed.), *The Handbook of Clinical Psychology.* Homewood, Ill.: Dow Jones-Irwin, 1983.

Lang, M., and Taylor, A. *The Making of a Mediator: Developing Artistry in Practice.* San Francisco: Jossey-Bass, 2000.

Lovenheim, P. *Becoming a Mediator: An Insider's Guide to Exploring Careers in Mediation.* San Francisco: Jossey-Bass, 2002.

Luborsky, L., Diguer, L., Luborsky, E., and Schmidt, K. A. "The Efficacy of Dynamic Versus Other Psychotherapies: Is It True That 'Everyone Has Won and All Must Have Prizes?'—An Update." In D. S. Janowsky (ed.), *Psychotherapy Indications and Outcomes.* Washington, D.C.: American Psychiatric Press, 1999.

Mosten, F. S. *Mediation Career Guide: A Strategic Approach to Building a Successful Practice.* San Francisco: Jossey-Bass, 2001.

Saposnek, D. T. *Mediating Child Custody Disputes: A Systematic Guide for Family Therapists, Court Counselors, Attorneys, and Judges.* San Francisco: Jossey-Bass, 1983.

Saposnek, D. T. "Aikido: A Systems Model for Maneuvering in Mediation." In D. T. Saposnek (ed.), *Applying Family Therapy Perspectives to Mediation* (*Mediation Quarterly* series, no. 14–15). San Francisco: Jossey-Bass, 1986.

Saposnek, D. T. "The Art of Family Mediation." *Mediation Quarterly*, 1993, *11*(1), 5–12.

Saposnek, D. T. *Mediating Child Custody Disputes: A Strategic Approach.* San Francisco: Jossey-Bass, 1998.

Saposnek, D. T., and Rose, C. "The Psychology of Divorce." In D. L. Crumbley and N. G. Apostolou (eds.), *Handbook of Financial Planning for Divorce and Separation.* New York: Wiley, 1990.

Watzlawick, P., Weakland, J. H., and Fisch, R. *Change: Principles of Problem Formation and Problem Resolution.* New York: Norton, 1974.

12

· ·

Tears

David A. Hoffman

On one of our happiest days of recent years, my wife and I cried. It was our daughter's bat mitzvah, celebrated with the usual wonderful mix of friends, relatives (both the close and seldom-seen varieties), and young adolescents. We cried as the service began, because this was our youngest child taking an important step toward adulthood. Joy, mixed with a touch of sadness, overwhelmed us as we reached for the Kleenex and tried not to be too obvious about it.

I was so worried about not being able to keep the tears in that when my wife and I got up to say a few words (at our synagogue, a speech from the bat mitzvah girl and her parents is part of the service), I talked about why I *always* cry at bar and bat mitzvah services, even if I don't know the family. There are really two reasons. One is a sentimental streak in me that makes me easy prey for long-distance-telephone commercials on TV; every time I see Jimmy Stewart return to his family at Christmas in *It's a Wonderful Life*, the tear ducts overflow. In a word, I'm a softy in the face of emotion.

The other reason, perhaps the more important one, is that for us older folks a bat mitzvah is a magical event. We enjoy simply being in the presence of a bar or bat mitzvah child. We love hearing the child chant the ancient Jewish melodies of prayer; we hear in that sound a piece of our past carried into the future. Bar and bat mitzvahs are magical, holy events because they rekindle in all of us the flame of hope and possibility. We look at this amazing child and see all that she might be and do in this world of ours that is so much in need of hope. A bat mitzvah represents the triumph of faith and commitment over cynicism and despair, and so we look at our daughter and we see the world anew. We see it, however, through a veil of tears because it seems almost too much to hope for. We are embarrassed by speaking aloud our fondest wish. In the wish is the possibility of both its fulfillment and its failure. Again, tears of sadness, tears of joy.

I grew up in a time when boys were taught that crying was a sign of weakness. You were a sissy if you cried—a crybaby. I remember the presidential candidacy of Ed Muskie (a New Englander who struck me at the time as one of the few politicians who valued principle over expediency) faltering in 1972 because of a few tears he shed at an emotional moment on the campaign trail. Today, some of the stigma associated with crying has abated; political candidates get credit in the press and with the public for a dignified show of emotion, even a little mistiness in the eyes, so long as they don't overdo it. President Clinton's ratings went up when he cried, and even General Norman Schwarzkopf got credit when he shed a few patriotic tears.

Of course, the messages imparted by our culture are different for men and women (no surprise). For women, crying is still considered a sign of weakness and perhaps sentimentality. For men, however, tears can, in some circumstances, be a show of strength—the culture tells us, paradoxically, that a man must be very sure of himself if he can let people see him cry. We even have a new term, coined by folksinger Christine Lavin, expressing both admiration and derision—for us "sensitive new age guys."

So I am ambivalent about my tears, and I am writing about them—and yours—in this chapter because as dispute resolvers we are constantly in the midst of emotion. I would like to make sense of why it is that in mediations and arbitrations I am sometimes close to the edge of tears, and a few times I have gone over the edge. At those moments, I look away and hope that the others in the room have not noticed. I am struggling, in those moments, to keep in some kind of balance the need to maintain the decorum of the process and yet at the same time honor the emotions in the room. These moments have come when:

- In a mediation, an elderly lawyer, sued by his clients, confessed that he had been a recovering alcoholic for thirty years, told me that his wife did not know about the lawsuit, and then looked me in the eye and said how much he appreciated the mediation and the settlement; "You're doing a wonderful thing here," he said, and I looked away because I thought my tears would embarrass him, and me.

- In a lengthy and bitter family business dispute, which tore apart two generations of a large family, the two matriarchs of the family met with my co-mediator and me and worked out a plan for settling the dispute, and then they stood and hugged each other for the first time in several years. There were no dry eyes in the room.

- In an arbitration of a Dalkon Shield case, a father testified that, when his wife got pregnant with the IUD in place, they decided not to abort because they are Catholic; when the baby arrived premature and stillborn, the medical staff literally threw the baby away with medical trash, and he had to recover the child so that he could perform a proper burial. His wife became infertile, their marriage ended, and he was in treatment for depression; even the advocate on the other side of the table looked stunned by this account.

- In a dispute between a doctor and nurse over the nurse's termination from her employment in the clinic of a homeless shelter, the parties exchanged mutual apologies, the nurse for having walked off the job in protest about the lack of medical supplies and the doctor for firing her. The doctor told the nurse how much he admired her idealism, and the nurse responded with admiration for the doctor's willingness to help the poor instead of pursuing a more lucrative practice. To this day, I sometimes get a little teary when I think of the way they expressed their profound respect for each other.

I could go on. Probably any of us could. Cases involving horrible injuries, horrible deaths. How do other professionals deal with these stories? Psychotherapists, lawyers, judges, and physicians face misery and raw emotion every day. Part of the answer is that in many professions tears are not permitted. Consider this account of a third-year medical student in Jeffrey Kottler's book *The Language of Tears*:

> I was sent in to take the vital signs of a cancer patient. I saw her lying in bed, bald, emaciated, tubes running in and out of her, and I just felt so sorry for her. After I took her blood pressure, I kept her hand in mine and we just cried together . . . until the resident burst in and demanded to know what the hell was going on: "And you want to be a doctor?" he said sarcastically. "If you are going to pull shit like this, why don't you just be a nurse!"

Or this description by an accountant:

> In order to make partner you have to be more ruthless than any of the other associates. . . . If I cried at work, I would be history. If I showed any feeling at all, it would be exploited in some way.

For many professionals, emotion is driven from the repertoire of expression.

On the other hand, my wife, a clinical social worker, tells me that although she is able to hold back her tears most of the time at work, when they occasionally well up they are often meaningful and helpful to her clients. I think the same has been true for me.

To be sure, there are times when tears would be counterproductive. If our role is to be neutral, our tears might be interpreted as a failure of impartiality. At the same time, one of the fundamental goals of both mediation and arbitration is to give people a meaningful opportunity to be heard. To listen well, with our hearts and our ears, means accessing those wellsprings of emotion that sometimes lead to tears. This is not always a matter of conscious choice and direction. Tears are mysterious and powerful because they often surprise us.

As professional dispute resolvers, we must learn to exercise appropriate discipline in our work. In addition, context is an important factor; becoming a bit tearful at the end of a successful mediation is obviously different from getting misty when one party is testifying in an arbitration. (Q: What should a defense lawyer do if the arbitrator is crying at the end of the plaintiff's testimony? A: Settle the case.)

Parties come to us to address their problems, not our own. But they come to us in part because mediation and arbitration typically offer a more humane setting for addressing those problems. Therefore, we should not be embarrassed about responding in a human way to the emotions in the room.

· · · · · · ·

A few years ago one of my partners at Hill & Barlow (the law firm where I practiced for seventeen years) retired. He was given more than the usual fanfare of speeches and accolades because his career had been particularly distinguished and his connection with the firm particularly deep. He stood before us, one of the most articulate courtroom advocates I have ever heard, and said that he did not think he could speak what was in his heart because he would become "unstuck." Instead he told a joke—a wonderful and memorable joke—that captured the spirit of the moment. But I felt a bit of loss there. Perhaps it's a generational thing; perhaps there is no way, given who he was and the era in which he had grown up, that he could risk becoming unstuck. But what an extraordinary gift that seventy-year-old partner would have given us if he had reached into that well of emotion and shared with us what was there, even if a few tears came up. Sometimes we must hold back, but I hope we reach a place in our culture where we can more fully accept and honor each other's tears as the tangible expression of the joys and sadness that life is made of.

Reflective Practice Questions

1. How comfortable are you with your own tears and those of others?

2. What is your instinctive response to others' tears? In what way, if any, have you had to modify that response in the context of your work as a dispute resolver?

3. How does the expression of emotion in a mediation—by the parties or the mediator—assist in the creation of the "sacred space" described in Sara Cobb's Chapter Nine?

13

Mindfulness Meditation and Mediation

Where the Transcendent Meets the Familiar

Daniel Bowling

The silence is deafening, but not loud enough. My own breathing sounds like a wind funnel on my favorite, deserted Sullivan's Island, South Carolina, beach in March. My heart is thumping like a jackhammer outside my office on Broad Street, and why did I have to sit behind someone with a deviated septum? And my body . . . I never realized that I could have so many aches and pains just from sitting. This meditation cushion feels like a stone. Only three days . . . seems like a month. My right side is burning like the red-hot poker my great-grandfather used to stoke the woodstove on cold nights in Pickens County.

And my mind . . . will it never stop wandering? Will these jumping-around thoughts never stop to allow me just to focus on my breath? Where is my breath anyway? How am I going to resolve that impossible environmental justice mediation? What if the burning on my right side is cancer? Why did we sell our beach house five years ago? No telling how much it's worth now. What is happening in the world? No newspaper since . . . Friday. Why did I say . . . to my wife before I left, knowing it would upset her like it always does? What a jerk. . . . The same stories and memories and worries keep winding, rewinding, and unwinding. How can my mind be so

*incredibly boring in the absence of external distraction? Am
I this boring when I speak? Six days to go. I will never make
it. Whose idea was this meditation retreat anyway?*

The Benefits of Meditation Practice

Why should any intelligent, mostly rational mediator submit himself or herself to nine days of a silent meditation retreat, making no
eye contact with anyone, alternating sitting and walking meditation from 5:00 A.M. to 10:00 P.M., with no reading or writing, not to
mention no other external forms of stimulation? Just for the
challenge, because it is certainly near the top of my hardest-things-
to-do list? Definitely not for the challenge. To gain peace? No,
because what is revealed is one's profound lack of peace. To be
taught how to meditate? Again no, because as with anything truly
worthwhile in life, meditation is an art that can only be experienced, and is experienced—the first time one ever sits even just for
five minutes, as one sits over and over, again and again, and
ultimately in every moment that one learns to be fully present to
the breath, right *now*.

Then what are the benefits of meditation, and how do those
benefits relate to practicing mediation or to living? Why should you
continue to read this chapter, when you undoubtedly have several
stacks of books and periodicals to read, not to mention e-mails?

As with exploring any art, the questions are more important
than the answers, especially in the beginning. Clarity about both
the questions in which to live and the unfolding of the answers
comes with time, patience, and persistent practice . . . over and
over, again and again.

The questions to ask in order to discover the benefits of a meditation practice and the potential impact on one's mediation or
other professional work are: What are you also thinking right now?
Where has your mind wandered as you read this chapter? Where is

your breath, right now . . . your body? Are you aware of either at this moment? Can you pay attention, and I mean really pay attention, to whatever you are doing, as you are doing it? Do you interview a client when you are interviewing a client, or does your mind take you away? Do you listen to your spouse, your children, your friends, and I mean really listen, when they need your attention?

Direct Experience Versus Thinking

Meditation is an ancient art and practice, untold thousands of years old. The Psalmist (46:10) tells us, "Be still and know that I am God." Vipassana or Insight or Mindfulness Meditation was originally delineated in the Buddha's first sermon, known as the Anapanasati Sutra, after his experience of enlightenment under a bodhi tree in India twenty-five hundred years ago. Although its origins are Buddhist, the practice is nonsectarian. Mindfulness Meditation is deceptively simple, yet it requires a lifetime of practice. The Buddha's first sermon outlined sixteen practices, divided into four sets, the first focusing on body awareness, the second on feelings in the body, the third on the mind, and the last on mental objects versus reality. All sixteen practices are grounded in focusing one's awareness on breathing in and breathing out. One does not practice Mindfulness Meditation only when sitting. The purpose of sitting meditation is to gain enough control over one's mind so that it is possible to be mindful throughout the day. To listen, when we are listening. To walk, when we are walking. To live, when we are living. To mediate, when we are mediating. To be fully and actually present, when we are physically present (Hanh, 1975).

Meditation has not remained a practice over so many centuries because it does not work. Few practice it, because it is profoundly challenging to confront how our "monkey" minds—so named by meditation teachers because our minds often leap from thought to thought in response to external stimuli—control us. What we call "thinking" is far too often simply the reactive meanderings of this monkey mind. Clear, nonreactive, thoughtful analysis is rare, but it does not have to be so. Our clients come to us as conflict resolvers for clear, nonreactive analysis and guidance. Obviously, a practice that develops our ability to provide what our clients seek has a direct and clear connection with excellence as a conflict resolver.

As mediators, we train others and ourselves by direct experience, rather than relying solely on lecture or study. We use role plays to elicit a form of direct experience. Meditation is learned the same way—only through direct experience. For example, through such direct experience, I learned why mediation does not work when a mediator offers solutions, especially early in the process; mediation works best when a mediator facilitates the parties in creating their own solutions. A separated husband and wife came to me for mediation regarding their marital home, mostly destroyed after a major hurricane. In the first session, they said they were struggling to afford their home and an apartment for the wife, who moved out following the hurricane. She wanted money to purchase her own home. They explained that their insurance claim was worth X amount, and they had an "as is" purchase offer for the marital home, which would net Y. The wife wanted to sell. The husband did not. X plus Y divided by two was easily sufficient for each to purchase their own house. The solution was so clear, I explained. The wife, naturally, loved my suggested solution. They never returned. Fortunately, I only occasionally forget this direct experiential lesson.

Similarly, I recall my direct experience of the fundamental cross-examination principle: "Don't ask the ultimate question." I was taught in law school, in trial advocacy books, and from experienced lawyers that the ultimate question asked the witness to tie the points of her cross-examination into a strong conclusion favoring one's client. I was taught that in skilled cross-examination, one draws out specific points from a witness that are helpful to one's client's case and ties them together only in closing argument to the jury, *never* by asking the ultimate question on cross-examination. Naturally, as a young public defender, I thought I understood—that is, until I actually asked an ultimate question to a witness in an armed robbery trial. As soon as the words left my mouth, I got it—too late. Before the witness could respond, however, I said, "I object, Your Honor." The prosecutor, no doubt recognizing my misstep, shouted out, "Mr. Bowling can't object to his own question." The judge, trying not to laugh, said, "Of course, he can't." In the confusion, the witness had not responded, and I quickly rephrased my question, taking the "ultimate" out of it. It was a narrow escape, but a powerful lesson. From then on I understood an ultimate question in a way my thinking mind had never allowed. The direct experience mattered, not the intellectual.

Both lessons were painful and embarrassing, which is often the case with direct experience. Likewise, it is painful and embarrassing to practice Mindfulness Meditation, and there is deep experiential learning, or insights. In meditation, the pain and embarrassment are—thankfully, since they are so frequent—internal experiences. The pain and embarrassment come with the realization of the power our monkey mind has in our lives and how it is the source of our suffering. The value in stress reduction, which has been proven scientifically, is very high, yet inconsequential compared with the true value. The reduction in blood pressure and heart rate are also proven, and again inconsequential.

> Where is your breath right now? Where have your thoughts wandered as you read? Notice how much or little you have been present, how much or little comparison you have made to what you already know, and how many or few judgments your thoughts have expressed. How valuable, really, are such thoughts?

Direct Experience Is Always Individual

Why practice meditation? Like realizing the nature of an ultimate question or the danger of offering early solutions in mediation, the answer must be lived. I hesitate to share my own answer because it is mine, and it may not be yours. Mine changes every few years. It may sound nonsensical. As with the ultimate question and offering early solutions, words are inadequate for direct experience. With that said, here it is.

I can't take this anymore. My body has finally relaxed. The hot poker is gone from my shoulder. The stories, however, are getting deeper. I've heard that when one is about to die, one's entire life flashes before the eyes. If that's true, this meditation retreat is an agonizingly slow death. After seven days, I'm still a teenager, having fantasy relationships with every female here. My friends told me I could not leave early, that after seven or eight days something happens to the mind. Now I know what they meant. I've discovered that I'm crazy. I'm certain that what is happening for me isn't happening for anyone else. They are all able to meditate. I'm not.

At lunch I watched a meditator stand near the bird feeder with her hand out, hoping a bird would light on her hand. How ridiculous, I judged, that will never happen in her lifetime. Close to fleeing the retreat, I decided to use a walking period to walk in the woods. It was comforting to hear birds singing—a noise, any noise to break the oppressing silence. As I walked, a wren flew ahead, landing on a branch and singing as I approached. Each time I got close, it flew ahead. I stopped and, without thinking, held out my hand. The wren lighted on it. Our eyes met. My monkey mind dropped into gear, and immediately the wren flew away. Only then did I recognize what had happened to my mind. I was far from crazy. My mind was quiet. Yet the same thoughts were arising. The difference? I was not holding onto them or believing them. The wren was a wren. My thoughts were thoughts. The difference? The wren was real. My thoughts were not, never had been, and never would be. My direct experience of life was real, but it was rare because my monkey mind got in the way over and over with its random, unclear thoughts. Through this "insight," I learned why Mindfulness Meditation is also called Insight Meditation.

In our overstimulated culture, where we seek to be occupied constantly, where we have MTV-syncopated media bombardment, it is difficult to distinguish the control our wandering, unclear monkey minds have. We rarely have new thoughts. Over time, as we practice Mindfulness Meditation, we see that we have "getting out of bed thoughts," "getting ready for work thoughts," "going to work thoughts," "avoiding a distasteful task thoughts," "talking to our spouse thoughts," and so on. As I said, what we call thinking is highly overrated. How many meetings have you sat through, knowing the statements certain people would make, regardless of the subject? Have you recognized that others are having a similar thought about what you will say? Our minds are in charge. They are on autopilot. We are not our minds. Through meditation, we can learn to turn off the autopilot and discover the quiet of true clarity. Then what we call thinking becomes wisdom.

Presence

In the quiet, we see our thoughts and release them, as we focus on the simplicity of breathing—our connection with life. By releasing thought and breath awareness, we become present. *Presence* brings peace (Bowling and Hoffman, 2000). It takes skill, experience, and knowledge to practice mediation. It takes presence, and the ability to bring peace to have a direct experience of the art of mediation. Practicing the art of mediation affords a mediator the opportunity to *be*, to create a healing connection with the client, to bring peace into the room, and to bring deeper fulfillment into one's practice.

Do you often find yourself in the future? Where are you right now, for example? Stress arises when we are somewhere different in our minds than we are in reality. Our mind takes us away from where we are, whenever our mind does not want to be where we are, which is a true measure of insanity. Spending hours or days in silence on a meditation cushion is a very sane approach to life. Our monkey mind constantly takes us to the past or to the future. Neither is real—never has been and never will be. To be in the present, we must release our futile attempt to create a better past. To be in the present, we must release our futile attempt to imagine our future into being. How can we be somewhere that we are not? Yet much of our life is filled with an attempt to be where we are not. That is not living (Tolle, 1997). We cannot develop presence in the past or the future. We can only be present in the present moment of *now*.

Mindfulness Meditation helps one to develop presence by training the mind to be present to the breath, no matter the circumstances. When one can be present to the breath, one begins to develop the ability to be present to one's deep and unconscious body pain. Only when we are present to our own pain can we be present to another's. When one can be present to one's own monkey mind patterns, one can be present to another's confusion and uncertainty. When one can be present to one's own anger, hurt, abuse, fear, one can be present to another's deepest suffering. When one can be present during one's own conflicts, one can be present during another's conflicts. Whenever we are mediating and our mind takes us away, wandering off into the imagined past or the future, we are actually resisting the conflict that is in the room. We cannot bring peace into the room, when we are resisting whatever is in the room, even on a subtle level. Through mindfulness practice, we learn to be present with all conflict.

Thinking

What we often call thinking prevents presence. How many times have you caught yourself failing to listen deeply to what someone was saying in mediation? We say, "I'm sorry. My mind wandered. Please repeat what you said." Those statements are deep denial. Yes, our mind wandered. It wandered when we were supposed to be listening deeply to a client. Would we willingly fail to serve our clients? What about when our mind "wanders" in the midst of a conflict with our spouse, partner, or child? We say, "I'm sorry, I was thinking about something else," or "I have a lot on my mind today," or "I got distracted." Each statement is actually a lie. How often each day does that occur? In our culture, we do not recognize that we have little control over our minds; rather, our monkey minds control us, most of the time. Meditation practice brings this recognition, this insight. It ends our culturally approved self-delusion. Only then can we begin to have small moments when we are in charge of our mind, when we can tell our monkey mind when it appears, "Thanks for sharing. Now I am returning to where I actually am, rather than to what you want to think about." Only then do we have even a chance to experience authentic being. Only then do we have a chance to bring peace into the room.

What we often call thinking is overrated because it is automatic and out of our control. With growing awareness from a dedicated meditation practice, we can distinguish our automatic thinking. We recognize its invalidity and the harm it creates in our lives. Only then are we able to use our minds, rather than our minds using us. We begin to expand our capacity to think clearly—think without a wandering mind, distinguishing our automatic thoughts from original thoughts. We learn to think when it is appropriate to think and to listen with full and deep presence when it is appropriate to listen. The arts of mediation and meditation begin to emerge.

Now—Where the Transcendent Meets the Familiar

There are certainly other ways to develop presence. Mindfulness Meditation is only one way. It is a way that has allowed me, from time to time, to experience the awesome quiet, the awesome heart of being. I commend it to you . . . now. Now is where the transcendent meets the familiar. The practice of mediation and meditation allow us, if we choose, direct experience of where the transcendent meets the familiar. What if we could reliably access those "magic moments" in mediation? What if we had insight into the subtle distinctions of being as presence? What if we were reliable for bringing peace into the room, for being peacemakers? Walking this pathway is to live a life worth living. Now is the only time to begin. Where is your mind? Where is your breath? Right now.

Cynicism and Futility: The Twin Pillars of Our Culture

Gandhi is often quoted as saying, "Be the change you wish to create in the world." One response to such a stirring aspiration is to dismiss it as impractical idealism—noble certainly, but irrelevant and impossible in our postmodern world with its intense demands on our time and energy. A second response is to believe that fulfilling such an admonition is only for the rarefied few—Gandhi, Martin Luther King Jr., Mother Teresa, the Dalai Lama, Black Elk, St. Teresa of Avila, Jelaluddin Balkhi Rumi, Rabia of Basra, Meister Eckhart, Shakespeare, St. Catherine of Siena, Mirabai, and other extraordinary human beings. Both responses are utterly disempowering of any personal or professional development. The implication is clear. I am who I am. The world is as it is, always has been, and will be. Real change is impossible.

These two attitudes are, in fact, classic retorts to life's challenges. They quash individual and global human development. We see a towering mountain and turn away with cynicism or futility. The summit is irrelevant or impossible—ironically the same barriers we mediators and our clients use to ignore and avoid resolving conflict. Cynicism and futility seem pervasive in our postmodern culture. How else to explain extraordinarily blatant corporate and political fraud, ever-decreasing voter turnout, denial of the impact of our growing environmental degradation, a debased and sexually focused entertainment industry, racism, ethnic wars, sexism, homophobia, child abuse, the growing and ignored gap between rich and poor, a bought-and-paid-for political system focused on narrow self-interest instead of the majesty of our Constitution and Bill of Rights, and decreasing worldwide humanitarian aid in the face of desperate need? The list is long and rapidly growing.

Sheltered by cynicism and futility, we allow our denial to grow. We can focus on "getting ours," forgetting that the smaller the world becomes, the more the ancient wisdom—that we are one, inter-connected in a great web of life—becomes practically relevant and not just epistemologically sound. Terrorism, plagues such as HIV-AIDS, and environmental degradation are here to teach us our interconnection, but so far we are poor students.

As mediators, we often confront cynicism and a sense of futility in our clients, as they confront what appears to be an impossible mountain of conflict that is outside their control, forced on them by another. We are limited in our ability to help these clients by our reluctance to release our own cynicism and futility—our fear of climbing the mountains of conflict in our own lives.

What if, instead of seeing only the mountain and the summit, we were able to distinguish the numerous plateaus and overlooks, valleys and ravines, streams and waterfalls, trees and shrubs that combine to create the mountain? The summit may be unattainable from our perspective at the base, but that first ravine appears to lead to that craggy overlook surrounded by red-leafed maples. I wonder what I could see if I sat by that waterfall?

The Contexts for Practicing Mindfulness Meditation and Mediation Are the Same: Being Is Presence

As we seek to unfold the dense mass of apparently impenetrable conflict our clients present in mediation, we know that the path-way crystallizes whenever we break down a challenge into smaller components, whenever we create previously unseen distinctions.

Gandhi admonishes us to be, not to do, or even to become. What is the distinction of being? Most of us recognize it when we see it, but the pathway—the subtle distinctions—remains a mystery. We misunderstand Shakespeare's famous, "To be or not to be, that is the question." For the same reason, we often dismiss presence as charisma, an innate quality that few of us have.

When one is being, others experience presence. Being is presence. Charisma is not necessarily being. Actors can project charisma. The distinction is authenticity, and we can be fooled. We can be taught to project charisma, as a skill or technique. Like many techniques, it is easier for some than for others. We cannot be taught authenticity, as a skill or technique. We can develop authenticity, but what is the developmental path? If there were no pathway, then we could not develop those personal qualities that call forth authentic presence. Those of us who have not learned to project charisma or who prefer authenticity would be doomed to cynicism and futility.

The absence of a pathway is not the problem. In fact, there are many pathways. Few, however, are willing to discover and then walk them far enough. Gandhi did not urge us to "be the change" to call forth even more cynicism and futility. He was urging us toward our highest potential as human beings. Unfortunately, for our postmodern, have-it-all-right-now culture, all such pathways are difficult, requiring dedication and commitment over time. Paradoxically, all pathways are also simple and clear. They can only be discovered and walked right now.

Being does not occur in the future. It always and only happens now. Similarly, development, both personal and professional, does not happen in the future. It only happens now—in this moment as you are reading these words and in the next moment and the next. As we allow our focus to move from the future to now, from the past to now, we slow down the pace of life. We see not only the summit, the Gandhian admonition, our clients' and our own conflicts, but also the pathways to the top, the challenging but not impossible steps of development, the distinctions within a conflict that lead to its resolution.

Being is not singular. An oak tree has no aspirations of becoming a maple, nor a rose an orchid. Only we humans lose ourselves in the futility of comparison leading inexorably to the suffering of becoming—becoming someone we are not. By contrast, being takes great joy in the multiple diversity of creation, with its numerous styles, countless techniques, and vast knowledge. Doing founders on the fundamentalist zealotry of one "right" approach. The efforts to define mediation as only possible through a single style, technique, or theory all miss the mark of what is the fundamental source of developing the ability to bring peace into the room. Being opens the heart to compassion and inclusion. There is no single path to the summit. Yet all paths lead to the summit. Conflict resolution soars through being.

Being is grounded in practice. A disciplined, committed practice of almost any kind benefits from being, and being expands practice. There are numerous ancient spiritual practices, which our postmodern world is beginning to embrace. My own inquiry into what it takes to develop the personal qualities that culminate in being has led me to explore many practices. My exploration is over, and I focus on Mindfulness Meditation. Although I can strongly endorse the practice and, as I have explained, in particular its relevance to mediation, I do not advocate it. I do, however, encourage adopting some daily practice, especially for anyone who is or aspires to become a conflict resolver. Develop a daily practice that encourages awareness of being, be it walking along a seashore, reading poetry, or spending time in silent meditation.

The development of being, as Gandhi said, leads to change. Likewise, change can lead to the development of being. Change takes place through time, but not within our cultural fixation on linear time as the only temporality; rather, it is within a developmental temporality that transcends and includes linear time. Time is rapid when it lives in a single dimension. Time slows down when we distinguish its multiple dimensions. Being unfolds as we sharpen our awareness of relational time, circumstantial time, reflective time, visionary time, integrative time, and, above all, eternal time. The time famine within which we typically live pulls for an excess of doing and blocks our openness to the developmental temporality that change requires (Eberle, 2003).

Both who we are as conflict resolvers and the process of conflict resolution are distorted by our cultural reduction of temporality to the single dimension of linear time. A consistent and focused inquiry into the nexus between our personal qualities as dispute resolvers and what happens in our practice is enriched by developmental time and the change in our being, which that temporality unfolds.

Being Is Presence: Creating a Life Worth Living

Gandhi's life and his admonition exemplify the power of intention, of focus, of commitment toward an ideal as the essence of what it means to live a fulfilled life. Idealism, grounded and balanced by clarity of vision, is the antidote to cynicism and futility. Aspiring to unfold one's being as a gift to oneself and more profoundly to everyone else in one's life links us to the highest idealism for our practice of conflict resolution. As our field gains wider acceptance by the mainstream culture, we must nurture idealism within ourselves to avoid the fate of most of our professions of origin. I firmly believe that the practice of mediation and other forms of conflict resolution cannot be both fulfilling and limited to the skills and techniques we learn and practice and the knowledge we acquire along the way. So limited, our practice becomes work, rather than a profession. When it includes an intention to nurture idealism by developing being, it becomes a calling.

G. K. Chesterton once quipped, "Angels can fly because they take themselves lightly." Perhaps because we are so heavy, we learn meditation and mediation by sitting and sitting. Knowledge and technique are heavy. More knowledge and technique are even heavier. Being requires emptiness, which founders on the rocky shoals of knowledge and technique, especially the right knowledge and technique. Hubris is heavier still. Those of us with degrees and experience and wisdom and especially recognition from others find it difficult to empty ourselves.

Thus the pathways of being are rarely discovered or followed to completion. The walk is lonely, leaving a life such as Gandhi's as a rare jewel—not because being is only granted to a few or because the pathways are unknown. Our times and our choice of profession, in my view, call for something more from us than more knowledge and technique. The world is desperate for peacemakers. Regardless of how far we walk up these ancient pathways, each of our lives is nonetheless a rare jewel. Choosing to polish that jewel sheds more light in our own lives and in the lives we encounter along the way. We may never face conflict at the level addressed by Gandhi, but the conflicts we face are no less life-altering for our clients. Imagine the potential of our collective impact on bringing peace to our planet, one conflict at a time.

For the sake of our children and the world we leave as our inheritance, I advocate commitment to a practice that develops being. My own commitment to Mindfulness Meditation practice and the inquiry it requires arose from my struggle with monumental conflict—my clients and my own. I offer this chapter as encouragement for choosing to awaken being, to stand for the ideals that are inherent in becoming peacemakers and thus to become the change you wish to see in the world.

Reflective Practice Questions

1. What connections do you see between a regular practice that focuses your attention on being rather than on doing and your ability to develop the personal qualities to which you aspire?

2. If you have a regular practice or discipline, what value does it bring to your life and your work as a dispute resolver?

3. What are the personal qualities that you aspire to master, and what practice or practices could you undertake to develop those qualities more fully?

References

Bowling, D., and Hoffman, D. "Bringing Peace into the Room: The Personal Qualities of the Mediator and Their Impact on the Mediation." *Negotiation Journal*, Jan. 2000, 16, 5–27.

Eberle, G. *Sacred Time and the Search for Meaning*. Boston: Shambhala, 2003.

Hanh, T. N. *The Miracle of Mindfulness: A Manual on Meditation*. Boston: Beacon Press, 1975.

Tolle, E. *The Power of Now*. Novato, Calif.: New World Library, 1997.

Suggestions for Further Reading

· ·

Benjamin, R. D. "The Constructive Uses of Deception: Skills, Strategies, and Techniques of the Folkloric Trickster Figure and Their Application by Mediators." *Mediation Quarterly*, Fall 1995, *13*(1), 3–18.

Benjamin, R. D. "The Mediator as Trickster: The Folkloric Figure as Professional Role Model." *Mediation Quarterly*, Winter 1995, *13*(2), 131–149.

Benjamin, R. D. "The Natural Mediator." *Mediation News* (Academy of Family Mediators), 1998, *18*(1), 8–9.

Capra, F. *The Web of Life*. New York: Anchor Books, 1996.

Cloke, K. *Mediation: Revenge and the Magic of Forgiveness*. Santa Monica, Calif.: Center for Dispute Resolution, 1994.

Cloke, K. *Mediating Dangerously: The Frontiers of Conflict Resolution*. New York: Wiley, 2001.

Cobb, S., and Rifkin, J. "Practice and Paradox: Deconstructing Neutrality in Mediation." *Law and Social Inquiry*, 1991, *16*(1), 25–63.

Eberle, G. *Sacred Time and the Search for Meaning*. Boston: Shambhala, 2003.

Gold, L. *Between Love and Hate: A Guide to Civilized Divorce*. New York: Plume/Penguin Books, 1992.

Gold, L. "Influencing Unconscious Influences." *Mediation Quarterly*, Fall 1993, *11*, 55–66.

Goleman, D. *Emotional Intelligence*. New York: Bantam Books, 1995.

Goleman, D. *Working with Emotional Intelligence*. New York: Bantam Books, 1998.

Hanh, T. N. *The Miracle of Mindfulness: A Manual on Meditation*. Boston: Beacon Press, 1975.

Hanh, T. N. *Being Peace*. Berkeley: Parallax Press, 1987.

Kabat-Zinn, J. *Wherever You Go, There You Are*. New York: Hyperion, 1994.

Kottler, J. *The Compleat Therapist*. San Francisco: Jossey-Bass, 1991.

Kottler, J. *The Language of Tears*. San Francisco: Jossey-Bass, 1996.

Lang, M., and Taylor, A. *The Making of a Mediator: Developing Artistry in Practice*. San Francisco: Jossey-Bass, 2000.

LeBaron, M. *Bridging Troubled Waters: Conflict Resolution from the Heart*. San Francisco: Jossey-Bass, 2002.

LeBaron, M. *Bridging Cultural Conflict: A New Approach for a Changing World*. San Francisco: Jossey-Bass, 2003.

Levine, S. *Getting to Resolution: Turning Conflict into Collaboration*. San Francisco: Berrett-Koehler, 1998.

Levine, S. *The Book of Agreement: Ten Essential Elements for Getting the Results You Want*. San Francisco: Berrett-Koehler, 2002.

Madonik, B. *I Hear What You Say, But What Are You Telling Me?: The Strategic Use of Nonverbal Communication in Mediation*. San Francisco: Jossey-Bass, 2001.

Maturana, H. R., and Varela, F. J. *The Tree of Knowledge: The Biological Roots of Human Understanding* (R. Paolucci, trans.). Boston: Shambhala (distributed by Random House), 1998.

Mayer, B. *The Dynamics of Conflict Resolution: A Practitioner's Guide*. San Francisco: Jossey-Bass, 2000.

Mindell, A. *The Leader as a Martial Artist: Techniques and Strategies for Resolving Conflict and Creating Community*. Portland, Oreg.: Lao Tse Press, 2000.

Richards, M. C. *Centering: In Pottery, Poetry, and the Person*. Middletown, Conn.: Wesleyan University Press, 1962.

Saposnek, D. T. "Aikido: A Systems Model for Maneuvering in Mediation." In D. T. Saposnek (ed.), *Applying Family Therapy Perspectives to Mediation* (*Mediation Quarterly* series, no. 14–15). San Francisco: Jossey-Bass, 1986.

Schön, D. *The Reflective Practitioner: How Professionals Think in Action*. New York: Basic Books, 1983.

Shafir, R. Z. *The Zen of Listening: Mindful Communication in the Age of Distraction*. Wheaton, Ill.: Theosophical, 2000.

Stone, D., Patton, B., and Heen, S. *Difficult Conversations: How to Discuss What Matters Most*. New York: Penguin Books, 1999.

Thompson, C. M. *The Congruent Life: Following the Inward Path to Fulfilling Work and Inspired Leadership*. San Francisco: Jossey-Bass, 2000.

Tolle, E. *The Power of Now: A Guide to Spiritual Enlightenment*. Novato, Calif.: New World Library, 1999.

Ury, W. *Getting to Peace*. New York: Viking Press, 1999.

Wilber, K. *No Boundary: Eastern and Western Approaches to Personal Growth*. Boston: Shambhala, 2001.

Wolman, R. *Thinking with Your Soul: Spiritual Intelligence and Why It Matters*. New York: Random House, 2001.

Notes

Chapter One

1. We recognize that there is considerable debate over the question of what constitutes success in a mediation. For example, although many would say that settlement of the dispute constitutes a successful outcome, others contend that empowerment and recognition, not settlement, are the hallmarks of success. See Bush and Folger (1994).

2. In the words of Jose Ortega y Gasset (1948), "The metaphor is probably the most fertile power possessed by man." (We are indebted to Albie Davis for alerting us to this quote.)

3. We acknowledge Ken Anbender for his contribution to these ideas concerning stages of development. To be sure, there are inherent limitations to any attempt to describe growth or change in a developmental framework. For example, personality and cultural differences may be a salient factor. In addition, the attempt to define a discrete set of stages in a process as fluid and complex as personal growth and change is inherently arbitrary.

4. A similar theme was sounded by mediator Ian Browde (1996), who describes this stage as a necessary step for mediators of the future. The changing nature of disputes, he writes, "requires us to learn to be different in many, and often fundamental ways. Those who have been used to, and even exceptionally skilled in mediating conflicts and disputes in the rapidly disappearing context, need to learn quickly how to mediate in the new one. The new context involves learning to actually *be* different."

5. Harvard Law School Professor Frank E. A. Sander first suggested this phenomenon to one of the authors as a placebo effect that must be separated from the salutary effects that court-connected ADR methods produce. We propose to call this phenomenon the "Sander effect."

6. An example of this phenomenon was discovered recently in a study of human pheromones—substances that the human body emits but that escape conscious detection. The effects of the pheromones on animals have been well established, but until recently the effects on humans were only a theory. A study performed at the University of Chicago showed that women who live together can alter the timing of each other's menstrual cycles. This phenomenon, known as "menstrual synchrony," had been reported for many years by women living in the same household but was not confirmed until 1998, when the results of a controlled study were published in the journal *Nature*. See Angier (1998).

7. See also writings on the subject of Buddhist meditation (for example, by Thich Nhat Hanh, 1987). It is probably no accident that the concept of integration resonates with teachings of yoga, as both authors of this chapter have been deeply influenced by that school of thought and practice, and one has done extensive yoga teaching. The Sanskrit word *yoga* means "yoke" or "union" and is similar to the concept of integration.

8. As noted earlier, systems thinking found expression in the field of psychology in the school of Gestalt psychotherapy, which was based on the premise that we perceive things not as isolated elements but as integrated, meaningfully organized wholes (Capra, 1996).

9. This fundamental shift in the way we view our participation in mediation is also suggested by the etymology of the word *conversation*. It derives from the Latin word *conversari*, meaning "to turn about with," made up of *vertere*, "to turn," plus *con*, "together, among." Thus conversation was originally the act of turning about among others. This is the basis by which the word came to be connected with physical intimacy and led to the ancient crime of "criminal conversation." Thus an *authentic* conversation is one in which we actually turn about with our partners in the conversation.

We are affected by an authentic conversation, just as we have an impact on others in an authentic conversation. Otherwise, we as mediators hold ourselves separate and apart from the mediation conversation, and the mediation will not be an integrated process.

Chapter Three

1. Bernie Mayer, Chris Moore, and Susan Carpenter told me about this in the early 1980s. I'm not sure if they actually invented the model or heard it from someone else. Regardless, the model has a certain elegance and sensibility that makes it pedagogically useful, which is one of the reasons it gets recited at the start of many mediation training programs.

2. The word *chunking* is sometimes used by language theorists to describe a way of parsing a text into syntactically correlated parts of words. It is also used by some communication trainers as a variation of actively listening, unpacking, and then reframing complex and emotion-charged statements. In this article, chunking refers to mental sequences that are stored in long-term memory and can be used to guide the short-term procedures we use in our work as mediators.

Chapter Seven

1. Frank Sander (1995) has also noted the risk that mediators may feel pressured by the tyranny of "settlement rate" statistics as a form of market pressure on them to promote settlement at the expense of other values.

2. For a dissenting opinion, taking issue with the conventional wisdom, see Green (1986).

3. See, for example, Mass. Unif. R. of Disp. Resol. 9(h); AAA-ABA-SPIDR Model Standards of Conduct for Mediators, Standard V.

4. For a useful summary of the scientific research on how emotion is expressed in a largely involuntary manner by the human face, see Gladwell (2002).

Chapter Nine

1. Although there may be a statistically significant relationship between the presence of an agreement and shifts in how parties relate to each other as the session ends, there is no research that documents a causal relationship. Furthermore, anecdotally, I have witnessed sessions in which agreements were reached without accompanying shifts in interaction patterns. Follow-up data on some of these cases show that the agreements hold, despite the absence of shifts in interaction at the time of the agreement. So agreements may be effective without the presence of any shifts in the quality of the relationship between parties. This would support the notion that conflict resolution is not coterminous with repair of ruptures in the social bond (Retzinger and Scheff, 2000).

2. Davis endeavors to account for the "magic" of the mediation process. I am not at all suggesting in this chapter that magic happens. On the contrary, I am hoping to show that what we take as magic is, in fact, a set of technical practices that yield shifts in interactional patterns.

3. Bush and Folger (1994). However, Bush and Folger do not construct this as a dynamic or systemic process but as an intrapsychic process within an individual.

4. Innes (1999); Pearson and Thoennes (1989). Even though these studies are ten years apart, the problems related to longitudinal research remain.

5. Loewenstein and Thompson (2000). Loewenstein and Thompson argue that the transfer of skills requires the development of comparisons through analogy. This research would suggest that the mediation process alone is not instrumental in the development of the ability to transfer skill sets from the session to other conflicts.

6. Although there is some acknowledgment within alternative dispute resolution (ADR) that disputes are moral contests between competing moral frames, there is very little research on how morality is negotiated (MacIntyre, 1989, pp. 8–10). MacIntyre states that there is no longer a unified or stable frame from which to assess morality,

once we grant that there are multiple realities, each with its own form of rationality and justice.

7. In a set of approximately thirty mediation sessions, videotaped and audiotaped for research, Janet Rifkin and I found that it was not at all uncommon for disputants to recommend to the mediator—often during a caucus—that the other should go see a therapist. This was not a systematic research finding, but more an incidental one. We never did any systematic research on this issue. There was a need expressed for the other to change, as well as to pay for some damage that was done. Furthermore, in some cases, parties made this recommendation for the other to go to therapy independent of whether or not there was an agreement reached.

8. On the basis of the discourse analytic research that Rifkin and I conducted on mediation sessions, we found that the first party to speak "colonizes" the discursive terrain, making it difficult for the second party to do anything other than defend itself (Cobb and Rifkin, 1991). Therefore I often conduct separate initial interviews when I am concerned over the volatility or the marginality of one or more parties. In this case, I was concerned about both, so I met with the parties separately.

9. I am not suggesting that all victims want their pain witnessed; on the contrary, many victims adopt the story of their victimizer and struggle to hide their pain. This is not to be confused with the social construction of victims, as the objects of weapons and the locations of wounds (Scarry, 1985).

10. The "body of the victim" is a phrase used by Andrew J. McKenna in his book *Violence and Difference* (1992); it invokes the visual imagery of the victim's body because speakers locate wounds (emotional and physical) on a specific person who is harmed. Thus "the body" is a site for making the victim present to others. It also makes obvious that the body is often in some way presented as marked by victimization, so the body of the victim becomes the record that victimization occurred.

11. McKenna describes Girard's work in a book that contains a section entitled "Tracing the Victim" (McKenna, 1992).

12. The case study is from a mediation session in southern California (1995); a transcript is on file with the author. "Steve" and "Beth" are pseudonyms.

13. This question was a strategic mistake on my part, as Beth had not yet been witnessed and, predictably, would use any opportunity to delegitimize Steve and elaborate her perspective. So although the first question allowed her to demonstrate competency in Steve's worldview, it would have been strategically better to end my witnessing of his view with a question asking him to demonstrate competency in her worldview:

> Steve, now that I think we know more of your perspective, and before Beth has her chance to speak, I would like you to signal, if you can, that you are at least a little familiar with her worldview, so I ask you this question: "Who in the firm would you think Beth would say is most at risk as a function of this conflict between the two of you?"

Answering this question requires him to put himself in her shoes before she begins to speak, reducing the "work" she has to do to elaborate her worldview. Thus, although it was useful to ask her to speak from Steve's worldview, it might have been better to ask him to do that as he finished laying himself out as the victim. However, in neither case would it have been useful to ask either one to then agree or disagree with the other as to whether the other in fact got it "right" regarding who they were the most worried about in the firm. Yet that is exactly what I asked Beth to do, with a predictably bad result. Sharing my hindsight hopefully will help others to avoid this mistake.

14. Inadvertently, I gave her an opportunity to delegitimize Steve. This followed quite predictably from my question, which, as I mention in note 15, was problematic, precisely because it opened the door to delegitimizing Steve.

15. I was careful to use this relational language of "betrayal," which was not Beth's word but reflected the familial and relational view that

Steve had of the problem. Beth nodded when I asked the question, signaling her alliance with me, perhaps because I linked betrayal (Steve's familial language) with "shut out" (Beth's language of "voice").

16. In a private session with me, Beth confessed that she was very frustrated with herself for acting like a "rebellious daughter," as she had long thought of herself as a very professional person.

17. These items emerged out of our interaction, so I played an important role in organizing a collective inquiry into what had worked in the past and how he could help it work in the future. Again, this kind of involvement is not, in my view, a sign of "bias" (a concept that implies that a value-free framework is possible), but rather a sign of the responsibility I take as a mediator for facilitating a quality of moral discussion that yields new plot lines, new roles, and new value sets (Rifkin and others, 1991).

18. They asked me to facilitate the meeting and I declined; instead I referred Steve and Beth to other professionals in my network.

19. When I probed for the nature of the "issues," Beth explained that Steve found it difficult to be one of three partners, and not the most important partner. He was continually "sneaking" into functional areas where he was not responsible, gathering information. Steve agreed to this description and explained it by noting that during his many years as the sole partner, he had to do it all by himself, so he was not used to working with others. Beth also used this frame, so that even though they saw Steve as behaving problematically, both saw it in the context of his past experience of being the only partner, and both agreed that change was difficult.

20. Accidents are not ritualized unless victims sue others for damages, in which case the telling of the violation becomes a public process in a courtroom setting.

21. I define "active listening" as a very passive activity, for it does little to evolve the content of the conversation. In fact, it continually anchors the very descriptions by which each party delegitimizes the other.

22. For a description of the "better formed" story, see Carlos E. Sluzki, "The 'Better-Formed' Story: Ethics and Aesthetic Practice" (unpublished manuscript on file with author). Sluzki provides a normative framework for discriminating narratives that internalize personal responsibility and increase options from narratives that reduce options and externalize personal responsibility. Here I am using Sluzki's normative framework for assessing the evolution of conflict stories in mediation.

23. I would differentiate these instances from those sessions where people simply agree to stop doing what they are doing already, as is the case with international cease-fires, for example. No new social rules are created; old social rules are simply reinvoked, usually with little success.

The Contributors

Daniel Bowling is a senior mediator and director of the Washington, D.C., office for RESOLVE, a public policy consensus-building organization. He was a cofounder of the first mediation organization in South Carolina, the Low Country Mediation Network. As executive director of the Society of Professionals in Dispute Resolution (SPIDR), he managed the merger among SPIDR, the Academy of Family Mediators, and the Conflict Resolution Education Network; he served as the first CEO of the Association for Conflict Resolution. He serves on the Policy Consensus Professional Advisory Council of the proposed U.S. Consensus Council for Search for Common Ground. He graduated from Furman University and Harvard Law School; was a member of one of the first public interest law firms, the Urban Law Institute; and served on the founding faculty of Antioch School of Law (the first law school to use an experiential pedagogy). He helped establish the Charleston County (South Carolina) public defender office, never lost a client to the death penalty, and was cited as one of the top criminal defense lawyers in the United States. He is a personal development coach and trainer and has practiced yoga and meditation for more than twenty-five years. He can be reached at dbowling@resolv.org.

David A. Hoffman is a member of The Boston Law Collaborative, LLC, a multidisciplinary firm that provides collaborative law and dispute

resolution services. Previously he was a member of the The New
Law Center, LLC, and a partner at the Boston firm of Hill & Barlow,
where he practiced for seventeen years. He serves as a mediator,
arbitrator, and case evaluator in cases ranging from complex commercial disputes to divorce, and he also serves as settlement counsel.
He is chair-elect of the ABA Section of Dispute Resolution, past
president of the New England chapter of the Association for Conflict Resolution, and cofounder of the Massachusetts Collaborative
Law Council. He has taught mediation, negotiation, and ADR at
Harvard Law School and Northeastern University Law School. He
is a graduate of Princeton University (B.A. 1970, *summa cum laude*),
Cornell University (M.A. 1974, in American studies), and Harvard
Law School (J.D. 1981, *magna cum laude*), where he was an editor
of the *Harvard Law Review*. Along with David Matz, he is the coau-
thor of the two-volume treatise *Massachusetts Alternative Dispute
Resolution* and has written a number of articles about ADR. He can
be reached at DHoffman@BostonLawCollaborative.com or via the
Web (www.BostonLawCollaborative.com).

Peter S. Adler is director of the Center for Science and Public Policy
at the Keystone Center, which applies consensus building and
cutting-edge scientific information to energy, environmental, and
health-related policy problems. His specialty is multiparty negotiation and problem solving. He mediates, writes, trains, and teaches
in diverse areas of conflict management. Prior to his appointment
at Keystone, he held senior executive positions with the Hawaii
Justice Foundation, the Hawaii Supreme Court's Center for ADR,
and the Neighborhood Justice Center. He was a Peace Corps
volunteer, an Outward Bound instructor, and president of the Society of Professionals in Dispute Resolution. He was awarded the
Roberston-Cunninghame Scholar in Residence Fellowship at the
University of New England, New South Wales, Australia; was a
Senior Fellow at the Western Justice Center; and was a consultant
to the U.S. Institute for Environmental Conflict Resolution. He

coauthored *Managing Scientific and Technical Information in Environmental Cases* (1999) and *Building Trust: 20 Things You Can Do to Help Environmental Stakeholder Groups Talk More Effectively About Science, Culture, Professional Knowledge, and Community Wisdom* (2002). He has written *Beyond Paradise* (1993) and *Oxtail Soup* (2000) and numerous articles and monographs. He can be reached at padler@keystone.org.

Robert D. Benjamin has been a practicing mediator since 1979, in all dispute contexts including health care, employment, civil and business, and family and divorce matters. He presents negotiation, mediation, and conflict management training courses and seminars nationally and internationally, including sessions in Russia, Eastern Europe, and South America. He is a Fellow at the Straus Institute for Conflict Resolution at the Pepperdine University School of Law and a visiting professor on the faculty of the Southern Methodist University Conflict Resolution Program. He is the former president of the Academy of Family Mediators, now merged with the Society of Professionals in Conflict Resolution to become the Association for Conflict Resolution, of which he is a member. He is the author of numerous articles and book contributions, and a regular columnist and editor for Mediate.com, an online publication, as well as a regular columnist and contributor to several ACR publications. He can be reached at rbenjamin@mediate.com; Web site www.rbenjamin.com.

Kenneth Cloke is director of the Center for Dispute Resolution and a mediator, arbitrator, consultant, and trainer specializing in resolving complex multiparty conflicts (on grievance and workplace, organizational, school, sexual harassment, discrimination, and public policy issues) and designing conflict resolution systems for organizations. He has written *Mediation: Revenge and the Magic of Forgiveness* and *Mediating Dangerously: The Frontiers of Conflict Resolution*. He is coauthor with Joan Goldsmith of *Thank God It's Monday! Fourteen Values We*

Need to Humanize the Way We Work; Resolving Conflicts at Work: A Complete Guide for Everyone on the Job; Resolving Personal Organizational Disputes: Stories of Transformation and Forgiveness; The End of Management and the Rise of Organizational Democracy; and *The Art of Waking People Up: Cultivating Awareness and Authenticity at Work.* He has a B.A. from the University of California, Berkeley; J.D. from the UC Boalt Law School; Ph.D. from UCLA; and LLM from UCLA Law School; he did postdoctoral work at Yale Law School and is a graduate from the National Judicial College. His university teaching includes law, mediation, history, and social sciences at Southwestern University School of Law, Pepperdine, Antioch, Occidental College, the University of Southern California, and UCLA. He has worked in Mexico, Germany, Zimbabwe, India, Pakistan, Cuba, China, the U.S.S.R., Georgia, Armenia, Brazil, Ireland, England, Canada, and Nicaragua. He can be reached at kcloke@aol.com.

Sara Cobb is director of the Institute for Conflict Analysis and Resolution (ICAR) at George Mason University. As a faculty member, she teaches theory, research, and practice-based courses on negotiation and the transformation of disputes. In her role as director, she provides liaison between ICAR and other private sector agencies and corporations at the national and international levels. She has a Ph.D. in communication from the University of Massachusetts, Amherst. Through her research, she has specialized in the analysis of conflict narratives and has contributed to the critique of "neutrality" in conflict resolution processes. She has published widely in communication studies and legal studies, supported by grants from the Ford Foundation and the UN High Commission on Refugees. She has held both administrative and academic positions at a variety of research institutions, including the Program on Negotiation at Harvard Law School; the University of California, Santa Barbara; and the University of Connecticut. She has consulted to a host of family-owned businesses in North and South America, as well as to private and public organizations, including the UN High Commission on Refugees,

La Caxia Bank, and Exxon, to name a few. She can be reached at scobb@gmu.edu.

Lois Gold is a founding board member and past president of the Academy of Family Mediators and has been prominently involved in the development of family mediation since the 1970s. She began the first divorce mediation service in Oregon in 1980 and currently maintains a private practice as a mediator and therapist in Portland. She holds a B.S. degree from the University of Pittsburgh and an M.S.W. from New York University, where she was awarded a National Institute of Mental Health fellowship. A former adjunct assistant professor at Portland State School of Social Work, she has published numerous articles in the area of divorce and the book *Between Love and Hate: A Guide to Civilized Divorce*. Her new book is *The Sacred Wound: Healing from the Death of a Child*, and she is working on a book on marriage titled *Bridging Differences: A Couples Guide to Resolving Conflict*. She has served on the board of several professional organizations, was a founding board member of the Oregon Mediation Association, and has been a trainer and consultant in conflict resolution for more than twenty years. She can be reached at www.loisgold.com.

Marvin E. Johnson is a nationally recognized mediator, arbitrator, and trainer with over twenty-seven years of dispute resolution experience. The Founder and Executive Director of the Center for Alternative Dispute Resolution, Mr. Johnson served as Professor of Labor Relations, Law, and Dispute Resolution at Bowie State University. He has a Bachelor of Science Degree in Business Administration from Kent State University and advanced degrees from the University of Wisconsin and Catholic University. Mr. Johnson produced and hosted the first biweekly cable TV program that addressed dispute resolution issues and has authored, coauthored, and edited many dispute resolution articles. In 1998, the Chief Judge of the Maryland Court of Appeals, Robert M. Bell, appointed

Mr. Johnson to the Maryland Alternative Dispute Resolution Commission. In 1999, President Clinton appointed Mr. Johnson to the Federal Service Impasses Panel, and in June 2000 he was appointed to the Foreign Service Impasse Disputes Panel. Maryland Governor Paris Glendening appointed Mr. Johnson to the Maryland State Labor Relations Board in July 2002. He holds leadership positions in several national dispute resolution organizations and professional groups, including serving on the Board of Directors of the Association for Conflict Resolution and the International Academy of Mediators. He can be reached at mejohnson@olg.com.

Michelle LeBaron is a writer, scholar, and practitioner of conflict resolution whose work on creative process design is used around the world. She is currently professor of law and director of the Nemetz Centre for Dispute Resolution at the Faculty of Law at the University of British Columbia, Canada. She is deeply committed to improving the quality of teaching, training, and practice in conflict resolution through holistic, relational approaches that take multiple ways of knowing into account. She has consulted and taught in North America, Europe, Africa, and Asia on a variety of topics, including spirituality, creativity, dialogue, psychological dimensions of conflict, family and organizational change management, and the integration of culture into political analysis and policy formulation. She is the author of numerous publications on bridging worldview and cultural differences in conflict, most recently *Bridging Cultural Conflicts: A New Approach for a Changing World* (Jossey-Bass, 2003) and *Bridging Troubled Waters: Conflict Resolution from the Heart* (Jossey-Bass, 2002). In addition to holding leadership positions in national and international conflict resolution organizations, she served as professor of conflict analysis and resolution at George Mason University, Fairfax, Virginia (1993–2003), and director of multiculturalism and dispute resolution at the University of Victoria, Canada (1990–1993). She can be reached atmlebaron@gmu.edu.

Stewart Levine is the founder of ResolutionWorks, a consulting and training organization dedicated to providing skills and ways of thinking people will need to thrive in the next millennium. He spent ten years practicing law before becoming an award-winning marketing executive at AT&T where he was recognized as a pioneer "intrapreneur." He uses his approach to form teams and joint ventures in a variety of situations. Organizations he has worked for, in the US and abroad include American Express; Chevron; Con-Agra; Deloitte & Touche; the D.C. Office of Corporation Counsel; EDS; General Motors; Oracle; Safeco; University of San Francisco; U.S. Depts. of Agriculture and the Navy. He was recently featured in an article about "Trend Setters" in the legal profession. His book *"Getting to Resolution: Turning Conflict into Collaboration"* (Berrett-Koehler 1998) was called "a must read" by *Law Practice Management Magazine*. It was an Executive Book Club Selection, featured by Executive Book Summaries, named one of the thirty Best Business Books of 1998, endorsed by Dr. Stephen Covey, and featured in *The Futurist* magazine. Mr. Levine's second book, *The Book of Agreement*, was released in fall 2002 and has been called "more practical than *Getting to Yes*."

Jonathan W. Reitman is a founding partner in Gosline, Reitman & Ainsworth, a mediation, arbitration, and consulting practice. He practiced employment and personal injury law for twelve years before becoming a full-time ADR practitioner in 1990. He is a frequent lecturer on negotiation, conflict resolution, and mediation. He has trained participants from fifteen countries on these topics in Bosnia and Herzegovina and the Republika of Srpska; Bologna, Italy; Tel Aviv and Haifa, Israel; and London. He has also taught an ADR course at law schools for seven years. He is former chair of the international sector of the Association for Conflict Resolution. He has facilitated strategic planning events for national organizations and served as the neutral facilitator for more than fifteen multiparty stakeholder processes and negotiated rule makings on a variety of public policy issues. He has mediated or arbitrated more than one thousand cases on an array of complex civil matters in the public and private sectors. He may be reached at jreitman@blazenetme.net or www.resolveconflict.com.

Lawrence R. Richard is a principal with Altman Weil, Inc., a consulting firm that provides a full range of management consulting services exclusively to the legal profession. A former practicing attorney, Dr. Richard earned his law degree from the University of Pennsylvania Law School and his Ph.D. degree in psychology from Temple University. He specializes in working with law firms to help improve communication and motivation, build teamwork, and train lawyers in leadership and management. He has published numerous articles and book chapters on law practice and behavioral science and is a frequently requested speaker at bar associations and law firm retreats.

Donald T. Saposnek is a clinical child psychologist, child custody mediator, family therapist, and author of the classic book *Mediating Child Custody Disputes* (1983; revised edition, 1998). He is the current editor of the Association for Conflict Resolution's *Family Mediation News* and of the family section of www.mediate.com. Saposnek has published extensively on child custody, mediation, and child psychology and is on the editorial boards of the *Family Court Review* and the *Conflict Resolution Quarterly* journals. He is a national and international trainer of mediation and teacher of child development; since 1977, he has been teaching on the psychology faculty at the University of California, Santa Cruz. He is a graduate of the University of California, Los Angeles (B.A. in 1966 in psychology), San Jose State University (M.A. in 1967 in psychology), and Ohio State University (Ph.D. in 1971 in clinical child and developmental psychology). In honor of his extensive contributions to the fields of divorce and child custody mediation, family systems theory, conflict resolution, and child psychology, he was the 2002 recipient of the international Association for Conflict Resolution's John M. Haynes Distinguished Mediator Award. Saposnek can be reached at dsaposnek@mediate.com or on the Web at www. mediate. com/dsaposnek.

Index

"systematic intuition" in, 91-93; technical-rational model of, 89-91; worlds of action/ideas combined in, 58. See also ADR (alternative dispute resolution); Mediation; Trickster model
Confused quality, 84-85
Congruence, 28, 198
Conscious competence, 64, 65
Cooley, J., 103, 110, 127
Cosgrave, P., 57
Courage, 242
Covey, S. R., 42
Creative disrupter role, 144
Crum, T. F., 118
Crying/tears, 257-262. See also Emotions
Cynicism/futility pillars, 272-273

D

Daives, B., 228
Dalai Lama, 272
D'Amasio, A. R., 99
Darwin, C., 31
Dass, R., 187
Davies, P., 31, 36
Davis, A. M., 216
de Chardin, T., 193
Deception: constructive vs. destructive, 124; ethics of, 125-127; natural history/dynamics of, 124-125; pursuit of the "noble lie" using, 128-130. See also Manipulation; Truth
Descartes, R., 99
Diamond, S., 93
Diguer, L., 246
DiLeo, D., 12
Direct experience: as always being individual, 267-269; thinking vs., 265-267
Directed intentionality: clarified for peacemaking/healing, 206; and intention of parties, 199-201
Disputes: creation of dissonance in, 113-114; honoring history of the, 239-240; importance of context in, 185-186; mediator's entry into each party's reality of, 112; metaphors and stories to reframe, 115-116; metastrategic thinking to transform, 123-124; using power of "mistakes" to transform, 119-120; questioning process used during, 118-119; reframing context of, 116;

relational field/context of, 185-186; resistance and paradox techniques used in, 116-118; ritual/drama of negotiation to transform, 120-123; role reversal technique used in, 160-161; structuring/managing negotiation process in, 120-123; transforming context of, 112-113; words and language to reframe, 114-115. See also Conflict
Dooling, D. M., 108, 113
Dossey, L., 192
Double witnessing, 229-230
Dunning, D., 61-62, 71
Dworkin, J., 25

E

Eberle, G., 276
Einstein, A., 201
Eliade, M., 102
Elster, J., 94
Embedded/indirect suggestions, 209-210
Emotional Intelligence (Goleman), 8
Emotions: encouraging expression of, 172; EQ (emotional intelligence) as recognizing one's, 152; honoring grief/loss, 208-209; importance to understanding conflict, 53-54; love, 236-237; mediator control over own, 249-250; role of mediator's self-awareness and, 23-24, 257-262. See also Crying/tears
Empathy: candor vs., 171; mediator's use of, 160, 250
EQ (emotional intelligence): definition of, 152; four clusters of, 155-163; implications for mediation, 154-155; importance for mediators of, 164; mediation style and capacity for, 250-251; as predictor for success, 8; principles of competencies of, 152-154; relevance to mediation work, 151
EQ (emotional intelligence) clusters: self-awareness, 156-157; self-management, 157-159; social awareness, 159-161; social skills, 161-163
EQ (emotional intelligence) principles: on self-awareness competencies, 153; on self-management competencies, 153; on social awareness competencies, 154; on social skills competencies, 154